THE JOURNAL OF AFRICAN AMERICAN HISTORY

Formerly *The Journal of Negro History*
Founded by Carter G. Woodson, January 1, 1916

V. P. Franklin, Editor

Published Quarterly by the
Association for the Study of African American Life and History

All print only subscriptions to *The Journal of African American History* are $65 per year individual, domestic; $25 per issue individual, domestic; $100 per year individual, international; $38 per issue individual, international; $150 per year institution, domestic; $38 per issue institution, domestic; $175 per year institution, international; and $44 per issue institution, international. Subscriptions to the online edition of the JAAH (ISSN 2153-5086) and the print plus online subscriptions can be obtained through JSTOR. For more information contact Sri Rajan, JSTOR Fulfillment Manager, 149 Fifth Avenue, 8th Floor, NY, NY 10010, or email: participation@jstor.org.

Manuscript submissions and correspondence concerning all editorial matters should be sent to the mailing address: V. P. Franklin, Editor, *The Journal of African American History,* University of California, Riverside, Graduate School of Education, 1207 Sproul Hall, 900 University Avenue, Riverside, CA 92521; telephone: 951-827-1976; e-mail: vpf1019@aol.com or jaah@jaah.org; website: www.jaah.org.

Three copies of each manuscript should be submitted in double-spaced typescript, no more than 35 pages in length (including the endnotes), and prepared using *The Chicago Manual of Style,* 15th Edition (University of Chicago Press, 2003). Manuscripts submitted for publication will be peer reviewed.

Subscription requests, books for review, advertising inquiries, changes of address, correspondence concerning membership in the Association for the Study of African American Life and History (ASALH), and all business matters should be sent to: Sylvia Y. Cyrus, Executive Director ASALH, 2225 Georgia Avenue, Suite 331, Washington, DC 20059; telephone: 202-865-0053; e-mail: info@asalh.net; website: www.asalh.org.

Change of Address: All address changes should be submitted to the ASALH national office as soon as possible. Please include the old and new addresses. Claims for undelivered copies must be made within three months following publication of an issue and should be submitted to ASALH. ASALH is required to pay a postage fee for all undeliverable journals. If your journal is returned to the national office, it will be re-mailed to you upon receipt of a check in the amount of $5.00 to cover the cost of re-mailing. ASALH does not assume responsibility for replacing missing issues when an address change has not been properly sent to the national office. Please send to Publications Coordinator, 2225 Georgia Avenue, Suite 331, Washington, DC 20059.

THE JOURNAL OF AFRICAN AMERICAN HISTORY

Formerly *The Journal of Negro History*
Founded by Carter G. Woodson, January 1, 1916

Editor: V. P. Franklin, University of California, Riverside

Associate Editors: Derrick P. Alridge, University of Georgia, Athens
                                Joyce Owens Anderson, Chicago State University

Managing Editor: Sylvia Y. Cyrus, ASALH

Editorial Assistants: Edward D. Collins and Stephanie Wilms

The Journal of African American History

Volume 96, No. 1 **Winter 2011**

Contents

W. E. B. DU BOIS AND THE GERMAN *ALLTAG,* 1892–1894 1
   Kenneth Barkin

"PEOPLE ALL OVER THE WORLD ARE SUPPORTING YOU": 14
   MALCOLM X, IDEOLOGICAL FORMATIONS, AND BLACK
   STUDENT ACTIVISM, 1960–1972
   Ibram H. Rogers

SYMPOSIUM

"THE LION OF ZION": LEON H. SULLIVAN AND THE PURSUIT 39
   OF SOCIAL AND ECONOMIC JUSTICE: INTRODUCTION
   V. P. Franklin

PAN-AFRICAN CONNECTIONS, TRANSNATIONAL EDUCATION, 44
   COLLECTIVE CULTURAL CAPITAL, AND OPPORTUNITIES
   INDUSTRIALIZATION CENTERS INTERNATIONAL
   V. P. Franklin

AMANDLA! THE SULLIVAN PRINCIPLES AND THE BATTLE TO END 62
   APARTHEID IN SOUTH AFRICA, 1975–1987
   James B. Stewart

THE PROGRESS MOVEMENT AND COMMUNITY DEVELOPMENT: 90
   THE ZION NON-PROFIT CHARITABLE TRUST
   Nathaniel Bracey

BOOK REVIEWS

Douglas Walter Bristol, Jr., *KNIGHTS OF THE RAZOR: BLACK BARBERS IN SLAVERY AND FREEDOM*   96
J. Brent Morris

Janice L. Sumler-Edmond, *THE SECRET TRUST OF ASPASIA CRUVELLIER MIRAULT: THE LIFE AND TRIALS OF A FREE WOMAN OF COLOR IN ANTEBELLUM GEORGIA*   98
Jacqueline A. Rouse

Carole C. Marks, *MOSES AND THE MONSTER AND MISS ANNE*   100
Linda A. Causey

LeeAnna Keith, *THE COLFAX MASSACRE: THE UNTOLD STORY OF BLACK POWER, WHITE TERROR, AND THE DEATH OF RECONSTRUCTION*   102
Charles Vincent

Christopher M. Span, *FROM COTTON FIELD TO SCHOOLHOUSE: AFRICAN AMERICAN EDUCATION IN MISSISSIPPI, 1862–1875*   105
Louis Ray

Angela Hornsby-Gutting, *BLACK MANHOOD AND COMMUNITY BUILDING IN NORTH CAROLINA, 1900–1930*   107
Daryl A. Carter

Andrew Napolitano, *DRED SCOTT'S REVENGE: A LEGAL HISTORY OF RACE AND FREEDOM IN AMERICA*   109
Zenobia V. Harris

Amy Bass, *THOSE ABOUT HIM REMAINED SILENT: THE BATTLE OVER W. E. B. DU BOIS*   111
Angela Jones

Edward J. Blum and Jason R. Young, eds., *THE SOULS OF W. E. B. DU BOIS: NEW ESSAYS AND REFLECTIONS*   114
Lawrence A. Burnley

Nathaniel Norment, Jr., ed., *THE ADDISON GAYLE, JR., READER*   116
Barbara L. Green

Vanessa Siddle Walker, *HELLO PROFESSOR: A BLACK PRINCIPAL AND PROFESSIONAL LEADERSHIP IN THE SEGREGATED SOUTH*
   Bettina L. Love
              118

Sherman A. Jackson, *ISLAM AND THE PROBLEM OF BLACK SUFFERING*
   Latif A. Tarik
              120

Alusine Jalloh and Toyin Falola, eds., *THE UNITED STATES AND WEST AFRICA: INTERACTIONS AND RELATIONS*
   Michael O. West
              123

Jehu J. Hanciles, *BEYOND CHRISTENDOM: GLOBALIZATION, AFRICAN MIGRATION, AND THE TRANSFORMATION OF THE WEST*
   Justin Williams
              125

Mary Frances Berry, *AND JUSTICE FOR ALL: THE UNITED STATES COMMISSION ON CIVIL RIGHTS AND THE CONTINUING STRUGGLE FOR FREEDOM IN AMERICA*
   W. Marvin Dulaney
              128

ANNOUNCEMENTS

Books Received—2010
              131

Carter G. Woodson Distinguished Lecturers, 2010–2011
              136

W. E. B. DU BOIS AND
THE GERMAN *ALLTAG*, 1892–1894

Kenneth Barkin

Courtesy of the Library of Congress, Washington, DC.

The best source for a study of W. E. B. Du Bois's two years in Germany is Du Bois himself. During his return to the United States from Germany he wrote, "As a student in Germany I built great castles in Spain and lived therein. I dreamed and loved, and wandered and sang. Then after two long years I dropped suddenly into Nigger-hating America."[1] Twenty-three years later in 1917, he pondered whether he should support Germany or the United States in World War I. He wrote, "I was seeing the Germany, which taught me the brotherhood of white and black pitted against America, which for me was the essence of Jim Crow."[2] Du Bois ultimately decided to support the United States, but not enthusiastically. In 1960, sixty-six years after leaving Germany, he explained to William Ingersoll of the Columbia University Oral History Project, who was conducting an interview with Du Bois at age 92 for their archives, "Germany was an extraordinary experi-

Kenneth Barkin is Professor Emeritus of History at the University of California, Riverside.

1

ence. . . . I began to believe white people were human."[3] Du Bois went on to say that he meant only European whites. He changed his mind frequently during his ninety-five years (who wouldn't?). But regarding Imperial Germany there was not a hint of change. In his most famous book *The Souls of Black Folk* (1903), he maintained that white racism was pervasive in his life with the exceptions of his childhood in Great Barrington, Massachusetts, and his experiences in Europe.[4] Since the only European nation he lived in for a significant amount of time was Imperial Germany, we have to assume that this was the nation to which he was referring. What strikes me as a historian is not only his praise for Germany but his contempt for the United States during the 1890s.

My intention is not to concentrate on his contact with Berlin professors, or the ideas he absorbed from their lectures and seminars over the three semesters he spent at the Humbolt University of Berlin. He never complained about Gustav Schmoller or Adolf Wagner, his major professors. Indeed, he praised them for accepting him into their over-filled seminars. Both mentors sent quite positive references to the officers of the Slater Fund about extending his stay for a second year, which they did; and for a third year, which was denied. Since Du Bois sought to prolong his stay in Germany, one is led to believe that he was happier in Berlin than he had ever been at Harvard.

For the purposes of this essay, *Alltag* can be translated as the everyday experiences, the ordinary, or perhaps the routine or normal that binds the individual with others who share a common culture and space. In order to answer my question about the *Alltag* in Du Bois's experience, one has to deal with two other questions. First, we have to examine his time at Harvard University where he spent four full years immediately preceding his Berlin years. Was he leaving Harvard with affectionate memories or with bitterness? The second question we have to address is: What did Du Bois know of Imperial Germany before he arrived there in the summer of 1892?

There is no question that he found Harvard stiff, even icy cold. Indeed, he never returned to Harvard after his years in Berlin.[5] Only one professor, William James, showed any genuine interest in one of Harvard's first black students. James regularly invited Du Bois for Sunday lunches and even sought to arrange a meeting of Du Bois with his brother, the novelist Henry James. His major professor, Albert Bushnell Hart, Du Bois told Ingersoll, "was very accurate in memory, names, and things, but he was not human. He was methodical. He was as dry as dust."[6] Compared to Fisk where he had spent three happy years and praised many of his teachers, the professors and students at Harvard made Du Bois feel he was an "invisible man."

This was also the case regarding the Harvard students. In his two major autobiographies and the oral history, Du Bois does not mention the name of any undergraduate or doctoral student with whom he had friendly relations. Bitterness best describes his mood at Harvard. He was turned down for the Harvard Glee Club, although he was convinced that his voice was superior to that of all but a few of the students who were accepted.[7] The clearest indication of Du Bois's disdain was his decision to move to Central Square, a mile away from the campus, so that he would have little contact with either students or faculty. The focus of his last years at Harvard was the African American community of Boston and Cambridge. However, his Harvard professors did come to his aid with references when he applied for a fellowship to study in Germany.[8]

The second question—What did Du Bois know about Germany before crossing the Atlantic?—has a surprising answer. He knew a great deal, and most of it was quite positive. At Fisk University, he studied German for three years and developed a close relationship with the German language professor Henry S. Bennett. He was a frequent visitor at the professor's home and often borrowed books from his private library. In the spring of 1888, at 20 years of age, Du Bois wrote two brief essays that centered on Germany and German immigrants to the United States. "Das Neue Vaterland" (The New Fatherland), written in German, was an appeal to German immigrants who were flooding into the United States in the 1880s.[9] He urged them to reject the racism of white southerners. African Americans, he pointed out, subscribed to the same Protestant religion as Germans from the eastern provinces of Prussia.[10]

Three months later, in June of 1888, Du Bois delivered the valedictory speech at Fisk University. The title of his speech was "Bismarck," and he showed genuine admiration for the achievements of the "Iron Chancellor." Otto von Bismarck had created a powerful nation in the center of Europe that no single nation alone could challenge. In an addendum Du Bois cautioned those who would emulate Bismarck because the political system of the German Empire was so complicated that only Bismarck could manage it. Without him, Du Bois thought the Kaiser's empire might collapse; a very precocious idea for a young black student of twenty who had never been to Europe. He went on to criticize Fredrich Hegel and a second philosopher, most likely Schopenhauer, both of whom had argued that Africans did not experience "emotions." Clearly, Du Bois was not uncritical of all things German, and certainly was not a fan of Hegel.[11]

Du Bois's desire to study in Germany was not unlike that of many contemporary educated Americans who sought an academic career.[12] German scholarship and training was a must for those pursuing a career in philosophy, history, or the social sciences. He applied to the John F. Slater Fund for the Education of Freedmen. His application for a fellowship was quickly turned down as unqualified. Thus, the fund had never granted a black student a fellowship, although according to its charter, that was the only purpose for its existence. Du Bois wrote a searing reply that implied that no African American could ever rely on any help from a white man.[13] Former U.S. President Rutherford Hayes, president of the Slater Fund, reconsidered his decision and awarded the fellowship for one year, part of which was to be paid back with interest. Du Bois would now get a glimpse of the United States from another continent with a different past.

The question for the historian is: What happened in those two years to compel Du Bois to praise Germany from the time of his return to the United States in 1894 until his interview with Ingersoll at Columbia in 1960? Even Du Bois's second novel, *Dark Princess: A Romance,* published in 1928, begins with a scene in Berlin in which the main character thinks to himself that, in contrast to the United States, he can go into any restaurant in the city and be served by a waiter.[14] I propose that it was primarily Du Bois's contact with Germans and other Europeans in everyday life, rather than his studies with German professors or his contact with students, that made a lasting impression on him. When Du Bois sought to compare Harvard professors with those in Berlin, he made the point that teaching was of much greater importance in American universities than in Berlin. German professors lectured in large classrooms, and they did not learn the names of the students. Only in the seminar room did the instructors get to know their students, and the students came into closer contact with their professors.[15]

Du Bois listed six or seven professors whose lectures he had attended, but only two professors conducted seminars in which he had enrolled. They did have a significant influence on his approach to economics and political economy. What I would like to stress, however, is that his experiences with Germans outside of the classroom were equally important, and in my view, more critical for the evolution of his thoughts about racism in the United States. It was the everyday experiences of living for twenty months in Berlin and his trips to many parts of Germany that gave him a foundation for rejecting the universality of racist practices found in everyday American life. It was in Germany that he realized that white Americans were out of tune, perhaps unique in the Western world, for the type of legal segregation that existed in so many spheres of life. They had created what one might call a unique American *Alltag* in the Western world, which included racialized practices of mob violence and lynching. This was an aspect of American "exceptionalism" that his professors at Harvard had ignored.[16]

Postcolonial theorists today term the United States a "settler colony" (usually the most violent) and similar in many respects, but not all, to South Africa, Australia, and New Zealand where race played an overwhelming role in day-to-day life.[17] The United States was somewhat different. It had imported in chains what might be called a substitute "indigenous population" in the Africans, since the vast majority of Native Americans were wiped out by disease and military conquest, and those who survived failed to adapt as an enslaved and exploited labor force for large-scale agricultural production. Justus Moeser, both a serious thinker and government official in the state of Osnabrueck, Germany, in the 18th century, was a major defender of the *Alltag* and a vociferous opponent of change based on "reason" or rationality. Moeser explained his view, clearly and distinctly: "When I come across some old custom, old habit which simply will not fit into the modern ways of reasoning, I keep turning around in my mind the idea that, after all, our forefathers were not fools, until I find some sensible reason for it."[18] In theory this allowed for some change, but in practice it led to continuity *uber alles.*

In his famous article on cockfighting in Bali, the anthropologist Clifford Geertz pointed to the shared assumptions accepted by all who wagered on cockfights—losers as well as winners. Departure from the rules led to expulsion from the community.[19] Du Bois learned on his first day in Europe that the difference in everyday life in Germany compared to that in the United States was like night and day for a black man. Much that Du Bois experienced in Europe struck him as normal such as Sunday church attendance, women minding the infants and young children, and men going to bars on payday to drink with their friends. But he also found much in Germany that was radically unfamiliar, requiring him to make comparisons, and reflect on American racial practices, which he loathed, but had reluctantly accepted as "normal" interracial relations in the Western world. To have challenged these, particularly in the U.S. South, could mean immediate death for a black man, woman, or child. Thus, what I am seeking to examine are the ordinary experiences of daily life that did not get one in trouble in Germany, but could be fatal in the world that Du Bois lived in during most of his adult years in the United States. The differences between university life in Cambridge or Nashville and Berlin paled in comparison with the differences in life on the streets, outside of academia. Those experiences had the greatest impact on Du Bois and led him to see Germany as a more humane and progressive society than the United States.

The first experience that left Du Bois in a daze occurred a day after his arrival in Europe on a small ship taking passengers down the Rhine from Rotterdam to Cologne.[20] He noticed a well-dressed woman with three daughters, between twelve and seventeen years of age, step on to the boat. There were many other passengers as well. The family moved toward him and he fled in another direction. Since it was a modest-sized riverboat, there was only so far he could go. Finally, he was cornered and the mother, a Dutch woman, introduced herself in German or English. After a while, Du Bois felt very relaxed, very comfortable conversing with her and the daughters and replying to their questions.[21] The mother then posed a question. They were approaching Duesseldorf where the boat would spend two hours. She and her older daughters wanted to walk around the city center, but the 12-year-old girl could not be talked into leaving the ship. The mother pointed out that she could not leave her alone. She asked Du Bois if he intended to stay on the ship, and if so, would he make sure that the 12-year-old did not get into trouble. Du Bois was shocked. He begged out of the task, but the Dutch woman refused to accept his negative response and he wound up being responsible for the young girl.

This was a startling introduction to Europe. It raised questions about his fundamental assumptions regarding race relations in the Western world. In his autobiography he listed this day in 1892 as critical for rethinking the issue of race. What had transpired was certainly not possible in the American *Alltag*. It would have led other passengers, or the captain of the ship, to intervene and convince the woman to stay on the ship, or force her daughter to join the family. In the U.S. South, it might have led to violence against the African American man or the white woman. This was the incident that Du Bois told Ingersoll could not happen in the United States in the 1960s. I believe he was correct in this judgment. It is possible that the woman noticed how well dressed Du Bois was, and that may have convinced her that he was a respectable and educated young man. He may have told her he was going to study at the University of Berlin. Nevertheless, I am doubtful that in 1892 any of those reasons would have led an American mother to leave her daughter with a young black man under similar circumstances.

Because Du Bois's spoken German needed improvement before the semester began, it was arranged, by his pastor in Great Barrington Evarts Scudder that he would live for six weeks or more in Eisenach with the Rev. Herr Rector Marbach and his family. They rented extra bedrooms in the summer to supplement the family's income. The German pastor's daughter, Dora, was four years younger than Du Bois and they got along exceedingly well, so much so that a visiting professor and his wife from Colorado felt it their duty to warn the Marbachs that their daughter was spending a good deal of her time with "a Negro." Du Bois overheard the conversation and fumed about white Americans who sought to spread their poisonous racism all over the globe. Apparently, Marbach and his wife ignored the Americans and did not in any way change their behavior toward Du Bois.[22]

Somewhat similar was Du Bois's experience at the opera in Vienna where an American woman glowered at him in the intermission.[23] When his stay in Eisenach came to an end, Dora Marbach proposed that they think about marriage. He asked when and she, according to Du Bois, said "*gleich*" (right now). He explained that it was impossible for the two of them to live in the United States. Decades later he confided to a friend that he had been deeply in love with Dora. The Marbachs had had an impact on his life and years later he would say that there was not one ounce of racism in that family.[24] When Du Bois arrived in Berlin, the housing office directed him to a street that Americans favored. He inquired about a street that had no Americans and rented a room on Oranienstrasse, free of his countrymen. He decided the style of American shoes was quite different from their German equivalent, and henceforth he avoided all students wearing what he came to think of as contaminated shoes.

Another example of the German *Alltag,* or at least the racial acceptance that Germans exhibited in everyday life, occurred on his birthday in 1893. Unbeknownst to him the elderly woman who managed his boarding house in Berlin, and brought him tea each evening, managed to find out his birth date. She arranged for all the students boarding in the building to be present at a modest birthday party on that day.[25] A cake or *torte* was presented to him and those attending sang "Happy Birthday" and received a piece of cake. Du Bois was deeply moved by this completely unforeseen event orchestrated by an elderly woman whom he had known only five months. He also received several birthday cards from Dora and three other friends he had made in Germany. After these three experiences Du Bois began to judge people more by their nationality and behavior than by their color.[26] These happy incidents did not happen at the University of Berlin, but in the Marbach house in Eisenach and a German boarding house on Oranienstrasse in Berlin.

Another part of the *Alltag* in Berlin was the frequent military parades that were sometimes led by Kaiser William II. Du Bois was occasionally in the crowd on these Sundays and one day the parade of marching soldiers stunned him. That evening he wrote in his notebook, "What did I see but one of my own, a full blooded and comely Negro marching with precision."[27] The first time I read this sentence I wondered if Du Bois was drunk when he wrote it. I could not conceive of a black "Unteroffizier" in the Prussian army any more than Du Bois could conceive of a woman leaving her 12-year-old daughter with him for two hours. It turns out that Du Bois was quite sober. Most likely the soldier was Gustav Sabac el Cher, who served as a corporal in the Prussian army from 1885 to 1909. He was a talented musician, born in Berlin, and late in life had a career as the conductor of a radio orchestra. An 1890 painting by the well-known painter Emil Doerstling of Sabac el Cher and his adoring girlfriend Gertrud, entitled "Happy in Love in Prussia," is now in the collection of the German National Museum in Berlin. The couple married eleven years later, and had two sons who, like their father, served in the military.[28]

One might conclude that this was a unique case, an unimportant artifact, or that all of this was surprisingly possible in the German *Alltag* in the 1890s. Du Bois may have been aware that the first black admitted to the U.S. military academy at West Point, John Chestnut Whittaker, was attacked viciously by his fellow cadets in 1880, survived, but was expelled from the college.[29] However, one black soldier in the Prussian army does not in any way excuse military attacks on the Ewe peoples in Togo, West Africa, in the 1890s, or the slaughter of Herero and

Nama peoples in German Southwest Africa in the first decade of the 20th century.[30] The Germans were quite cruel toward the African peoples in their colonial territories. Although the Germans claimed large amounts of territory in Africa and sought to use the native peoples as exploited workers producing cotton and other staples for the European market, following World War I they were stripped of these colonial possessions.[31] Here, I should add that Du Bois had no contact with the German elite or "official Germany"; his positive experiences were with the common people. Indeed, for the most part they were with women and men of all ages.

But there was one incident that was serious and indisputably racial. One Saturday morning Du Bois visited the city of Luebeck, apparently with a young woman whom he had met at a socialist party meeting. Historian Manning Marable, who has done more to study Du Bois's private life than any other scholar, believes that Du Bois was having a serious love affair with a woman named "Amelia," with whom he either lived or spent a good deal of time in a rented room. On that Saturday morning they strolled to the market in the city center. As they approached the stands laden with vegetables, several young men or teenagers spotted them and began to shout loudly, and then advance toward them still shouting. Du Bois and his companion were shocked, and ran back to their hotel. They closed the door behind them and the incident came to an end without physical harm. There is no question that Du Bois was shaken by the incident. Clearly it was racially motivated, and, most likely it was a result of his being with a German woman.[32] This immediate and visceral reaction of the youths was not part of the German *Alltag* that he had experienced during the previous year. In the United States he could have possibly been lynched. He was presumably dressed in his formal suit with cane and gloves. This did not prevent the youths' aggressiveness. Most likely race simply trumped dress in his case. All of his experiences of the previous year caused Du Bois to find the incident bewildering.

It should have been a warning to him that such prejudice could also be part of the German *Alltag*. Now that he was thoroughly comfortable in Germany, he had experienced an event that he had anticipated a year earlier, but that had not transpired. Some Germans had now indicated that his behavior was unacceptable and, perhaps he himself viewed it as unacceptable. Toward the end of his years in Berlin, Du Bois undertook alone a *Harzreise,* a winter journey to the Harz Mountains in Germany, which demonstrated that he still had faith in the tolerance of Germans (as long as he was not with a German woman). Since he did not dwell on this racial incident, it is my impression that he decided to ignore this experience, to judge it as unique, and he would not allow a bunch of thugs to spoil all of his positive interracial experiences during the previous year.

Thus, while we know that Du Bois did not travel alone during his first year in

Berlin, he gradually grew more confident that there were not hordes of racists in the forests waiting for a well-dressed African American. One wishes there was more information about that weekend in Luebeck. We know that interracial marriage was possible since Gustav Sabac el Cher married Gertrud in 1901 and the couple had two children. Such marriages were banned in more than thirty American states; and in at least twelve states, interracial couples were banned from living there, even when they were married elsewhere. These laws were not ruled unconstitutional by the U.S. Supreme Court until 1967.[33]

We have here four experiences (mostly with ordinary Germans) that must have led to serious reflection by Du Bois. None of the positive ones could have transpired in the United States where in the 1890s the lynching of African Americans increased dramatically in the South and West. In one of the lectures that Du Bois attended, German historian Heinrich von Treitschke announced that he learned from the newspaper that morning that in the previous year, 130 Americans had been sentenced to the death penalty by judges after being convicted in trials by jury; whereas 191 people were killed by lynching. Later figures compiled for the year 1892 indicated that 205 people were lynched. For the two years Du Bois was in Germany, it was estimated that 405 Americans (nearly all African Americans) were lynched.[34] This kind of mob violence was not part of the German or Western European *Alltag* in the late 19th century, and one would have to hark back to the burning of witches in the 16th and 17th centuries to find a European experience similar to that of the United States. It must have impressed this young exchange student who heard this quite nasty, anti-Semitic, ultra-nationalist professor, Treitschke, suggest that the American South was not part of Western civilization.

A few additional comparisons are instructive and take the issue of race in Germany beyond one example of Du Bois's experiences. In 1911 a young black Harvard graduate, Alain Leroy Locke, chose to spend a year at the University of Berlin, following two years at Oxford University in England on a Rhodes Fellowship. Like Du Bois, Locke spent a good deal of his spare money on his clothing, but unlike Du Bois, he was homosexual. He found Berlin as tolerant of black people as Du Bois had over a decade earlier, perhaps even more so. Although he returned to the United States after his year in Germany and later played a major role in the "New Negro Renaissance" in the 1920s, Locke returned to Germany regularly for visits. He visited in the summers of 1913 and 1914, and annually between 1919 and 1935. The most likely reason is that Berliners were much more tolerant than Americans in the sphere of sexuality, particularly during the years of the Weimar Republic in the 1920s, and there was a sizeable homosexual subculture that Locke had linked up with in the German capital. There is also the possibility that he had a long lasting relationship with one lover that made the trips appealing. One has to assume that Locke's sexual relationships were interracial. He was as comfortable in Berlin as Du Bois had been; his visits ceased when the Nuremberg laws of 1935 were issued.[35]

A comparison can also be made of the experiences of Du Bois and Hans Massaquoi, an Afro-German who was born in 1926 to an African father and a German mother. He remained with his mother in a working-class section of Hamburg, Germany, until after World War II. Massaquoi's important book *Witness to Destiny* appeared in 2001.[36] What strikes the reader immediately are some parallels with the experiences of Locke and Du Bois in Germany, although there are significant differences as well. Massaquoi did not have a lover, but a close relationship with a young German woman, Gretchen, in the working-class section of the city. Gretchen was the aggressor as Dora had been with Du Bois. Gretchen's mother was quite aware of the relationship and had no objections. Massaquoi's virginity ended with a German prostitute in the early 1940s. This happened in Nazi Germany with nobody paying much attention to Hitler's racial ideology in Hamburg's infamous red light district. Another surprising similarity occurred when Massaquoi took dancing lessons in his neighborhood. When the director informed his pupils that there would be a *Damenwahl* (ladies' choice), Massaquoi sought to leave as Du Bois had from a church dance in Eisenach a half century earlier.[37] The young women chose Hans for dances, as they had Du Bois, before he could get away. In 1932 only 27 percent of Hamburgers voted for the Nazis, 10 percent less than the national average, and in the working-class communities of Hamburg, it was considerably lower. Perhaps Du Bois, Locke, and Massaquoi all had the good fortune to live in large cosmopolitan cities where tolerance was more widespread than in villages or small German towns.[38]

There are other possible explanations for Du Bois and Locke assimilating into German culture with a minimum of difficulty. The different histories of Germany and the United States may be of greatest importance. On the one hand, the United States had legalized slavery from the colonial era to the Civil War, and this was followed by a century of legal segregation and racialized oppression. On the other hand, while Prussia had serfdom for centuries, there was no slavery based on race. Prussia, unlike other European nations such as France, Portugal, the Netherlands, and Britain, did not participate in the lucrative transatlantic slave trade. The Prussian "Great Elector" brought a few Africans into the country, primarily for their musical talents, as did later monarchs. Nevertheless, Prussia and most of the states of the former Holy Roman Empire had little experience with African people.[39]

Another possibility relates to dress. After a few months in Berlin, Du Bois made the decision to dress like a member of the *Bildungsbuergertum*, with gloves, a cane, and occasionally spats. Dress may have been one reason he was as acceptable as he was in Germany. In a nation in which sumptuary laws had existed for centuries, Du Bois and Locke projected two messages. First, both had light-brown skin color, which signified to the Germans that they were foreigners, outsiders, and non-Europeans. But their dress could be read as that of an elite, if not European then perhaps American or African. Most importantly, they both spoke German. Thus they presented mixed messages to the typical, nonacademic German. These were not men dressed for physical labor; thus, the German observer got two messages and most decided to proceed carefully. This was *terra incognita.*

Perhaps Du Bois would have been treated well even if he had studied in Britain, France, or the Netherlands. Thus the question might be: Was the German response in actuality a European response? There is some indication that this explanation might have validity. Du Bois did travel to Paris years later and claimed that Paris was extremely tolerant. Locke spent time in Paris and London, but preferred Germany to England, even after spending two years at Oxford University. The Germans had the advantage of being more committed to learning, and less, Locke wrote, to the culture of hunting, shooting, horse racing, and sherry.[40] As for Du Bois, he considered Imperial Germany in the 1890s a racial paradise compared to the United States at *fin de siècle,* and he continued to write and say this from 1894 until his death in 1963.

NOTES

[1]W. E. B. Du Bois wrote this to his friend Dollar while on a boat back to the United States in 1894. See "Berlin Sketches," (microfilm) reel 87, frame 167, W. E. B. Du Bois Papers, University of Massachusetts, Amherst (hereafter, Du Bois Papers). He also included the words in *The Autobiography of W. E. B. Du Bois,* ed. Herbert Aptheker (New York, 1968), 83.

[2]W. E. B. Du Bois, "My Evolving Program for Negro Freedom," in *What the Negro Wants*, ed. Rayford Logan (New York, 1944), 31–70.

[3]In 1960 Du Bois submitted to a series of interviews with William Ingersoll, who was head of the Oral History Project at Columbia University, entitled "The Reminiscences of W. E. B. Du Bois." Ingersoll was very critical of Du Bois's praise of Imperial Germany. This resulted in the 92-year-old Du Bois saying, "In Germany I had a very interesting time. I began to realize that white people were human." The "Reminiscences of W. E. B Du Bois," Oral History Center, Columbia University (New York, 1963), 114–17 (hereafter, Ingersoll interview).

[4]Du Bois, *The Souls of Black Folk* (New York, 1903), 7.

[5]Du Bois told Ingersoll that his doctoral advisor at Harvard, Albert Hart, was "not human." Ibid. 90. He added, "My human contacts at Harvard were narrow." "Harvard Notes," reel 87, frame 476, Du Bois Papers.

[6]Ibid.

[7]Ibid., His failure to make the Harvard Glee Club convinced Du Bois that racial discrimination existed at Harvard.

[8]In his autobiography Du Bois, some fifty years later, could not control his anger at the Slater Fund for his rejection. His emotional letter convinced President Hayes to reconsider and, ultimately to change his mind once three of Harvard's major professors supported Du Bois strongly.

[9]W. E. B. Du Bois, "The New Fatherland," and Kenneth Barkin, "Introduction: Germany on His Mind: 'Das

Neue Vaterland,'" *The Journal of African American History* 91 (Fall 2006): 444–50.

[10]More than 1.5 million Germans, mainly from the eastern provinces of Prussia emigrated to the United States in the 1870s and 1880s. For a more detailed discussion of the emigration, see Kenneth Barkin, *The Controversy Over German Industrialization* (Chicago, IL, 1970).

[11]Bismarck Commencement Speech, Fisk University, June, 1888, Du Bois Papers. Du Bois's praise of Bismarck was limited. He wrote that the empire's strength was in a man, not in institutions. For a 20-year-old to recognize one of Bismarck's major failings while he was still in power was remarkable.

[12]Between 1870 and 1914 many bright young educated Americans were attracted to "the lure of the Germany university" rather than Oxford for study because German universities were considered superior in their scholarship and much less expensive than Oxford and Cambridge. The latter also provided no graduate training. See, Lawrence R. Veysey, *The Emergence of the American University* (Chicago, IL, 1965), 125–33.

[13]W. E. B. Du Bois to Rutherford B. Hayes, 19 April 1891 and 25 May 1891, in *The Correspondence of W. E. B. Du Bois, Volume I, Selections, 1877–1934*, ed. Herbert Aptheker (Amherst, MA, 1973), 10–17.

[14]W. E. B. Du Bois, *Dark Princess: A Romance* (New York, 1928), 7. The impact of Germany was still powerful thirty-four years after his departure in 1894. The novel begins with a description of the civility of Germans toward black people.

[15]Daniel Fallon, *The German University: A Heroic Ideal in Conflict with the Modern World* (Boulder, CO, 1980); Thomas Weber, *Our Friend "The Enemy": Elite Education in Britain and Germany Before World War I* (Stanford, CA, 2008).

[16]For a recent analysis of the unique aspects of lynching and mob violence in the United States, see Ashley M. Howard, "Lynching and Mob Violence: Challenging Dominant Perspectives," *The Journal of African American History* 95 (Spring 2010): 248–56.

[17]Bill Ashcroft, Gareth Griffins, and Helen Tiffin, eds., *Post Colonial Studies: The Key Concepts* (London, 2003); and Patrick Williams and Laura Chrisman, eds., *Colonial Discourse/Post Colonial Theory* (New York, 1994).

[18]See Karl Mannheim, "Conservative Thought," in *Karl Mannheim's Essays on Sociology, and Social Psychology*, ed. Paul Kecskemeti (London, 1953), 74–114; see also Jonathan Knudsen, *Justus Moeser and the German Enlightenment* (Cambridge, MA, 1986).

[19]Clifford Geertz, "Deep Play: Notes on the Balinese Cockfight," in *The Interpretation of Culture* (New York, 1973), 412–53.

[20]In his writings Du Bois points to the day on the Rhine River as the critical one that forced him to rethink his understanding of race. His passionate comments in *What the Negro Wants* some fifty-two years after the event underscores its importance for his subsequent thinking on race. Du Bois, "My Evolving Program for Negro Education." Also see Ingersoll interview, 101–103, 159.

[21]Du Bois also refers to "laughing, singing, and eating together" with the Dutch family. In the oral history he told Ingersoll, "I felt like crying when we left." Ingersoll interview, 159.

[22]W. E. B. Du Bois, *The Autobiography of W. E. B. Du Bois: A Soliloquy on Viewing My Life from the Last Decade of Its First Century*, ed. Herbert Aptheker (New York, 1968), 160–62.

[23]At the opera in Vienna Du Bois claims Americans were indignant and resentful. "I kept away from Americans always." Ingersoll interview, 98.

[24]Manning Marable, *W. E. B. Du Bois: Black Radical* (Boston, MA, 1986), 19.

[25]Du Bois wrote in his notebook that Frau Braun made tea every evening and a cake on his birthday, and added that he "experienced the most pleasant companionship with the students living in the boarding house." "Berlin Sketches," reel 87, frames 467 and 497, Du Bois Papers.

[26]W. E. B. Du Bois, *Against Racism: Unpublished Essays, Papers, and Addresses, 1887–1961* (Amherst, MA, 1985). On a page titled "Celebrating My 25th Birthday," he wrote, "I went to bed after one of the happiest days of my life," 27.

[27]Du Bois Notebooks, "Berlin Sketches: Parade in Berlin," reel 87, frame 498, Du Bois Papers.

[28]Information on Emil Doerstling, Gustav Sabac el Cher, and the painting "Happy in Love in Prussia" can be found at http://hojja-nusreddin.livejournal.com/1782217.html.

[29]"Righting a Historical Wrong: West Point Cadet Drummed Out of School More Than a Century Ago Gets Posthumous Commission," *Ebony*, October 1995.

[30]For a recent detailed study of the Germans and their military and economic operations in Africa in the 1890s and early 1900s, see Andrew Zimmerman, *Alabama in Africa: Booker T. Washington, the German Empire, and the Globalization of the New South* (Princeton, NJ, 2010).

[31]There is no question that how African peoples or any minority are treated in their home country is quite separate from government policies in their colonial empire. See Isabel V. Hull, *Absolute Destruction: Military Culture and the Practices of War in Imperial Germany* (Ithaca, NY, 2006). Also worthy of attention is Helmut Walser Smith, *The Continuities of German History* (Cambridge, UK, 2008), 197–203.

[32]Most likely Amelia was with Du Bois in Luebeck. See, Du Bois, "Berlin Sketches," reel 87, frame 500–503, Du Bois Papers.

[33]Peggy Pascoe, *What Comes Naturally: Miscegenation Law and the Making of Race in America* (New York, 2009).

[34]Heinrich von Treitschke was right to be appalled. On lynching, see Ralph Ginzburg, *100 Years of Lynchings* (1962; rept., Baltimore, MD, 1996), who estimated that 4,733 people in the United States suffered this form of torture and death between 1880 and 1950; see also Philip Dray, *At the Hands of Persons Unknown: The Lynching of Black America* (New York, 2002), who reported that between 1882 and 1944, over 3,710 African Americans were lynched in the United States.

[35]Russell J. Linnemann, *Alain Locke: Reflections on a Renaissance Man* (Baton Rouge, LA, 1982); Leonard Harris and Charles Molesworth, *Alain L. Locke: Biography of a Philosopher* (Chicago, IL, 2010); see also Hubert Kennedy, *Homosexuality and Male-Bonding in Pre-Nazi Germany: The Gay Movement, the Youth Movement and Male Bonding Before Hitler's Rise* (New York, 1992); Otto Friedrich, *Before the Deluge: A Portrait of Berlin in the 1920s* (New York, 1995); and Peter Gay, *Weimar Culture: The Outsider as Insider* (New York, 2001).

[36]Hans Massaquoi, *Witness to Destiny: Growing Up Black in Nazi Germany* (New York, 2001).

[37]Ibid., 166–77. Massaquoi, like Du Bois, was frightened of dance in Germany in which the females choose their partners (*Damenwahl*), although both found young German women competing to dance with them. Both went to prostitutes while in Germany; in Massaquoi's case it was in Nazi Germany during World War II.

[38]For a detailed discussion of these issues, see Kenneth Barkin, "African Americans, Afro-Germans, White Americans, and Germans—Essay Review," *The Journal of African American History* 94 (Spring 2009): 253–65.

[39]James Charles Roy, *Vanished Kingdom: Travels Through the History of Prussia* (New York, 2000), 105–62; Christopher Clark, *Iron Kingdom: The Rise and Downfall of Prussia, 1600–1947* (Cambridge, MA, 2009); and Eric D. Brose, *German History, 1789–1871: From the Holy Roman Empire to the Bismarckian Reich* (Oxford, UK, 1997).

[40]Harris and Molesworth, *Alain L. Locke,* 92–106; and Irek Malgorzata, "From Berlin to Harlem: Felix von Luschan, Alain Locke, and the New Negro," *The Black Columbiad: Defining Moments in African American Literature and Culture,* ed. Werner Sollors and Maria Diedrich (Cambridge, MA, 1995), 174–84.

"PEOPLE ALL OVER THE WORLD ARE SUPPORTING YOU": MALCOLM X, IDEOLOGICAL FORMATIONS, AND BLACK STUDENT ACTIVISM, 1960–1972

Ibram H. Rogers

George Breitman, editor of *Malcolm X Speaks*, lecturing at a memorial meeting sponsored by the Militant Labor Forum in New York on 11 February 1966, almost a year after Malcolm X was assassinated, discussed that segment of U.S. society in which Malcolm's ideas were "taking root." They were budding "especially among the young people," Breitman declared, "those in their twenties and late teens, and younger even than that."[1] An unidentified faculty member at Tougaloo College, the private black college in Mississippi, informed College Press Service reporter Walter Grant in 1968 that "Malcolm X is more popular than Jesus Christ here. The students actually worship him."[2] Malcolm's young widow Betty Shabazz was quoted in *Ebony* magazine in 1969 saying that Malcolm's ideology had blossomed into the advancing Black Power Movement, striking "a responsive chord among black people in general, but particularly black youths."[3] In 1971 *Chicago Tribune* columnist Vernon Jarrett announced that Malcolm still held the mantel as "probably . . . the most quoted of all modern black spokesman . . . among black leaders of high school and college age."[4]

In the late 1950s and early 1960s as the national spokesman for the Nation of Islam (NOI), Malcolm X became a nationally recognized figure through his organizing activities for the NOI, and his constant and forceful ridiculing of the southern, integrationist, and nonviolent Civil Rights Movement. His rise to prominence was greatly aided by his public lambasting of whites as "devils," and the CBS television documentary, "The Hate That Hate Produced," broadcast nationally in 1959. Malcolm impressed students with his fiery speeches, quick wit, striking analogies, glorification of black people and Africa in general, and down-to-earth yet scholarly presentations. But most students were not attracted to his religious ideology since it was wrapped in the Nation of Islam's theology, which deified Elijah Muhammad, who shunned political activism, preached a strict moral code, denigrated women, denounced all whites as inherently evil, and advocated complete "separation of the races." However, over the years Malcolm's rhetoric

---

Ibram H. Rogers is Assistant Professor of African American History at SUNY College at Oneonta in New York.

became more secularized and matured politically, with those elements that intoxicated black and white students coming to the fore. By 1964 Malcolm had not only left the Nation of Islam after a prolonged suspension and life-changing religious experience in the holy city of Mecca, but had dropped the NOI theology, had become an orthodox Muslim, and had founded the Muslim Mosque Inc. and the Organization of Afro-American Unity (OAAU). With these new organizations, Malcolm began developing and sharing his ideas about black national and international unity, self-determination, self defense, and cultural pride. The boldness of his rhetoric was still attractive and his logic continued to persuade. His love of black people and social justice remained and his authenticity and honesty were even more apparent. This expansive ideological perspective struck a responsive chord among African peoples and African American students throughout the United States.[5]

Over the last forty years, the scholarly literature on Malcolm X has offered similar assessments of his powerful impact on black youth in the Black Power era in the late 1960s and early 1970s. In one of the early studies on black student activism, Anthony Orum classified Malcolm as one of the originators of the movement. Frederick Harper, Jeffrey Ogbar, and Alphonse Pinckney alluded to Malcolm's widespread appeal among African Americans, especially the youth. Clayborne Carson discussed Malcolm's influence on the radicalized Student Nonviolent Coordinating Committee (SNCC) in the late 1960s, while Peniel Joseph, Donald Cunnigen, Donald Alexander Downs, and Richard P. McCormick pointed to Malcolm's impact on black campus activists at Cornell, Rutgers, and other colleges and universities. Wayne Glasker described the student activists at the University of Pennsylvania in the late 1960s as the "ideological children of Malcolm X." William W. Sales concluded that "by 1967–68, on previously all-white northern and southern campuses, a black student movement was born, consciously identified with the thought of Malcolm X." And William L. Van Deburg found that members of black student unions (BSUs) were "greatly influenced by the writings of Malcolm X."[6]

None of these authors, however, specifically explored Malcolm's remarkable contribution to black student ideologies and activism during the 1960s and early 1970s. In other words, this idea of Malcolm's impact has become generally accepted in historical writings, but there is little in the historiography that fully documents that influence in the actual statements, activities, and organizations formed by African American and other students during those years. There are numerous references to Malcolm's inspirational role for black students found in the various studies of the 1960s. Through an examination of the historical literature, as well as the periodicals and primary source materials, this essay identifies Malcolm's foundational status in the ideological configurations for African

American youth, especially college students in the 1960s. Crucial in these configurations were Malcolm's boldness, honesty, charisma, logical claims, confrontational behavior towards whites, personal story of redemption, revered status as a martyr, and radical ideological perspectives. Malcolm inspired black cultural nationalists who emphasized cultural revitalization, as well as revolutionary nationalists plotting the destruction of the capitalist system in the United States. A wide range of black groups and individuals found Malcolm's words and actions challenging, providing substantive and justifiable reasons to organize. Although the writings and speeches of Frantz Fanon, Dr. Martin Luther King, Jr., Mao Tse-Tung, Robert F. Williams, Karl Marx, Albert Camus, James Baldwin, W. E. B. Du Bois, and others played an important role in formulating the ideologies of students pursuing Black Power and self-determination during those years, for many Malcolm X became their ideological father.

During this era of Black Power, student activism operated on two fronts—in the community and on the campus. Students (and former students) belonged to organizations such as SNCC, the Congress of Racial Equality (CORE), Revolutionary Action Movement (RAM), and the Black Panther Party (BPP) that targeted issues and problems facing the African American community. During the black campus movement between 1965 and 1972, BSUs were organized at predominantly white institutions; and at black universities the student government associations (SGAs) attempted to make their educational experiences more "relevant" to themselves and their communities and pursued initiatives such as Black Studies programs.[7] In both spaces, the community and the campus, many of the principal objectives and tactics were grounded in Malcolm's ideology.

This essay explores the dissemination of Malcolm's ideological perspectives among black and white students through his speaking engagements at numerous colleges and universities throughout the United States. Malcolm chose specifically to focus on black youth because he viewed this segment of the African American community as a vanguard revolutionary force. I also describe how Malcolm's ideology blossomed into the philosophical foundation of the leaders of two important student-led Black Power organizations—Stokely Carmichael (Kwame Ture) of SNCC, and Huey P. Newton of the Black Panther Party.[8] And finally, Malcolm's ideas took on new life among students pursuing Black Power on college campuses in the late 1960s and early 1970s.

MALCOLM X ON CAMPUS

Malcolm X purposefully sought to spread his ideas among African American students by speaking at numerous colleges and universities across the nation and other venues with large student audiences. In the last years of his life, he predicted that black youth would be at the forefront of any radical black mass movement, and by the time of his death young people were beginning to make him their prophet. In an interview on 19 March 1964 after he left the Nation of Islam, Malcolm indicated that his "accent will be upon youth." Malcolm and his associates by this time had already issued a call for college students around the nation "to launch their own independent studies of the race problem," so they could devise an "action program geared to their thinking." At variance with traditional left-wing Marxist thought that considered the white working class as the faction with the most revolutionary potential, Malcolm in his speeches positioned black students as the chief change agents because this "new generation" had less of a stake than adults "in this corrupt system and therefore [could] look at it more objectively."[9] To his way of thinking, black adults, including the working class, were tied to the older and more conservative civil rights establishment. Malcolm consciously sought to ideologically nurture this "new generation of black people who [had] come on the scene" because they were "disenchanted" and "disillusioned over the system," and were "willing to do something about it." They had reached the point of no return "out of frustration and hopelessness."[10] After traveling to Africa in April 1964 where he was personally welcomed by crowds of students at African universities, Malcolm internationalized his appeal to students at the first Organization of Afro-American Unity (OAAU) rally on 29 November 1964. "The students all over the world are the ones who bring about a change; old people don't bring about a change."[11]

Malcolm X believed that black students were aggravated and desperate, discontented and cynical, and ready to pursue radical change. Deciding to ideologically adopt and nurture rebellious youth, Malcolm embraced as many opportunities as possible to speak to students at colleges and universities and in the last year of his life, he was second only to Republican presidential candidate Senator Barry Goldwater as the most requested speaker.[12] White students also clamored to hear Malcolm, but these hundreds of lectures were critical in the ideological formation of African American students, whose ideas and actions were greatly influenced by Malcolm's historical and contemporary analysis. Black students were eager to hear him and Malcolm came to relish his role as "master teacher," as he "appealed to their sense of justice." As Benjamin Karim, Malcolm's assistant minister, recalled, "He invited them to open their minds, to think, to call upon their knowledge and logic in order to see the fallacies of America's past and to imagine its future possibilities."[13]

Radical black nationalist students enrolled in colleges and universities in the early 1960s were often critical of civil rights groups' nonviolent methods, and sought a new line of thought and action. This small band of activists would soon reach a critical mass in number and influence and transform the black student movement from civil rights concerns to Black Power activism. They were found jockeying for positions of leadership in SGAs at black colleges, campus chapters of the NAACP, CORE, SNCC, and other civil rights organizations and cultural groups, and they were able to use these organizational ties and resources to invite Malcolm to their campuses.[14] Like BSUs that emerged in the late 1960s, these student groups used their meager funds to bring to campus people who were known to educate and electrify their audiences. For example, at the University of Southern California on 23 March 1958, Malcolm decried African Americans' "wretched condition," which was "the by-product of the hypocrisy which [was] skillfully cloaked in the disguise of Western Democracy."[15] At an interracial seminar at Boston University in March 1960, with hundreds of Harvard University and Massachusetts Institute of Technology students in attendance, Malcolm denounced the hypocrisy of black and white liberals who offered excuses for racist violence in the North and the South.[16] According to Queens College student Gay E. Plair in 1960, Malcolm facilitated a "challenging and stimulating discussion" there, which prompted the Queens NAACP to invite him back to speak to that group in 1961.[17] The University of Pennsylvania, Princeton University, University of California, Berkeley, and Upsala, Hunter, and Morehouse colleges were only some of the college campuses Malcolm visited in 1960 and 1961.[18]

One of his most highly publicized appearances was at the Harvard University Law School Forum on 24 March 1961 where Malcolm addressed an overflow crowd in the university's largest auditorium. "As your colleges and universities turn out an ever-increasing number of so-called Negro graduates with education equal to yours," Malcolm declared, "they will automatically increase their demands for equality in everything else."[19] In early 1962 Malcolm lectured at Antioch College and at New York University where he stimulated "countless corridor conversations" and the African American Club asked him to come back later in the year.[20] Also in 1962 Malcolm accepted an invitation to speak at Michigan State University that came from Ayo C. Azikiwe, the leader of the university's African Students Association and son of the future Nigerian president Nnamdi Azikiwe.[21] In addition to Michigan State, Malcolm addressed students at Oakland University, Columbia University, Long Island University, Jersey City State, Trinity, Adelphi, St. Francis, Williams, and Smith colleges in 1962.[22]

The list of college campuses Malcolm visited in 1963 is even longer.[23] In addition to his trips to Africa and the Middle East in 1964, Malcolm was invited to speak at the University of Chicago, University of Connecticut, Cornell University, Wisconsin State at Whitewater, Tuskegee Institute, and Columbia University.[24] His invitation to speak at Yale University in 1964 came from Yale student and future presidential candidate John Kerry, who wrote: "May I stress how much we would like to have you come." Malcolm's invitation to speak at

Harvard University in 1964 came from Professor Henry A. Kissinger, who later served as Richard Nixon's secretary of state.[25]

Many of Malcolm's speaking engagements at colleges and universities involved debates, and on those occasions Malcolm leaned on the debating skills he honed while in prison. At Yale University in 1960 Malcolm debated Herbert Wright, the NAACP national youth secretary.[26] The following year, Malcolm was matched up with Herbert Wright again, this time at City College of New York in an event hosted by the campus NAACP, where over three hundred people heard Malcolm famously declare, "[I]t'll take more than a cup of tea in a white restaurant to make us happy."[27] On 17 March 1961 at Clark College in Atlanta, Malcolm was paired with the famed Morehouse theology and philosophy professor, Rev. Samuel Williams.[28] At Rutgers University, student Edwin Stevens reported that Malcolm "outclassed" political science professor Neal Brown in a debate hosted by the NAACP in 1961, which "awakened and delighted the apathetic and sleeping among us."[29] At Morgan State College in Baltimore in March 1962, Malcolm faced off against historian August Meier, an occasion Morgan State student G. Fraser Williams believed "will surely be recorded as one of the most memorable ones in the history of our . . . campus."[30] At Cornell University in 1962, Malcolm debated CORE's chairman James Farmer in an exchange dubbed "Separation versus Integration." Historian Donald Anthony Downs concluded that "though Malcolm's message was strange for the Cornell of that time, it was about to grow in influence as new students arrived on campus."[31]

Malcolm's most famous public debate was with Bayard Rustin, internationally known peace activist and advisor to Dr. Martin Luther King. The debate took place on 31 October 1961 at Howard University's 1,500-seat Crampton Auditorium with hundreds more standing outside wanting to enter. Renowned sociologist E. Franklin Frazier moderated the debate, titled "Integration or Separation." The event was hosted by Howard's student government and the Nonviolent Action Group (NAG), an organization affiliated with SNCC. Stokely Carmichael, a member of NAG, would bring Malcolm's version of black nationalism to the ideological foreground in SNCC in the late 1960s. "The black man in America will never be equal to the white man as long as he attempts to force himself into his house," Malcolm argued at one point. "The real problem is that the anemic Negro leader, who survives and sometimes thrives off of gifts from white people, is dependent upon the white man whom he gives false information about the masses of black people." Malcolm's captivating performance permanently etched itself in the minds of many Howard students. Carmichael explained decades later, "To this very day, whenever—and wherever—I meet people who were at Howard with us, that is what they seem to remember first." For Carmichael, it was a decisive moment in his ideological development. At the time, a "European theoretical context" anchored his political worldview. But what "Malcolm demonstrated that night . . . was the raw power, the visceral potency of the group, our unarticulated collective blackness. . . . I'll never forget it." Malcolm's storied impact led one unidentified professor to tell reporters, "Howard will never be the same. I feel a reluctance to face my class tomorrow."[32]

Malcolm also spoke to many student groups not affiliated with colleges. He participated in the 1962 "Frontiers Seminar" organized by the National Student Christian Federation, which, according to the group's leader Evelyn C. Fortna, "meant a tremendous amount to [those] young people."[33] In 1963 Malcolm spoke at an "in service to youth" program hosted by VISTA, the domestic Peace Corps program.[34] That year students asked Malcolm to speak at the Northeast Regional Methodist Student Movement Conference, as did the Boston branch of the Pan-African Students' Organization.[35] Representatives of New York City's Young Women's Christian Association declared, "[We] shall long remember" Malcolm's participation in a panel on 13 November 1963.[36]

In the last few months of his life in particular, Malcolm reached out to black student activists working in the South. At the Hotel Theresa in Harlem on 31 December 1964, Malcolm shared his ideas with a delegation of thirty-seven teenage SNCC activists from McComb, Mississippi. Malcolm impressed upon the students to take control of their ideological development, refrain from practicing nonviolence with people who do not practice it with them, and to avoid the inactivity of many of his generation who "sat around like a knot on a wall while the whole world was fighting for its human rights," a direct criticism of the older civil rights leadership. According to Stokely Carmichael, Malcolm made "a hell of an impression" on these students. "The youth came back elated, just elated, talking about nothing but Malcolm."[37]

On 3 February 1965 Malcolm X spoke to 3,000 students at Tuskegee Institute in Alabama: "I'm not willing to sit and wait on God to come. If he doesn't come soon, it will be too late. I believe in religion, but a religion that includes political, economic, and social action designed to eliminate some of these things, and make a paradise here on earth while we're waiting for the other."[38] After leaving Tuskegee, Malcolm traveled to nearby Selma, Alabama, where SNCC organizers had invited him to speak. Malcolm lectured to 300 young civil rights organizers at Brown Chapel AME Church, expounding on the differences between the "house Negro and field Negro" mentalities.[39] With these two important speeches, Malcolm ideologically nurtured those in Alabama pursuing black self-determination. In 1965 the growing disagreements and resentments between Dr. King and SNCC activists over the Selma to Montgomery march, the organizing of the all-black Lowndes County Freedom Organization, and the rise in popularity of militant SNCC activist Sammy Younge, Jr., who was killed in 1966, further radicalized black student workers. Those SNCC members who had moved away from Dr. King's nonviolent strategies by 1965 more closely identified with the positions taken by Malcolm X. Even though Black Power was launched into the political mainstream during the James Meredith march in Mississippi in June 1966, the groundwork had been laid in Alabama and other locations by Malcolm X in the preceding years.

Malcolm X at Tuskegee Institute, February 1965.
Courtesy of Tuskegee University Library and Archives.

On 18 February 1965, three days before Malcolm was murdered, he spoke to 1,500 students at Barnard College and Columbia University. This was his last major speech before his ideological offspring. It was also his last public speech, and Malcolm conveyed the fearlessness, the demands for justice and equality, and the flexibility of tactics that would all come to dominate student activism in the Black Power era. "I would rather be dead than have someone deprive me of my rights," he declared. "[The African American] must take any means necessary to secure his full rights as an individual human being. Our demands are just, and we will use any means to get them."[40]

Before his death, Malcolm had every reason to believe he had succeeded in one of his final goals—the creation of a radicalized cohort of black students. As he told Vassar College administrator C. H. L. Pennock in 1962, "Student groups throughout America are showing great interest."[41] After Malcolm spoke at these schools, many students sent him letters conveying their support for his ideological positions.[42] Robert Johann, a 21-year-old from New Jersey, who had just been diagnosed with an incurable illness, asked Malcolm for a card with his autograph: "You have always been a great hero of mine. I mean every word of this."[43] University of New Hampshire's Joseph B. Axenroth informed Malcolm that he agreed "with everything" Malcolm had shared in an earlier letter.[44] In 1963 Malcolm instructed Muslim student Martin Miller that college students were "beginning to see that more than 'education' [stood] between them and the White man."[45] Shortly after Malcolm spoke at her unidentified college in 1963, Maxine Sprott dispatched a letter: "Because I am worried about the future and realizing that worry without action accomplishes nothing, I decided to write you to find out just what *I* can do."[46] Lou Holland praised Malcolm's use of cogent analogies and apt metaphors when he spoke at his school.[47] Anne Donaldson, representing her peers at the University of Bridgeport, told Malcolm they "thoroughly enjoyed" his speech there.[48]

Malcolm received numerous requests from students seeking information about his ideological positions to include in their class projects and seminar papers. A night school student at City College sent Malcolm a questionnaire for a class project in 1962. "I feel that I can benefit as well as educate myself in understanding what you as a leader are trying to do for our people," Marva J. King wrote.[49] In the early 1960s Malcolm received written requests for information for research papers from students at Wells College, St. Bonaventure University, Allegheny College, Washington University, and other schools.[50] Requesting an interview for an oral report in an English class in 1963, Carole Hewitt, a high school senior, told Malcolm, "I have attended a few of your meetings and I am quite impressed."[51] Leonard C. Simmons, a social work student at Case Western Reserve University in Cleveland, Ohio, wanted Malcolm to describe the workings of the Muslims' rehabilitation program for prisoners, drug addicts, and alcoholics.[52] Charged with asking an outstanding individual about the best verse in the Old Testament, Michael Blatt, a ninth grader at a school in New Jersey, sought out Malcolm's view as well.[53]

When he decided to leave the Nation of Islam in 1964 and organize the Muslim Mosque Inc. and later the Organization of Afro-American Unity, many students informed Malcolm about their willingness to join his newly proposed "united front."[54] In an April 1964 speech Malcolm announced he would attempt to forge a "black nationalist party," and reported that he received a great deal of mail from college students "who expressed complete sympathy and support and a desire to take an active part in any kind of political action based on black nationalism, designed to correct or eliminate immediately evils that our people have suffered here for 400 years."[55] These sentiments were echoed in a letter to a Bay Area psychology student Eleanor Mason in March 1964.[56] Michigan State University's Ayo C. Azikiwe, who had stayed in touch after Malcolm spoke at his school in 1962, gave Malcolm his "blessing in [his] new move to uphold the dignity of the black [man]."[57]

MALCOLM'S IMPACT ON BLACK LEADERS AND ORGANIZATIONS

A new generation of young black leaders was inspired by Malcolm X either directly through reading his words, or hearing one of Malcolm's many lectures at colleges and universities and other locations across the country; or indirectly from other individuals or groups that passed on the information. Stokely Carmichael and Huey P. Newton were two of the most prominent leaders of the Black Power Movement who were directly inspired by Malcolm X. Two years after graduating from Howard University, Carmichael assumed leadership of SNCC in 1966; and Huey Newton, along with Bobby Seale, founded the Black Panther Party that same year. Carmichael and Newton had heard Malcolm speak in the early 1960s, but the NOI theology was unattractive to both. Yet, as they developed ideologically and as Malcolm changed and disavowed much of the NOI theology, adding and refining ideas of black nationalism and self-defense, Carmichael and Newton became Malcolm's disciples, as did thousands of black youth by the late 1960s.

In the spring of 1966, Stokely Carmichael became the chairman of SNCC, and by the summer of that year, he became nationally known as the major exponent of "Black Power." Carmichael spent the next few years speaking about and defending his ideological principles. As Carmichael grew in prominence, so did the comparisons to Malcolm X. Filmmaker Charles Hartman in 1966 wanted to document Carmichael's tour of Africa and his meetings with African leaders and students in a film, since Malcolm's description of his trips to Africa was "one of the most fascinating parts of his autobiography."[58] In 1967 Rev. Albert Cleage, a fiery black nationalist preacher in Detroit and friend of Malcolm, declared, "Malcolm X laid the entire foundation for everything Stokely Carmichael says."[59] By 1967

Carmichael had become the "poster boy" for black student activism, with Malcolm X looming in the background.

Malcolm's tutelage began when Carmichael was a teenager growing up in New York City. Along with other great public speakers, Malcolm X became a "street-corner orator" in Harlem in the late 1950s speaking to thousands. As a high school student, Carmichael heard about Malcolm's chastisement of Harlem youngsters shooting craps on 135th Street, outside of the New York Public Library's Schomburg Collection, instead of going inside and studying their history and culture. This impressed upon Carmichael the importance of the Schomburg Collection. Later, when Carmichael enrolled at Howard University, he packed into the television room with his peers to watch programs featuring Malcolm X and novelist and social critic James Baldwin. The "attitudes" of Carmichael and his peers were "informed by their examples," Carmichael recalled. "I don't know if these two brothers ever fully understood just how much they meant, how crucially important, how painfully necessary, their kind of bold representation in those times was for our age set."[60]

When Malcolm left the Nation of Islam and founded the Muslim Mosque Inc., James Shabazz, Malcolm's secretary, notified SNCC organizers that Malcolm wanted to work with the organization.[61] During the last three months of his life, Malcolm spoke directly to SNCC members on at least three occasions. These meetings were central in the growth and development of SNCC's black members and their movement toward Malcolm's ideological positions.[62] SNCC teachers required the students in their freedom schools in Mississippi to read Malcolm's autobiography and his most famous speeches.[63] Historian Clayborne Carson observed, "As the thrust of SNCC's activities shifted from desegregation to political rights, its philosophical commitment to nonviolent direct action gave way to a secular, humanistic radicalism influenced by Marx, Camus, and Malcolm X."[64] Cleveland Sellers, who helped spearhead that ideological shift, also made reference to the move in 1966 of SNCC's black organizers toward "Malcolm X in terms of [their] thinking, [their] orientation."[65]

When SNCC leaders traveled to Africa in 1964, they could not ignore the profound influence Malcolm had on young Africans. As they traveled from country to country, SNCC leaders were continuously asked about their organization's relationship to Malcolm X. John Lewis, SNCC chairman at the time, later recalled, "[Malcolm] became a measuring rod in every one of our encounters."[66] When SNCC members arrived at their hotel in Kenya, they encountered Malcolm who had just come from Tanzania. SNCC leaders and Malcolm conferred at the hotel for the next two days.[67] Malcolm told them, "Don't give up. This is an ongoing struggle. People are changing . . . people all over the world are supporting you."[68] After this meeting in which Malcolm shared with them his ideas about

Pan-African cooperation, and his plans to go before the United Nations to denounce the racist practices in the United States, SNCC leaders began to "place stronger emphasis on developing alliances with African liberation organizations that were fighting colonialism, and with progressive African states."[69] Through this exchange of ideas and the influence of Malcolm's writings, SNCC members grew more aware of the international implications of African American oppression.[70]

In 1964 the Revolutionary Action Movement's (RAM) Max Stanford (later Muhammad Ahmad) helped to organize at Fisk University the first "Afro-American Student Conference on Black Nationalism." The Afro-American Student Movement (ASM), a group affiliated with SNCC and led by Michele Paul and Betty Rush, hosted the conference. According to Ahmad, "The consensus of the conferees was that African-Americans needed to control their own neighborhoods, similar to what Malcolm X was teaching at the time." The students declared support for Malcolm's vision of taking the case of U.S. African Americans before the United Nations. They called for a "cultural revolution" and increased emphasis on Pan-Africanism. Several of the conference's "Thirteen Points for Implementation" resembled the "Basic Aims and Objectives" of Malcolm's OAAU.[71]

The conference led to a major policy decision by SNCC chairman John Lewis.[72] Early in 1965 Lewis added Ronald Snellings (later Askia Mohammed Toure) and Max Stanford to the Mississippi field staff so they could experiment with building a "black self-defense project," a clear reflection of Malcolm's urging SNCC organizers to engage in self-defense. For example, on 5 July 1964 at the second rally of his Organization of Afro-American Unity, Malcolm publicized his recommendation to SNCC that an armed contingent of brothers be sent to the South to protect civil rights workers if the federal government was unwilling to do it.[73] According to Ahmad, the militant nationalists revolted against the Mississippi leadership, including legendary SNCC organizer Bob Moses and many progressive whites. The revolutionary nationalists argued that whites should not be used to organize, empower, and educate black communities in Mississippi, and instead they should organize in the white community to "divide the white racist front." These militant nationalist members on SNCC's Mississippi field staff met in the early summer of 1965 to discuss shifting the principles of the student organization to, among other things, armed self defense and an alliance with RAM.[74]

By the summer of 1965 many of the newer members of SNCC were not reading Mahatma Gandhi and Henry David Thoreau, but *The Ballot or the Bullet* and *Malcolm X Speaks*.[75] According to Gloria House, they began talking about Malcolm's ideas. "We internalized them and we were moving out of this consciousness towards what later was coined Black Power."[76] Then with the launching of the Lowndes County Freedom Organization in Alabama, an independent black political organization along the lines Malcolm had envisioned, a group of SNCC's black members presented a position paper at a 1966 staff meeting calling for the expulsion of whites in favor of their working in white communities. Carmichael soon replaced Lewis as SNCC's chairperson, and by June 1966 Carmichael was calling for "Black Power."[77]

By 1966 SNCC as an organization became an embodiment of ideological positions associated with Malcolm X.[78] SNCC members reprinted and circulated Malcolm's writings, as well as articles about him and his work such as John Henrik Clarke's essay "Malcolm X—The Man and His Mission" and SNCC's report "The Murder of Malcolm X."[79] The members began to advocate and practice black self-defense, economic and political self-determination, cultural pride, and Pan-Africanism. After "carefully" reading *Malcolm X Speaks* and Malcolm's "criticism of the term *civil rights*, and his advocacy of *human rights* in its place," James Forman formulated a resolution adopted at a June 1967 SNCC staff meeting. It was resolved that SNCC was a "human rights" organization, "working for the liberation not only of black people in the United States, but of all oppressed peoples, especially those in Africa, Asia, and Latin America."[80]

At various points in time, Black Panther leaders Bobby Seale and Eldridge Cleaver claimed that Huey P. Newton was "the heir of Malcolm X."[81] An unidentified contributor to *The Black Panther* newspaper declared, "Huey P. Newton . . . is the man who went forth and implemented all of the things that Malcolm X talked about and what Malcolm was teaching."[82] As was the case with Stokely Carmichael, Newton came under the influence of Malcolm X at a young age. In his memoir Newton described how he taught himself to read while in high school, and like Malcolm, the acquisition of literacy "changed forever" the course of Newton's life and a "whole new world opened up." Newton first heard Malcolm speak in the early 1960s at McClymonds High School in Oakland during a conference sponsored by the Bay Area's Afro-American Association, a black nationalist student group. "Malcolm X impressed me with his logic and with his disciplined and dedicated mind," Newton explained. "Here was a man who combined the world of the streets and the world of the scholar, a man so widely read he could give better lectures and cite more evidence than many college professors." After this first encounter, Newton visited Muslim mosques in Oakland and San Francisco and talked to black Muslims, but he did not join the Nation of Islam.[83] However, Newton did heed Malcolm's call for African Americans to learn their history. Malcolm's admonition served as a spark for the decision to demand the offering of a black history course at Merritt College where Newton was a member of the Soul Student Advisory Council (SSAC) in 1966.

While in SSAC, Newton suggested that the group organize a symbolic demonstration on Malcolm's birthday (May 19) and invite armed community members to campus displaying their weapons of self-defense. When SSAC leaders rejected this idea, Newton and Bobby Seale realized this group did not reflect Malcolm's goals, so they left the organization and subsequently organized "the Black Panther Party for Self Defense" (BPP).[84] Unlike SNCC, the party attempted to pursue Malcolm's goals and strategies from the beginning. In 1966 when Newton and Seale were shaping the philosophy of the Black Panther Party, they read and studied carefully the speeches and writings of Malcolm X. According to Newton, Malcolm was the chief inspiration for the formation, mission, and program of the Black Panther Party.

> Malcolm's influence was ever-present. We continue to believe that the Black Panther Party exists in the spirit of Malcolm. . . . The words on this page cannot convey the effect that Malcolm has had on the Black Panther Party. . . . As far as I am concerned, the Party is a living testament to his life's work.[85]

The Black Panther Party's famous "Ten-Point Program" reflected the Nation of Islam's platform published every week in *Muhammad Speaks*.[86] Moreover, one can find that Malcolm fully supported all ten points of the BPP program at various points in his public career. Malcolm preached black self-determination (point one); and he often chided American governmental and economic leaders for failing to provide decent employment opportunities for African Americans (point two).[87] He questioned the ability of black people to thrive in a capitalist economy, given their exploited status (point three); and he condemned the inadequate housing conditions in Harlem and black neighborhoods across the country (point four).[88] Throughout his public career Malcolm emphasized the importance of studying and learning about black history and culture (point five).[89] And beginning when he was a spokesperson for the Nation of Islam, he often chastised African Americans who participated in U.S. military operations, particularly those launched against oppressed colored peoples (point six).[90] Malcolm responded with passion and determination to incidences of police brutality against black Muslims in Harlem in 1957 and Los Angeles in 1962 (point seven).[91] Having spent many years in the U.S. prison system, Malcolm demanded prison reform and institutional change (points eight and nine).[92] The BPP's call for the United Nations or other international bodies to intercede on behalf of oppressed African Americans (point ten) mirrored Malcolm's objectives for the OAAU.[93]

Modeled after *Muhammad Speaks*, launched by Malcolm X in 1960, *The Black Panther* newspaper, founded in 1967, pledged its "allegiance" to Malcolm.[94] For most Black Panthers, Malcolm was their "prophet," who served as "the fore runner of the Afro-American struggle"; and "the Black Panther Party is an organizational manifestation of the teachings of Brother Malcolm X."[95] As "the heirs of Malcolm X," the Panther newspaper honored him regularly and announced memorials and commemorations in issues published near the dates of his birth and assassination.[96] For example, in February 1967 the Panthers publicized and participated in the week-long commemoration held in the Bay Area, which opened with a speech by Malcolm's widow, Betty Shabazz.[97] In May 1969 after Malcolm's birthday, an unidentified contributor to the newspaper declared, "We of the BLACK PANTHER PARTY and Black People all over the nation say 'Power' to Brother Malcolm and his death will not have been in vain."[98] Another Panther wrote in 1971, "Malcolm taught us and begged us to take hold of our lives, over which only we ourselves should have control. That was his gift, ongoing, even now, as our struggle develops each year."[99]

Throughout the BPP's existence, Malcolm X's autobiography and *Malcolm X Speaks* were required readings for its youthful members and were used as texts in the political education classes.[100] Editorial writers in *The Black Panther* often quoted Malcolm X, and the paper published excerpts from his speeches.[101] In November 1968 Freddie Anderson rebuked the mainstream press for not reporting on the "genocidal killing" of black people by white cops. And even "when they do," Anderson argued, "it's put in the middle of the papers or in the back. And as Malcolm X once said, 'they make the victim look like the criminal, and the criminal look like the victim.'"[102] In reflecting on the origin of the BPP, one Panther reporter declared, "Our Party looked at history and decided that the old ways weren't good enough; . . . that black people must organize themselves, support themselves and defend themselves, like Malcolm X said: 'There can be no black-white unity until there is black unity.'"[103]

MALCOLM X AND BLACK STUDENT ACTIVISM

In the late 1960s while black youth in SNCC, the Black Panther Party, and other community-based organizations were studying Malcolm's messages and acting to achieve the goals he sought, black students on campuses across the United States organized among themselves to make higher education more relevant to their needs and aspirations. Nothing demonstrated Malcolm's impact on black higher education more than the development of two colleges named in his honor— Chicago's Malcolm X College and Malcolm X Liberation University (MXLU) in Durham, North Carolina. Formerly Crane Junior College, Malcolm X College was named after the Black Power pioneer in 1969 to "serve as a catalytic agent to synthesize the varied components of the community into a viable force for liberation"; and it remains in operation as a two-year college.[104] Likewise, Malcolm X

Liberation University was organized by black students in North Carolina who believed that their schools could not address their demands for a more relevant education.[105] A portrait of Malcolm was painted at the main entrance to Malcolm X Liberation University and the painting included the statement that this was a school for members of "a new generation of black people who have become disenchanted with the entire system and who are ready now and willing to do something about it." Opened with fifty-nine students in the fall of 1969, it was, according to its director Howard Fuller, "a nation-building school, a school for people who want to build an independent African nation and who want to be doing things right things now."[106]

Some of the students who traced the beginnings of their own activism directly to Malcolm's influence recorded their responses to the news of his assassination on 21 February 1965. In *Seize the Time*, Bobby Seale began his personal narrative and account of the origins of the Black Panther Party with the death of Malcolm X.

> When Malcolm X was killed in 1965, I ran down the street. I went to my mother's house, and I got six loose red bricks from the garden. I got the corner, and broke the motherfuckers in half. . . . Every time I saw a paddy roll by in a car, I picked up one of the half-bricks, and threw it at the motherfuckers. I threw about half the bricks, and then I cried like a baby. I was righteously crying. I was pissed off and mad.[107]

Like scores of black students across the country, Andrea Coaxum of Boston University wept when she learned of Malcolm X's murder.[108] Many black students organized and held services and rallies in Malcolm's honor such as the ones at Southern Illinois University and San Francisco State College.[109]

The urban insurrections, the War on Poverty, and expanded financial aid programs from the federal government led to increasing numbers of African American students enrolled in U.S. colleges and universities in the second half of the 1960s.[110] These new students were welcomed by many of the initiators of the black campus movement who had heard Malcolm speak in the early 1960s and had become committed to his program for black advancement. For example, Gwen Patton, who heard Malcolm's speech at Tuskegee in February 1965, became Tuskegee's SGA president in the fall of that year and led her student body in demanding and protesting for a more relevant "black" education.[111] These pioneers were joined in the late 1960s by a critical mass of black student activists who created organizations and demanded spaces on predominantly white campuses for black students to meet and organize ongoing activities.[112] Many believe that the nation's first BSU was formed at San Francisco State College in the spring of 1966. James Garrett, one of the organizers of this BSU and a former member of SNCC, remembered that he and his comrades specifically chose the term "black" to harness a particular wave of consciousness spreading across the United States at that time—a wave unleashed by the teachings of Malcolm X. "There was a national consciousness that was developing and consolidating," Garrett recalled. "Blackness was the new consciousness or the consolidation of a consciousness that came from Malcolm X."[113] Over the next few years, hundreds of BSUs were formed, or preexisting groups were renamed, adding "black" or "Afro-American" to their titles.

At the height of black student activism, from the assassination of Dr. King in April 1968 through the end of the 1968–1969 school year, "the philosophy of Malcolm X" inspired many of the black student activists' "demands."[114] Reflecting Malcolm's commitment to self-determination, these students demanded "separate facilities in which to conduct alternative educational and cultural activities." Historian William Van Deburg noted that these separate facilities included living, dining, and meeting areas, autonomous departments of Black Studies, along with demands for more black students, faculty, coaches, players, administrators, and resources.[115]

In a speech in London on 11 February 1965, Malcolm declared, "If something is yours by right, then you fight for it or shut up. If you can't fight for it, then forget it."[116] Following this advice, when university administrators failed to move immediately on students' demands, they often demonstrated their willingness to "fight for it" by occupying campus offices and buildings, and organizing demonstrations and strikes. The spirit of Malcolm X hovered over these demonstrations. At Howard University in April 1965, campus activists marched on their administration building to protest the autocratic practices and policies of university administrators. As Jerrold Roy, a chronicler of the Howard protests, explained, "Malcolm X's impact on the Howard student movement loomed larger after his death than when he was alive."[117]

In November 1967 at Central State University in Wilberforce, Ohio, the black student group "Unity for Unity" led a boycott of classes and pickets around campus in support of the college's non-academic workers who went on strike for higher wages and employer-funded life insurance. The students also demanded black history courses for academic credit, and asked that Malcolm's autobiography and *Malcolm X Speaks* be added to the university's library.[118] In March 1968 when more than 1,200 students took over Howard University's administration building, they gained control of the university speaker-system and played recordings of Malcolm's speeches and read from his autobiography.[119] A few days before Dr. King's assassination on 4 April 1968, students at Cheyney State College in Pennsylvania issued their demand to change the school "from a Negro institution to a black one," and called for "more emphasis on writers like W. E. B. Du Bois, James Baldwin, and Malcolm X, than [William] Shakespeare and [Henry

Wadsworth] Longfellow."[120] When students at Columbia University in New York City occupied buildings in April 1968, black students seized Hamilton Hall and hung posters of Malcolm outside the main entrance and a cardboard sign proclaiming "Malcolm X University, Founded 1968 A.D."[121]

In October 1968 twelve black student activists at the University of California, Santa Barbara, barricaded themselves inside North Hall, renaming it "Malcolm X Hall," and refused to come out until their eight demands for a "more relevant education" were met. When the BSU members at San Francisco State College held a press conference in early November 1968, before the four-and-a-half month student strike, BSU chairman Ben Stewart credited "Brother Malcolm X, by his courageous life and character," with laying the "foundation for the struggle." In January 1969, sixty-four black students at Brandeis University in Medford, Massachusetts, barricaded themselves inside a building, issued their demands, and then draped a huge sheet from a second story window that displayed a photograph of Malcolm, declaring the building to be part of "Malcolm X University." When they walked out of the building eleven days later, all of the students wore badges displaying the figure of Malcolm X.[122]

At Voorhees College in Denmark, South Carolina, seventy-five black student activists, armed with guns and knives, took over the administration building in March 1969, and proclaimed the institution "the liberated Malcolm X University," plastered the walls with posters of Malcolm, and issued a list of demands, including the establishment of a Black Studies department.[123] More than 1,000 students boycotted classes in February 1969 to support a demand for a new college at University of California, Santa Cruz, to be named in honor of Malcolm X. Later that month, at Duke University in Durham, North Carolina, forty-eight black students entered the administration building, walked to the central records section, told the clerical workers they had to leave, nailed the doors shut, threatened to burn university records if the police were called, and renamed the area "Malcolm X Liberation School."[124] At West Virginia State University, the historically black school in Institute, student activists seized an administration building in March 1970 after college officials refused to name a dormitory after Malcolm X.[125] These spaces were seized by students to convert them into places where their ideological goals would be pursued. Malcolm X personified what they understood as "relevant" in their lives and the world around them. It was a tribute to their ideological father figure whose words inspired them to claim those spaces to demand social and educational change.

The creation of Black Studies programs became the institutional manifestation of this educational change. However, even before courses were offered and departments organized, black students were reading Malcolm's works on their own. In the summer of 1966, there were 220 government-financed Upward Bound programs set up on college campuses to improve the academic skills of high school students, and in many of these courses *The Autobiography of Malcolm X* was required reading.[126] In the fall of 1966, black students at Wesleyan University in Middletown, Connecticut, founded a reading group and together read *The Autobiography of Malcolm X*.[127] In the spring of 1967, Malcolm's autobiography was one of the two most widely read books among black students. The other was Claude Brown's *Manchild in the Promised Land*.[128] When Black Studies courses began to be offered on many campuses in 1968, the speeches and the autobiography of Malcolm X were studied systematically.[129] Black campus groups read excerpts from his speeches at their meetings and engaged in long and serious discussions on the significance of his words and teachings.[130] And many black students, like Clarence Thomas, a freshman at the College of the Holy Cross in Worchester, Massachusetts, in 1968, and later U.S. Supreme Court Justice, participated in tributes and commemorations and hung huge posters of Malcolm X in their dormitory rooms.[131]

CONCLUSION

Since assassins killed Malcolm X only about a year after he left the Nation of Islam, he did not have enough time to implement many of the ideas that became so inspiring to African American students and many others. Through remembering their past encounters with Malcolm, hearing Malcolm's continuous admonitions to the "new generation" to rebel, hearing recordings of his speeches, and reading the autobiography, black students and other Black Power activists were inspired to put Malcolm's ideas into action. They were his "natural constituency" when he was alive, and they became his constituent legacy after his death. Malcolm X became the ideological father for black student activists during the Black Power era; their "Black and Shining Prince" who sat on his rhetorical throne.

During a period when students demanded authenticity and respected boldness, they deemed Malcolm the boldest and the most genuine. In an era of standing up to white America and standing for black love, no one appeared to stand higher and stronger than Malcolm X. For the disaffected, disillusioned, dissatisfied black youth across the ideological spectrum, Malcolm became a reflection of boldness, honesty, confrontational behavior, fearless dedication, unvarying defense of self, black pride, the veneration of Africa, black unity, and willingness to make the ultimate sacrifice. To the youth, no other leader could boast so strikingly *all* of these qualities. "Malcolm was the only figure of that generation, the only one, who had the natural authority, the style, language, and charisma, to lead and discipline rank-and-file urban youth," Stokely Carmichael declared. "The only one who commanded that kind of respect."[132]

NOTES

I would like to thank V. P. Franklin, Muhammad Ahmad, Weckea Lilly, and the anonymous reviewers for *The Journal of African American History* for offering their extremely helpful comments that assisted me in improving this article.

[1]George Breitman, "Appendix E, On the First Anniversary of Malcolm X's Death," in *The Last Year of Malcolm X: The Evolution of a Revolutionary*, ed. George Breitman (New York, 1967), 151–152.

[2]*The Reflector*, 19 March 1968.

[3]Betty Shabazz, "The Legacy of My Husband, Malcolm X," *Ebony*, June 1969, 173.

[4]*Chicago Tribune*, 21 February 1971.

[5]Basic biographical information on Malcolm X can be found in Malcolm X and Alex Haley, *The Autobiography of Malcolm X* (New York, 1965); Bruce Perry, *Malcolm: The Life of the Man Who Changed Black America* (Barrytown, NY, 1992); Manning Marable, *Malcolm X: A Life of Reinvention* (New York, 2011).

[6]Anthony M. Orum, *Black Students in Protest: A Study of the Origins of the Black Student Movement* (Washington, DC, 1968), 80–81; *Sun Reporter*, 27 December 1969; James Turner, "Black Students and Their Changing Perspective," *Ebony*, August 1969, 135; Frederick Harper, *Black Students: White Campus* (Washington, DC, 1975), 9; Jeffrey O. G. Ogbar, *Black Power: Radical Politics and African American Identity* (Baltimore, 2004), 136; Alphonso Pinkney, *Red, Black, and Green: Black Nationalism in the United States* (New York, 1976), 64; Clayborne Carson, *In Struggle: SNCC and the Black Awakening of the 1960s* (Cambridge, MA, 1981), 3; Peniel E. Joseph, *Waiting 'Til the Midnight Hour: A Narrative History of Black Power in America* (New York, 2006), 92; Donald Cunnigen, "Malcolm X's Influence on the Black Nationalist Movement of Southern Black College Students," *Western Journal of Black Studies* 17 (Spring 1993): 32; Donald Alexander Downs, *Cornell '69: Liberalism and the Crisis of the American University* (Ithaca, NY, 1999), 4; Richard P. McCormick, *The Black Student Protest Movement at Rutgers* (New Brunswick, NJ, 1990), 5; Wayne Glasker, *Black Students in the Ivory Tower: African American Student Activism at the University of Pennsylvania, 1967–1990* (Amherst, MA, 2002), 38; William W. Sales, Jr., *From Civil Rights to Black Liberation: Malcolm X and the Organization of Afro-American Unity* (Boston, MA, 1994), 169; William L. Van Deburg, *New Day in Babylon: The Black Power Movement and American Culture, 1965–1975* (Chicago, IL, 1992), 71.

[7]For more information on the black campus movement, see Ibram Rogers, "The Black Campus Movement: An Afrocentric Narrative History of the Struggle to Diversify Higher Education, 1965–1972," Ph.D. diss., Temple University, 2009.

[8]A similar examination could be given on Maxwell Stanford, a leader of RAM, and Maulana Karenga, the founder of the US Organization, two college graduates who led powerful Black Power organizations in the 1960s. See Scot Brown, *Fighting for US: Maulana Karenga, The US Organization and Black Cultural Nationalism* (New York, 2003) and Muhammad Ahmad (Maxwell Stanford, Jr.), *We Will Return in the Whirlwind: Black Radical Organizations, 1960–1975* (Chicago, IL, 2007).

[9]Malcolm X, "Interview by A. B. Spellman," in *By Any Means Necessary: Speeches, Interviews, and a Letter by Malcolm X*, ed. George Breitman (New York, 1970), 6.

[10]Malcolm X, "The Black Revolution," in *Malcolm X Speaks: Selected Speeches and Statements*, ed. George Breitman (New York, 1965), 56; Malcolm X, "Appeal to African Heads of State," in *Malcolm X Speaks*, 76.

[11]Malcolm X, "OAAU Homecoming Rally," in *By Any Means Necessary*, 142.

[12]Malcolm X, "The Harvard Law School Forum of December 16, 1964," in *Malcolm X: Speeches at Harvard*, ed. Archie Epps (New York, 1991), 161.

[13]Benjamin Karim, Peter Skutches, and David Gallen, *Remember Malcolm: The Story of Malcolm X from Inside the Muslim Mosque by His Assistant Minister Benjamin Karim* (New York, 1992), 128.

[14]Some students were denied their request to bring Malcolm, though. For example, see *Afro-American*, 20 May

1961; *Washington Post*, 14 February 1961.

[15]*New York Amsterdam News*, 5 April 1958.

[16]*New York Amsterdam News*, 5 March 1960.

[17]Gay E. Plair to Malcolm X, 8 September 1961, box 3, folder 17, Malcolm X Collection: Papers, 1948–1965, Schomburg Center for Research in Black Culture, New York Public Library, New York, NY (hereafter, Malcolm Collection); Gay Plair to Malcolm X, 24 September 1961, box 3, folder 17, Malcolm Collection.

[18]"Statement," 25 January 1963, box 4, folder 4; Morroe Berger to Malcolm X, 19 September 1961; John Shenis to Malcolm X, 15 December 1961, box 3, folder 17, Malcolm Collection; *Afro-American*, 20 May 1961; *Pittsburg Courier*, 25 February 1961.

[19]Malcolm X, "The Harvard Law School Forum of March 24, 1961," in *Malcolm X: Speeches at Harvard*, 130; *New York Amsterdam News*, 8 April 1961.

[20]H. Lawrence Ross to Malcolm X, 8 February 1962, box 4, folder 3; Audrey Johnson to Malcolm X, 31 August 1962, box 3, folder 17; and Sharon Philbrick to Malcolm X, 23 April 1962, box 4, folder 3, Malcolm Collection.

[21]Malcolm X to Ayo C. Azikiwe, 10 November 1962, box 3, folder 3, Malcolm Collection.

[22]Gerald M. Harris to Malcolm X, 17 September 1962, box 3, folder 8; John Hartman to Malcolm X, 12 February 1962; J. Haywood Harrison to Malcolm X, 13 March 1962; Arthur Lipman to Malcolm X, 9 April 1962; Maher Kamel to Malcolm X, 17 May 1962; Maher Kamel to Malcolm X, 31 July 1962; N. J. Block to Malcolm X, 21 August 1962; Malcolm J. Arth to Malcolm X, 27 August 1962; Thomas F. Burke, Jr., to Malcolm X, 24 September 1962; Robert A. Spivey to Malcolm X, 27 September 1962; Charles Richter to Malcolm X, 13 October 1962; Alexandra Corman to Malcolm X, 18 December 1962, box 3, folder 17, Malcolm Collection.

[23]Among the colleges and universities Malcolm visited in 1963 were Trenton State, City College of New York, Columbia, Amherst College, Brandeis University, Bates College, Lincoln (PA), Ohio University, Rochester Institute of Technology, Friends World College, Syracuse University, Bellarmine College, Wayne State, University of Michigan, Michigan State, Princeton, University of Hartford, Brooklyn College, DePauw, Oberlin, Michigan at Flint, Worcester Polytechnic, Middlebury College, Bowdoin, New York University, Skidmore College, and Dickinson College. See Douglas Harris to Malcolm X, 23 September 1963 and Kathryn Edmonds to Malcolm X, 2 October 1963, box 4, folder 4; Hugh Hawkins to Malcolm X, 29 January 1963; Oliver Fein to Malcolm X, 6 February 1963; Edward Pearlmutter to Malcolm X, n.d.; Pamela Young to Malcolm X; Sylvester Murray to Malcolm X, 13 April 1963; Richard Fernandez to Malcolm X, 17 April 1963; Mike Thelwell to Malcolm X, 16 July 1963; Robert A. Osofoky to Malcolm X, 27 August 1963; Joseph V. Aprile to Malcolm X, 1 September 1963; Ron Jameson to Malcolm X, 2 September 1963; Morroe Berger to Malcolm X, 18 September 1963; William J. Jacobs to Malcolm X, 21 September 1963; Anthony S. to Malcolm X, 25 September 1963; Phil Brown to Malcolm X, 3 October 1963; Carolyn S. Ensor to Malcolm X, 9 October 1963; E. Boundzeki to Malcolm X, 10 October 1963; William Shedd to Malcolm X, 18 October 1963; Lawrence F. Hull to Malcolm X, 29 October 1963; Anne Donaldson to Malcolm X, 30 October 1963; Robert Coults to Malcolm X, 30 October 1963; Donald A. Goldsmith to Malcolm X, 31 October 1963; Irving Kirsch to Malik Shabazz, 8 November 1963; Christine A. to Malcolm X, 18 October 1963, box 3, folder 18; Joseph R. Washington, Jr., 23 January 1963, box 3, folder 19, Malcolm Collection.

[24]Malcolm X to Charles Keil, 21 March 1964, box 3, folder 4; Richard Levinson to Malcolm X, 8 January 1964; William L. England to Malcolm X, 10 March 1964; Jeffrey Cohlberg to Malcolm X, 14 August 1964; Charles J. Graham to Malcolm X, 18 August 1964; Clara Henning to Malcolm X, 24 November 1964, box 3, folder 19, Malcolm Collection.

[25]John F. Kerry to Malcolm X, 15 August 1964; Henry A. Kissinger to Malcolm X, 5 June 1964, box 3, folder 19, Malcolm Collection.

[26]*New Pittsburg Courier*, 29 October 1960.

[27]*New Pittsburg Courier*, 10 March 1961.

[28]*New Pittsburgh Courier*, 25 February 1961.

[29]Edwin Stevens to Malcolm X, 10 November 1961, box 4, folder 3, Malcolm Collection; *Afro-American*, 18 November 1961.

[30]August Meier, "The Black Muslims: A Critique," n.d., box 4, folder 3; G. Fraser Williams to Malcolm X, 2 April 1962, box 3, folder 17, Malcolm Collection.

[31]Downs, *Cornell '69*, 46.

[32]Stokely Carmichael and Ekwueme Michael Thelwell, *Ready for Revolution: The Life and Struggles of Stokely Carmichael (Kwame Ture)* (New York, 2003), 253, 259–60; *Tri-State Defender*, 18 November 1961. For official letter of thanks from Howard student body, see Michael Winston to Malcolm X, 7 November 1961, box 3, folder 17, Malcolm Collection.

[33]Evelyn C. Fortna to Malcolm X, 30 April 1962, box 4, folder 1, Malcolm Collection.

[34]George W. Broadfield to Malcolm X, 14 October 1963, box 3, folder 18, Malcolm Collection.

[35]Charles W. Estus to Malcolm X, 29 June 1963; Aggrey S. Awori to Malcolm X, 6 November 1963, box 3, folder 18, Malcolm Collection.

[36]Hortense Bowery and Sioux Nichols Taylor to Malcolm X, 15 November 1963, box 4, folder 1, Malcolm Collection.

[37]Malcolm X, "To Mississippi Youth," in *Malcolm X Speaks: Selected Speeches and Statements*, 137, 139, 145; Carmichael and Thelwell, *Ready for Revolution,* 440.

[38]Malcolm X, "Elijah Is Willing to Sit and Wait—I'm Not," in *February 1965: The Final Speeches*, ed. Steve Clark (New York, 1993), 22.

[39]Malcolm X, "The House Negro and the Field Negro," in *February 1965 The Final Speeches*, 27.

[40]Malcolm X, "A Global Rebellion of the Oppressed against the Oppressor," in *February 1965 The Final Speeches*, 177–178.

[41]Malik Shabazz to C. H. L. Pennock, 22 March 1962, box 3, folder 4, Malcolm Collection.

[42]Ahmed Siddik Osman to Malcolm X, 13 September 1963, box 4, folder 4, Malcolm Collection.

[43]Robert Johann to Malcolm X, 15 March 1964, box 4, folder 5, Malcolm Collection.

[44]Joseph B. Axenroth to Malcolm X, 23 September 1963, box 4, folder 4, Malcolm Collection.

[45]Malik Shabazz to Martin Miller, 6 December 1963, box 3, folder 4, Malcolm Collection.

[46]Maxine Sprott to Malcolm X, 19 November 1963, box 4, folder 4, Malcolm Collection.

[47]Lou Holland to Malcolm X, n.d., box 4, folder 7, Malcolm Collection.

[48]Anne Donaldson to Malcolm X, 22 November 1963, box 3, folder 18, Malcolm Collection.

[49]Marva J. King to Malcolm X, 9 December 1962, box 4, folder 3, Malcolm Collection.

[50]Judith Hummer to Malcolm X, 27 September 1961; Charles Douglas Cary to Malcolm X, 4 April 1963; Marguerite E. Allen to Malcolm X, n.d., box 4, folder 7; Jeff Kane to Malcolm X, 19 February 1962; Willard Hunter to Malcolm X, 29 March 1962, box 3, folder 17; Barbara L. to Malcolm X, 23 October 1963, box 3, folder 18, Malcolm Collection.

[51]Carole Hewitt to Malcolm X, 21 October 1963, box 4, folder 7, Malcolm Collection.

[52]Leonard C. Simmons to Malcolm X, 21 October 1963, box 4, folder 7, Malcolm Collection; see also, V. P. Franklin, "Malcolm X and the Resurrection of the Dead," in *Living Our Stories, Telling Our Truths: Autobiography and the Making of the African American Intellectual Tradition* (New York, 1995), 319–46.

[53]Michael Blatt to Malcolm X, [n.d.] November 1963, box 4, folder 7, Malcolm Collection.

[54]Malcolm X, "Interview by A. B. Spellman," 6–7; Malcolm X, "The Leverett House Forum of March 18, 1964," 143.

[55]Malcolm X, "The Black Revolution," in *Malcolm X Speaks: Selected Speeches and Statements*, 47.

[56]Malcolm X to Eleanor Mason, 21 March 1964, box 3, folder 4, Malcolm Collection.

[57]Ayo Azikiwe to Malcolm X, 25 March 1964, box 3, folder 3, Malcolm Collection.

[58]Charles Hartman to Stokely Carmichael, 10 August 1966, reel 2, no. 52, Student Nonviolent Coordinating Committee Papers, 1959–1972, Paley Library, Temple University, Philadelphia, PA (hereafter, SNCC Papers).

[59]Reverend Albert Cleage, "Myths About Malcolm X," in *Malcolm X: The Man and His Times*, ed. John Henrik Clarke (Trenton, NJ, 1990), 24.

[60]Carmichael and Thelwell, *Ready for Revolution*, 100, 105, 588, 254–55, 730.

[61]James Shabazz to John Lewis, 15 May 1964, reel 5, no. 53, SNCC Papers.

[62]"Black Power," in *A Circle of Trust: Remembering SNCC*, ed. Cheryl Lynn Greenberg (New Brunswick, NJ,

1996), 160.

[63]"Freedom School Reading List," n.d., reel 55, no. 74; "Straight from Brother Malcolm," n.d., reel 55, no. 74, SNCC Papers.

[64]Carson, *In Struggle*, 3.

[65]Greenberg, "Black Power," 159.

[66]John Lewis and Michael D'Orso, *Walking with the Wind: A Memoir of the Movement* (San Diego, CA, 1993), 297.

[67]John Lewis and Donald Harris, "The Trip," 14 December 1964, reel 1, no. 37, SNCC Papers.

[68]Lewis and D'Orso, *Walking with the Wind*, 297. For more information on the Pan-Africanism of SNCC, see Fanon Che Wilkins, "The Making of Black Internationalists: SNCC and Africa Before the Launching of Black Power, 1960–1965," *The Journal of African American History* 92 (Fall 2007): 468–90.

[69]Ahmad, *We Will Return in the Whirlwind*, 26.

[70]Cleveland Sellers and Robert Terrell, *The River of No Return: The Autobiography of a Black Militant and the Life and Death of SNCC* (New York, 1973), 187.

[71]Sales, *From Civil Rights to Black Liberation*, 129–30; Ahmad, *We Will Return in the Whirlwind*, 115–18.

[72]Ibid., 130.

[73]Ahmad, *We Will Return in the Whirlwind*, 54; Malcolm X, "Second OAAU Rally," in *By Any Means Necessary*, 101.

[74]Ahmad, *We Will Return in the Whirlwind*, 55.

[75]"Bibliography," n.d., reel 55, no. 74, SNCC Papers; Lewis and D'Orso, *Walking with the Wind*, 364–65.

[76]Greenberg, "Black Power," 161.

[77]Cheryl Lynn Greenberg, "Introduction," in *A Circle of Trust: Remembering SNCC*, 11; Lewis and D'Orso, *Walking with the Wind*, 381.

[78]Sellers and Terrell, *The River of No Return*, 188.

[79]John Henrik Clarke, "Malcolm X—The Man and His Mission," n.d., reel 63, no. 31; "The Murder of Malcolm X," February 1967, reel 22, no. 253; "Newsletter Published by the Student Nonviolent Coordinating Committee of Alabama," n.d., reel 3, no. 73, SNCC Papers.

[80]James Forman, *The Making of Black Revolutionaries: A Personal Account* (New York, 1972), 440.

[81]Bobby Seale, *Seize the Time: The Story of the Black Panther Party and Huey P. Newton* (New York, 1970), 4; Mumia Abu-Jamal, "A Life in the Party: An Historical and Retrospective Examination of the Projections and Legacies of the Black Panther Party," in *Liberation, Imagination, and the Black Panther Party: A New Look at the Panthers and Their Legacy*, ed. Kathleen Cleaver and George Katsiaficas (New York, 2001), 40.

[82]*Black Panther*, 28 February 1970. For other statements from writers in *The Black Panther* newspaper, see *Black Panther*, 19 May 1970 and 16 October 1976.

[83]Huey P. Newton and J. Herman Black, *Revolutionary Suicide* (New York, 1973), 53, 55, 71.

[84]Seale, *Seize the Time*, 30–31, 34. This situation probably contributed to one of the major disagreements the BPP leaders had with Malcolm. Although Malcolm held up students as "the ones that bring about change," the party placed the lumpenproletariat in that role. For discussion of these issues, see Ollie A. Johnson, "Explaining the Demise of the Black Panther Party: The Role of Internal Factors"; Chris Booker, "Lumpenization: A Critical Error for the Black Panther Party," in *The Black Panther Party Reconsidered,* ed. Charles Jones (Baltimore, MD, 1998), 337–414; and V. P. Franklin, "Jackanapes: Reflections on the Legacy of the Black Panther Party for the Hip Hop Generation," *The Journal of African American History* 92 (Fall 1997): 553–60.

[85]Newton and Black, *Revolutionary Suicide*, 113.

[86]Jane Rhodes, *Framing the Black Panthers: The Spectacular Rise of a Black Power Icon* (New York, 2007), 7.

[87]Malcolm observed: "The political philosophy of black nationalism means that the black man should control the politics and the politicians of his own community. . . . The economic philosophy of black nationalism . . . only means that we should control the economy of our community." See Malcolm X, "The Ballot or the Bullet," in *Malcolm X Speaks: Selected Speeches and Statements*, 38. And he declared, "The masses of our

people still have bad housing, bad schools and inferior jobs, jobs that don't compensate with sufficient salaries for them to carry on their life in this world." See Malcolm X, "After the Bombing," in *Malcolm X Speaks: Selected Speeches and Statements*, 174.

[88]Malcolm believed that "all of the countries that are emerging today from under the shackles of colonialism are turning toward socialism." "I don't think it's an accident," he said. "Most of the countries that were colonial powers were capitalist countries, and the last bulwark of capitalism today is America. It's impossible for a white person to believe in capitalism and not believe in racism. [He] can't have capitalism without racism." See Malcolm X, "The Harlem 'Hate-Gang Scare,'" in *Malcolm X Speaks: Selected Speeches and Statements*, 69. With regard to poor housing in Harlem, Malcolm pointed out: "These bad housing conditions that continue to exist up there keep our people victims of health problems—high infant and adult mortality rates, higher in Harlem than any other party of the city." See Malcolm X, "Prospects for Freedom in 1965," in *Malcolm X Speaks: Selected Speeches and Statements*, 155.

[89]Malcolm declared, "The social philosophy of Black Nationalism says that we must eliminate the vices and evils that exist in our society, and that we must stress the cultural roots of our forefathers, that will lend dignity and make the black man cease to be ashamed of himself. We have to teach our people something about our cultural roots. We have to teach them something of their glorious civilizations before they were kidnapped by your grandfathers and brought over to this country." See Malcolm X, "The Leverett House Forum of March 18, 1964," 142.

[90]Malcolm believed, "If you're dumb enough to go, that's up to you. If you're dumb enough to fight for someone who means you no good; if you're dumb enough to fight for something that you have never gotten; if you are dumb enough to be as dumb as your other brothers who went into Korea and came back and still caught hell; if you're dumb enough to follow in the footsteps of your older brothers during World War II, who fought all over the South Pacific, like Isaac Woodard, who came back here to this country and got his eyes punched out by police right here in this country; if you are dumb enough [given] what you know about the white man today to let him stick his uniform on you and send you overseas to fight, well, you go the hell on and fight. But I'm not that dumb." Malcolm made this statement at the Black Front Unity Rally in Harlem on 10 August 1963.

[91]Malcolm said: "If we're going to talk about police brutality, it's because police brutality exists. Why does it exist? Because our people in this particular society live in a police state. A black man in America lives in a police state. He doesn't live in any democracy, he lives in a police state." See Malcolm X, "The Harlem 'Hate-Gang Scare,'" 66.

[92]"I'm not against law; I'm not against law enforcement," Malcolm made clear. "You need law to survive and you need law enforcement to have an intelligent, peaceful society; but we have to live in these places and suffer the type of conditions that exist from others who lack understanding and who lack any human feeling." Ibid., 67.

[93]Malcolm concluded, "When you expand the civil-rights struggle to the level of human rights, you can then take the case of the black man in this country before the nations in the U.N. You can take it before the General Assembly. You can take Uncle Sam before a world court." See Malcolm X, "The Ballot or the Bullet," in *Malcolm X Speaks*, 34.

[94]Rhodes, *Framing the Black Panthers*, 97; Geronimo ji Jaga, "Every nation struggling to be free has a right to struggle, a duty to struggle," in Cleaver and Katsiaficas, *Liberation, Imagination, and the Black Panther Party*, 75; *Black Panther*, 23 November 1967, 4 October 1969, 18 October 1969, 15 August 1970, 21 August 1970, 25 September 1971, 26 May 1973, 22 January 1977.

[95]*Black Panther*, 16 March 1968, 15 November 1969, 31 May 1970.

[96]*Black Panther*, 15 August 1970.

[97]Earl Anthony, *Picking Up the Gun: A Report on the Black Panthers* (New York, 1970), 3–4.

[98]*Black Panther*, 3 March 1969.

[99]"Malcolm: Black Shining Prince, People's Servant," *Black Panther*, 26 February 1971.

[100]*Black Panther*, 26 October 1968, 16 November 1968, 21 December 1968, 31 May 1969; William Lee Brent, *Long Time Gone: A Black Panther's True-Life Story of His Skyjacking and Twenty-five Years in Cuba* (New York, 1996), 96.

[101]See *Black Panther*, 25 April 1970, 31 May 1970, 7 December 1972, 18 March 1972, 19 May 1973, 11 March 1978, 18 February 1978, February 19–March 4, 1979, 28 February 1970, 21 March 1970.

[102]*Black Panther*, 16 November 1968.

[103]*Black Panther*, 25 May 1969.

[104]Van Deburg, *New Day in Babylon*, 71, 80–81.

[105]"Malcolm X Liberation University Information and Application," n.d., reel 43, no. 94, SNCC Papers; *New York Times*, 14 September 1969.

[106]*New York Times*, 28 October 1969.

[107]Seale, *Seize the Time*, 3.

[108]*Bay State Banner*, 5 September 1968.

[109]*Chicago Daily Defender*, 25 February 1965; William Barlow and Peter Shapiro, *An End to Silence: The San Francisco State College Student Movement in the '60s* (New York, 1971), 84.

[110]Darlene Clark Hine, William C. Hine, and Stanley Harrold, *The African-American Odyssey: Volume Two, Since 1965* (Upper Saddle River, NJ, 2003), 562.

[111]Gwen Patton, telephone interview with author, 16 May 2010.

[112]Malcolm X, "The Ballot or the Bullet," 41.

[113]Ibram H. Rogers, "Remembering the Black Campus Movement: An Oral History Interview with James P. Garrett," *The Journal of Pan-African Studies* 2 (June 2009): 32.

[114]Frederick D. Harper, "The Influence of Malcolm X on Black Militancy," *Journal of Black Studies* 1 (June 1971): 401.

[115]Van Deburg, *New Day in Babylon*, 72.

[116]Malcolm X, "The oppressed masses of the world cry out for action against the common oppressor," 53.

[117]Jerrold Roy, "Student Activism and the Historically Black University: Hampton Institute and Howard University, 1960–1972," Ph.D. diss., Harvard University, 2000, 104–05.

[118]*New York Times*, 15 November 1967; *New York Amsterdam News*, 2 December 1967.

[119]*New Republic*, 13 April 1968.

[120]*Philadelphia Tribune*, 2 April 1968.

[121]*Life*, 10 May 1968; see also Stephan Bradley, "'Gym Crow Must Go!' Black Student Activism at Columbia University, 1967–1968," *The Journal of African American History* 88 (Spring 2003): 163–81; and *Harlem v. Columbia University: Black Student Power in the Late 1960s* (Urbana, IL, 2009).

[122]Dikran Karagueuzian, *Blow It Up: The Black Student Revolt at San Francisco State College and the Emergence of Dr. Hayakawa* (Boston, MA, 1971), 92–93; Ione D. Vargus, *Revival of Ideology: The Afro-American Society Movement* (San Francisco, CA, 1977), 105, 125.

[123]*New York Times*, 29 April 1969.

[124]Permanent Subcommittee on Investigations of the Committee on Government Operations, United States Senate, *Staff Study of Campus Riots and Disorders, October 1967–May 1969* (Washington, DC, 1969), 30; Allan Kornberg and Joel Smith, "'It Ain't Over Yet': Activism in a Southern University," in *Black Power and Student Rebellion*, ed. James McEvoy and Abraham Miller (Belmont, CA, 1969), 107–09.

[125]*Washington Post*, 7 May 1970.

[126]*Bay State Banner*, 13 August 1966.

[127]Alford A. Young, *Revolt of the Privileged: The Coming Together of the Black Community at Wesleyan University, 1965–1976* (Middletown, CT, 1988), 21–22.

[128]*New York Times*, 26 February 1967.

[129]Harper, *Black Students: White Campus*, 10.

[130]Conrad M. Dyer, "Protest and the Politics of Open Admissions: The Impact of the Black and Puerto Rican Students' Community (of City College)," Ph.D. diss., City College of New York, 1990, 83.

[131]*New Yorker*, 27 September 1993.

[132]Carmichael and Thelwell, *Ready for Revolution*, 441.

SYMPOSIUM

"THE LION OF ZION": LEON H. SULLIVAN AND THE PURSUIT OF SOCIAL AND ECONOMIC JUSTICE

INTRODUCTION

V. P. Franklin

> I was beholden to no one but God, Zion [Baptist Church], and [my wife] Grace. My church made me free, so much so that in Philadelphia, I was called "the Lion of Zion."
> —Leon H. Sullivan, 1998[1]

In recounting the history of the Civil Rights Movement in the United States, there are some locations that cannot be left out of the story. Montgomery, Birmingham, Selma, and Lowndes County, Alabama; Jackson and Greenwood, Mississippi; Albany and Atlanta, Georgia, are places that are essential to the story of "the Movement." While many would add Philadelphia, Mississippi, the site of the horrible murders of civil rights workers James Chaney, Andrew Goodman, and Michael Schwerner at the beginning of the "Freedom Summer" campaigns in June 1964, it is likely that few would make room for Philadelphia, Pennsylvania, in the list of cities that contributed to the end of apartheid, American style.

Adding the "City of Brotherly Love and Sisterly Affection" to the overall story of the Civil Rights Movement, however, would allow historians and other researchers to address a perspective that has arisen among some researchers of the most important movement for social change in the United States in the 20th century. Some historians and social scientists have raised the issue of the "unfinished business" or "lost promise" of the Civil Rights Movement. These authors suggest that rather than pursuing issues of "economic justice" that were associated with the Communist Party and the organized labor movement in the 1930s and in World War II, the NAACP and other civil rights organizations decided to pursue the desegregation of public education and accommodations and black voting rights. These authors note that it was only in the last years of his life that Dr. Martin Luther King, Jr., took up the issue of economic and employment discrimination with his support of the Memphis sanitation workers' strike and the "Poor People's

Campaign" in 1967 and 1968. With the advent of the Black Power Movement, the civil rights coalition splintered and demands for economic justice were drowned out in the cries for Black Power, Chicano Power, Women's and Gay Liberation; and the rise of "identity politics" in the 1970s.[2]

The public career of Rev. Leon H. Sullivan, the pastor of Zion Baptist Church in Philadelphia, not only involved direct connections with civil rights campaigns launched by the NAACP and Dr. King's Southern Christian Leadership Conference (SCLC), but also focused on economic justice issues for African American workers, the expansion of black business enterprises, and the internationalization of the social justice and economic empowerment issues closely associated with the Civil Rights and Black Power movements. In the wake of the launching of the Montgomery Bus Boycott, African American ministers in Philadelphia organized a boycott of businesses that refused to hire black and other minority workers. Between 1960 and 1963 the "Selective Patronage Campaign" led by Rev. Leon Sullivan and the "400 Ministers" was successful in opening up employment opportunities for black workers in hundreds of businesses that previously hired "whites only." But what happened in Philadelphia inspired boycotts in New York City and in other northern cities, and the movement for economic justice for decades. "As a result of the success of the selective patronage program in Philadelphia," Sullivan recalled, "I came to know Dr. Martin Luther King Jr. as an associate and friend." More importantly, "the concept of selective patronage became the 'economic arm' of the Southern Christian Leadership Conference" with the launching of "Operation Breadbasket" in 1967 under the leadership of Rev. Jesse Jackson, who subsequently organized People United to Save Humanity (PUSH).[3]

The successful boycott led to an increase in employment opportunities for African Americans in Philadelphia, but the problem soon arose of the lack of availability of black workers with the skills and training needed by local industries. As Leon Sullivan put it, "integration without preparation led to frustration."[4] Thus he decided to create a training program for disadvantaged workers. Raising funds through his congregation and the Philadelphia black community, and with equipment donated by local industries, Sullivan opened the first Opportunities Industrialization Center (OIC) in North Philadelphia in January 1964. With financial support from contributions by African Americans locally and nationally, the Ford Foundation and the Office of Economic Opportunity that supported programs in Lyndon Johnson's "War on Poverty," OICs were opened throughout the United States. With the launching of the "Philadelphia Plan" by the Nixon administration in 1969, which historians consider "the first fully developed Affirmative Action program in the United States," builders who received federal contracts were required to seek out and hire skilled minorities in the building trades, and many of these workers received their training from OIC.[5] By 1980, OIC programs had opened in over a hundred U.S. cities and in eight African nations.[6]

"Pan-African Connections, Transnational Education, Collective Cultural Capital, and Opportunities Industrialization Centers International" examines the transfer of educational programs by and for U.S. African Americans to African colonial territories and nations. From the late 19th century the European imperial powers had been interested in introducing the Hampton-Tuskegee form of industrial education into their African colonial territories because they believed these colonized peoples needed to be "educated for work." The Phelps Stokes Fund was intimately involved in the promulgation of industrial education, Tuskegee-style, in East, West, and Southern Africa in the early decades of the 20th century. However, the evidence reveals that these programs were tied to the introduction of exploitative labor practices in colonial territories and were resisted and often rejected by the Africans themselves. This was in stark contrast with the introduction of OIC programs on the African continent. Not only did Africans seek out Rev. Sullivan and inquire about how they could open these vocational training centers in their cities, they raised the cultural capital collectively to support the implementation and maintenance of the OIC programs. The activities of Opportunities Industrialization Centers International (OICI) and Rev. Sullivan's philanthropic organization, the International Foundation for Education and Self-Help (IFESH), founded in 1988, represent the internationalization of the economic justice goals associated with the U.S. Civil Rights and Black Power movements.

The "social justice" objectives of the Civil Rights and Black Power movements were pursued through the implementation of the "Sullivan Principles" in the Republic of South Africa. "Amandla! The Sullivan Principles and the Battle to End Apartheid in South Africa, 1975–1987" by James B. Stewart examines the history of the implementation of the Sullivan Principles that has been ignored by earlier researchers of anti-apartheid activism in the United States. As a member of the board of directors of General Motors (GM), Sullivan developed the principles for GM and other U.S. firms operating in South Africa to ensure that "petty apartheid" was not part of the daily practices of these corporations. With the rise of the divestment campaigns and the demands for economic sanctions against the government of South Africa, the adoption of the Sullivan Principles allowed U.S. companies to demonstrate that they were not participating in South Africa's racially oppressive practices in their workplaces. Some anti-apartheid activists were critical of the Sullivan Principles because they believed their adoption allowed the continued operation of U.S. businesses in South Africa in the face of increasing demands that these companies withdraw from the country altogether. Using archival materials and other sources, Stewart makes it clear that Leon Sullivan was supportive of demands for divestment and sanctions from the beginning, and his principles were aimed at improving the day-to-day conditions for black South African workers at U.S. companies operating in South Africa. The Sullivan Principles were an important weapon in the arsenal of international activism that led to victory in the battle against apartheid in South Africa.

In his pursuit of economic justice, Leon Sullivan launched his "community investment cooperation movement" in 1962, known as the "10–36 Plan," in which he asked members of his congregation to invest $10.00 a month for thirty-six months "to build housing and shopping centers and businesses." Over four thousand people agreed to participate and provided the financial support for Zion Investment Associates (ZIA), which soon obtained financing for the construction of Zion Gardens Apartment Complex and Progress Plaza Shopping Center, and the opening of many black-owned businesses in Philadelphia. At the same time, Sullivan believed it was important to instill the lessons of charity and philanthropy in those who profited from their investments in successful ZIA-funded business enterprises associated with the "Progress Movement." Nathaniel Bracey's "The Progress Movement and Community Development: The Zion Non-Profit Charitable Trust" (ZNPCT) describes the foundation's activities from its formation in 1966 to the present. The trust not only provided funds and secured grants for the management training of the owners and supervisors of the businesses supported through ZIA's investments, but it also worked with tenant groups seeking support to rehabilitate their homes and those interested in building housing for the elderly and disabled.

Leon Sullivan believed that "even the lofty goal of freedom and peace for the world is ours to grasp or turn away." "I stake that claim, not as an idealist," he declared, "but as a person of simple faith, faith in God who has proved time and again through my life that he is capable of moving mountains."[7] Hopefully, this symposium on "the Lion of Zion" represents the beginning of the assessments by historians, educators, social scientists, and others of the monumental accomplishments of Leon H. Sullivan, whose legacy lives on in the numerous institutions, centers, and programs that trace their origins to his religious faith, civil rights activism, educational vision, and economic commitments.

NOTES

[1]Leon H. Sullivan, *Moving Mountains: The Principles and Purposes of Leon Sullivan* (Valley Forge, PA, 1998), 116.

[2]Michael J. Klarman, *Unfinished Business: Racial Equality in American History* (New York, 2007); Risa L. Goluboff, *The Lost Promise of Civil Rights* (Cambridge, MA, 2007); Clint Bolick, *Unfinished Business: A Civil Rights Strategy for America's Third Century* (San Francisco, CA, 1991). See also James T. Patterson, Brown v. Board of Education: *A Civil Rights Milestone and Its Troubled History* (New York, 2002); Michael J. Klarman, *From Jim Crow to Civil Rights: The Supreme Court and the Struggle for Racial Equality* (New York, 2006); and Mikel Holt, *Not "Free at Last": The Unfinished Business of the Civil Rights Movement: Our Battle for School Choice* (Ithaca, NY, 1999).

[3]Sullivan, *Moving Mountains,* 25; Adam Fairclough, *To Redeem the Soul of America: The Southern Christian Leadership Conference and Martin Luther King, Jr.* (Athens, GA, 1987), 349–351; Stacy Kinlock Sewell, "The 'Not Buying Power' of the Black Community: Urban Boycotts and Equal Employment Opportunity, 1960–1964," *The Journal of African American History* 89 (Spring 2004): 135–52. The best account of Jesse Jackson and the beginnings of the PUSH organization is Barbara Reynolds, *Jesse Jackson: The Man, the Movement, and the Myth* (Chicago, IL, 1975).

[4]Sullivan, *Moving Mountains*, 14.

[5]Quote from Guian McKee, *The Problem of Jobs: Liberalism, Race, and Deindustrialization in Philadelphia* (Chicago, IL, 2008), 211. For analyses of the Philadelphia Plan, see also Hugh Davis Graham, *The Civil Rights Era: Origins and Development of National Policy, 1960–1972* (New York, 1990), 125–62; and *Civil Rights and the Presidency: Race, Gender, and American Politics, 1960–1972* (New York, 1992), 150–69; Thomas Sugrue, "Affirmative Action from Below: The Building Trades and the Politics of Racial Equality in the North, 1945–1969," *Journal of American History* 91 (June 2004): 155–70.

[6]V. P. Franklin, "Opportunities Industrialization Centers: Collective Cultural Capital, Philanthropy, and Public-Private Partnerships in the Provision of Supplementary Education," in *Educating Comprehensively: Varieties of Educational Experiences,* ed. Linda J. Lin, Herve Verenne, and Edmund W. Gordon (Lewiston, NY, 2011), forthcoming.

[7]Sullivan, *Moving Mountains*, 194.

PAN-AFRICAN CONNECTIONS, TRANSNATIONAL EDUCATION, COLLECTIVE CULTURAL CAPITAL, AND OPPORTUNITIES INDUSTRIALIZATION CENTERS INTERNATIONAL

V. P. Franklin

> When I plan for the future, my thoughts turn eventually to Africa. . . . I envision a bridge from America to Africa over which one day my children and my black brothers and black sisters will move freely from one side to the other and back again. The Bible has said, "The day will come when Ethiopia shall stretch forth her hands again," and I know that day is coming, though I shall not live to see it. The time is not far off when black technicians, artisans, and craftsmen by the thousands and tens of thousands will visit a flourishing Africa, helping to mold that continent into a new greatness glorious to see.
>
> —Leon H. Sullivan, *Build Brother Build* (1969)[1]

The educational programs put in place by and for African Americans in the United States were at times exported to their brothers and sisters in Africa in the 20th century. When the vocational education program created by Rev. Leon Sullivan's Opportunities Industrialization Centers (OIC) was transferred to many African nations in the 1970s, it was dependent upon the collective cultural capital and philanthropy raised by the people themselves in Nigeria, Ghana, Ethiopia, Kenya, and other nations for its successful implementation. This was a very different situation from the early decades of the 20th century when the Hampton-Tuskegee form of black industrial education was introduced and promoted by European colonial powers and by the Phelps Stokes Fund in the United States in the 1920s and 1930s and implemented in European colonies in West, East, and Southern Africa. Indeed, many Africans rejected the educational programs trumpeted by Booker T. Washington and the imperial powers and preferred to support missionary schools and independent African schools that provided training in English, French, and other local and foreign languages, literary studies, mathematics, and higher education.

Beginning with General Samuel Armstrong, the founder of Hampton Institute in Virginia in 1867, and continued by Booker T. Washington at Tuskegee Institute and at a number of "little Tuskegees" opened in various parts of the American South in the late 19th century, a distinctive form of "Negro industrial education" was developed for African Americans. The curriculum consisted of basic literacy skills; character education; rudimentary training in several trades, including carpentry, agriculture, and printing; as well as large amounts of manual labor. The social purposes to be served by the Hampton-Tuskegee form of industrial education were to instill discipline, develop a commitment to agriculture, and provide a corps of conservative teachers and leaders for southern black public and private schools and communities. The training that was provided at Hampton and Tuskegee was not intended to produce highly skilled workers who could compete with white workers in the industrial workplace, although many students were attracted to the schools because of the promise of industrial training. Because the training provided at Hampton and Tuskegee accommodated the social and racial realities of southern life, and was aimed at making sure that southern black workers remained in the South as agricultural laborers, these institutions received great support from northern philanthropic foundations such as the John D. Rockefeller's General Education Board, the Andrew Carnegie Foundation, the John Slater Fund, the Phelps Stokes Fund, the Anna T. Jeanes Foundation, and the Rosenwald Fund. Despite the fact that African Americans sought various types of schooling, especially literary studies and higher education comparable to that available to white students, these foundations provided funding specifically for elementary and secondary forms of industrial education, along the lines of Hampton and Tuskegee.[2]

During the Civil War when the supply of high-quality Upland cotton produced in the U.S. South was no longer being supplied to textile mills in the United Kingdom, France, Germany, and other European nations, these countries attempted to find viable substitutes. The British turned to India for cotton and Indian producers hoped to provide a substitute. But the short-staple cotton grown in India was only a short-term substitute for U.S. cotton, and following the war, the United States continued to be the major supplier for European textile manufacturers.[3] With the carving up of the African continent by the European powers in the 1880s, and the widespread belief that the only way to produce the Upland cotton that came out of the South was with "the Negro and a mule," the European imperialists began to investigate the possibilities of introducing cotton production into their African colonial territories.

TUSKEGEE IN AFRICA

Booker T. Washington, the principal of Tuskegee Institute in Alabama, received national and international recognition for his industrial education program, and he gained enormous influence over the black educational institutions interested in receiving financial aid from the major philanthropic foundations. Through the highly publicized "farmers conferences" held at Tuskegee Institute annually, Washington claimed to be bringing black farmers the latest information on agricultural techniques and equipment that would greatly improve their farming practices and increase their yields of cotton and other staple crops for the local and national markets. On the basis of the national recognition he achieved after his famous speech at the Cotton States Exposition in 1895, Washington received inquiries from various European nations about the potentiality of introducing his educational program and agricultural techniques in other parts of the world.[4]

The Germans were claiming and taking control of huge amounts of land in western and southwestern Africa in the 1880s and 1890s, and contacted Washington to learn more about his educational and agricultural programs. German officials eventually entered into an arrangement to have African Americans from Tuskegee travel to the German-controlled territory of Togo in West Africa and set up schools to train the Togolese people to raise Upland cotton, similar to that produced in the U.S. South, for the German and European markets. In *Alabama in Africa: Booker T. Washington, the German Empire, and the Globalization of the New South*, Andrew Zimmerman described the military conquest and economic subjugation of the Ewe peoples in Togo in 1895.

> The German state established political and economic control in Togo, less with the construction of Ewe ethnic identities, than with direct military force accompanied by economic transformations that robbed many Africans of their previous independence. Establishing African cotton cultivation for export to European industry played a central role in the process. . . . The Tuskegee expedition followed German conquests, establishing cotton farming to consolidate colonial rule in the aftermath of the military conflicts.[5]

Mirroring the racist ideologies and practices coming out of the "New South," the Germans believed that, as was the case with black southerners, it was necessary to reduce the Africans to a state of economic dependency, and they sought to work with the educators from Tuskegee to "impose a 'Negro' identity from New South ideology, first on the Ewe, and later on Africans throughout Togo." Three black educators from Tuskegee—James Nathan Calloway, John Wilfrey Robinson, and Shephard Lincoln Harris—arrived in January 1901, and eventually set up their school in Notse. While the Notse graduates were able to set up farms to produce cotton for the export market, it was at great cost. Zimmerman concluded that "the [Tuskegee] expedition succeeded in creating a cotton export market in Togo because it sent Africans backward along lines of progress commonly accepted by Germans, Africans, and Americans: from literate office work to agricultural labor, from domesticity to social disintegration, from prosperity to poverty, from skilled work to forced labor, and from freedom to domination."[6]

Missionary schools had been set up in Togo beginning in 1892 by Protestant and Catholic groups where they offered English language, reading and writing, arithmetic, and other subjects that prepared the graduates for white-collar positions. While the mission school graduates were needed for the colonial administration, they were universally disparaged by the Germans as "dandies" because they "challenged the singularity and superiority of European culture and the uniquely European face of political and economic authority in Africa."[7] However, unlike the Togolese Tuskegee at Notse that aimed at "subverting Togolese aspirations for literacy and white collar employment to make them a subject 'Negro' peasant population," the mission schools were very popular; though in 1897 there were only 15, but by 1911 there were over 140 mission schools.[8] Reports of atrocities committed as part of the military conquests carried out in East Africa and in Southwest Africa made their way to the German parliament in 1906, 1907, and afterward. At the same time, Kaiser Wilhelm II sought to reform the colonial practices. However, following Germany's defeat in World War I, the African territories were taken away, and in the postwar period the British, Belgians, and French attempted to emulate the German agricultural "success" in Togo with the assistance of U.S. foundations.

The Phelps Stokes Fund was organized in 1910 under the terms of the will of Caroline Phelps Stokes, and Booker T. Washington was contacted about what needed to be done in the area of schooling for African Americans. Eventually, the Phelps Stokes Fund would promote Tuskegee-style industrial education in the southern United States *and* in European colonies in Africa. With regard to black education in the U.S. South, Washington recommended a survey of the entire field of "Negro education" for the purpose of determining those schools worthy of financial assistance from northern philanthropies. According to Washington and Thomas Jesse Jones, a Welshman who had taught at Hampton Institute and was hired by the Phelps Stokes Fund to carry out the survey, the only schools worthy of support were those committed to the Hampton-Tuskegee form of industrial education. With additional support from the U.S. Bureau of Education, in 1917 Jones's two-volume report was published, *Negro Education: A Study of the Private and Higher Schools for Colored People of the United States*. The report basically condemned all black independent schools offering literary studies and praised Tuskegee, Hampton, and the "little Tuskegees" that offered primarily farming, gardening, basic literacy training, and "rural studies." This survey made it more difficult for black schools providing academic or college preparatory studies to receive financial support from northern philanthropic foundations. For example, Jones criticized the numerous small black "colleges," pointing out that this was a misnomer since the vast majority of the students were enrolled in secondary level courses. Jones failed to point out that the reason for the large number of secondary students was the absence of public or private secondary schools for black southerners and thus institutions of higher education had to provide those preparatory courses of study needed for college entrance.[9]

Recent research has revealed that hundreds of public and private schools opened in the North and the South before and after the Civil War by and for African Americans were supported through materials and funds provided by the local African American communities. *Cultural Capital and Black Education: African American Communities and the Funding of Black Schooling, 1865 to the Present* included case studies of the "collective cultural capital" that was raised to support African American education. When a business enterprise such as the opening of a school is considered important for the economic, social, or cultural development of an entire group, that institution or enterprise could also draw on cultural capital from members of that group. Historically, educational institutions opened by women, Roman Catholics, Jews, and various Protestant denominations could obtain financial donations and other forms of support—collective cultural capital—from members of the group because the contributors understood that the institution created would benefit not just the individuals who attended these schools, but the entire group.[10] In addition to the schools and educational institutions examined in *Cultural Capital and Black Education*, other studies have documented the important role played by African American communities in supporting their schools, particularly during the period of legal racial segregation.[11] In the case of the over 5,300 "Rosenwald schools" built for African American students in the South between 1912 and 1932 through the activities of the Julius Rosenwald Fund, these schools would not have been built without the financial support from the African American communities where they were located. In *The Rosenwald Schools of the American South,* Mary Hoffschwelle documented the history of these institutions and reported that at least one-third of the financial resources came from the local African American communities, which often provided more money and other resources than the Rosenwald Fund. Hoffschwelle also provided detailed information on the raising of collective cultural capital by black southerners to support the Rosenwald schools.[12]

In the same period that the Rosenwald Fund was involved in the campaign to open elementary and secondary schools that would provide industrial *and* academic training to black southerners, the Phelps Stokes Fund sponsored international commissions to examine and make recommendations for the most appropriate forms of "native education" in the European colonies in Africa. *Education in Africa: A Study of West, South, and Equatorial Africa by the African Education Commission* was published in 1922; and *Education in East Africa: A Study of East, Central, and South Africa by the Second African Commission* was published in 1925. These two reports were also written by Thomas Jesse Jones and he made it clear that the objectives of the commissions were "to study and report upon industrial education adapted to the needs of the African." The major theme found in the Phelps Stokes Fund reports was the "adaptation" of educational programs to conditions for Africans, who were located primarily in villages in rural areas.[13]

In addition to sponsoring international commissions that recommended the incorporation of Tuskegee-style industrial education in missionary schools and in schools sponsored by colonial governments, the Phelps Stokes Fund also sponsored visits by African missionary and colonial officials to Hampton, Tuskegee, and other black schools in the United States that specialized in "Negro industrial education." Beginning in 1907 the Anna T. Jeanes Fund began supporting "Jeanes teachers" in the U.S. South who taught and supervised agricultural education and programs in all-black schools in rural areas. Education researcher Phyllis McClure reported that between 1907 and 1958 the Jeanes Fund subsidized the salaries of over 2,400 black teachers.[14] The Phelps Stokes Fund also sponsored the training of "Anna Jeanes Teachers" or "village teachers" in several African colonies who traveled to rural "village" or "bush" schools to provide specialized courses in agriculture and gardening. The fourth area where the Phelps Stokes Fund engaged in transnational activities to spread the Tuskegee-style industrial education was the sponsoring of African students to travel to and receive training at Hampton and Tuskegee institutes.[15]

Historian Kenneth J. King examined the Phelps Stokes Fund's transnational program to introduce industrial education into missionary and government schools in Africa in *Pan-Africanism and Education: A Study of Race, Philanthropy, and Education in the Southern States of America and East Africa* and concluded that there was a serious disconnect between the provisioning of industrial education in missionary and government-sponsored schools and Africans' desire for academic education, literary studies, and higher education. While the Africans sought college and university education that would prepare them for leadership positions and eventually self-determination, the Phelps Stokes Fund offered Tuskegee-style industrial education.[16]

The industrial emphasis in missionary schools, which in some instances was first introduced in the 19th century as a way to produce goods and services to support the missionary activities, meant that Africans interested in literary studies had to found and support independent schools through the cultural capital supplied by Africans themselves. For example, the Phelps Stokes report on East Africa was received well by European settlers in Kenya because as King points out, "many of those [Europeans] who gave evidence to the commission had little doubt that industrial education should produce semi-skilled illiterate artisans to work for white farmers, builders, and planters." However, when Local Native Councils were established in Kenya in 1925, "Africans immediately began taxing themselves for an education that would be out of missionary control. . . . By 1929 they presented the new Director of Education . . . with the problem of more than 50,000 pounds raised by voluntary taxes specifically for non-mission education." King went on to note that "the growth of the Kenya Independent Schools was greatly a reaction to the government's unwillingness to use Local Native Council money for secondary education."[17]

Similarly, African Americans in the U.S. South during this period raised collective cultural capital to support black private and public schools that provided literary studies and secondary education for black students. Those founders of independent black schools who introduced industrial education classes before 1915 in hopes of securing funds from the major white philanthropies, but who remained committed to academic and college preparatory education, were exposed in 1917 by the Thomas Jesse Jones report, "Negro Education." Black southerners were supportive of the efforts, spearheaded by Booker T. Washington and the various philanthropies, to provide Hampton-Tuskegee-style industrial education in black private and public schools, as long as there was the alternative of enrolling in schools that offered the same traditional academic courses available in schools for whites. Africans in colonial Kenya, Uganda, Southern Rhodesia, and other areas were generally hostile to the attempts to introduce Tuskegee-style industrial education into the missionary and government-sponsored "native schools" because this type of training would not prepare them for leadership positions they sought in the colonial government and eventually for self-determination.

The Phelps Stokes Fund was involved in another educational enterprise in an attempt to spread the Booker T. Washington form of industrial education to Africa. Olivia Elveston Stokes set aside in her will $50,000 specifically for the opening of a Booker T. Washington Institute in Africa. The New York State Colonization Society (NYSCS), an affiliate of the Phelps Stokes Fund, supported the visit by Benjamin Brawley and his wife to Liberia in 1920 to investigate the possibility of opening an institute in Liberia. In the 1920s there were only three secondary schools barely operating in Liberia—Liberia College, the College of West Africa, and Monrovia College—and none offered Tuskegee-style industrial education. Using funds from the Phelps Stokes Fund, the NYSCS chartered the Booker T. Washington Institute (BTWI) in Liberia in November 1928. Donald Spivey in *The Politics of Miseducation: The Booker T. Washington Institute of Liberia, 1929–1984* traced the history of this school and described the myriad problems it faced because of the policies and practices it pursued. The first three principals were southern white men who fully subscribed to the idea that the Africans should be "educated for work." Under their leadership the school developed a close relationship with the white officials of the Firestone Rubber Company, which maintained large-scale operations in Liberia and was accused in the 1930s of engaging in labor abuse and "slavery" in Liberia by the League of Nations.[18] The students who attended BTWI were members of the indigenous ethnic groups and *not* the children of the Americo-Liberian elites, and they came to despise the institution because as part of their education they were required to engage in "dangerous and exploitative" work on road-building projects for the government to fulfill its obligations to the Firestone Company.

Even with the appointment of the first black principal, Walter C. Wynn, in May 1946, Spivey pointed out that the students' "days of conscription into service as forced laborers for the Liberian government were not over. Students were still required to work on various government projects against their will and faulted [BTWI] for not intervening on their behalf."[19] This situation did not improve until students who lost limbs while on the road-building projects filed lawsuits against the school. The conditions at BTWI continued to deteriorate even after Wynn was replaced by another black principal, Howard Hill. Finally in January 1954, the school was taken over by government of Liberia and became the industrial institute for the University of Liberia, established in 1951. Even after it was taken over by the government, Spivey concluded that "the underlying mission of the Booker T. Washington Institute remained basically unchanged. The school's commitment to training natives to assume a prescribed and subservient role in Liberian society was only slightly altered."[20] The educational activities and programs at BTWI in Liberia throughout most of its history continued the pattern of offering industrial training to prepare Africans to work for colonial administrations and foreign corporations interested in profiting from the exploitation of African labor.

OIC TRAINING PROGRAMS:
FROM NATIONAL TO TRANSNATIONAL

With regard to the transnational industrial education programs offered to Africans in the 1970s through Opportunities Industrialization Centers International (OICI), the organizers depended on cultural capital raised by the Africans themselves, who were to eventually take over total funding for the centers. Opportunities Industrialization Centers (OIC) grew out of the need to train black workers for the various industries that sought to desegregate their workforces following widespread civil rights protests in Philadelphia in the early 1960s. Whereas in Montgomery, Alabama, in December 1955 the African American community under the leadership of Dr. Martin Luther King, Jr., and the Montgomery Improvement Association organized the boycott of the buses and other public transportation because of Jim Crow practices, the objective in Philadelphia was to desegregate factories and industries where no black or minority workers were employed. Beginning in 1960 black ministers in Philadelphia came together in a group called "400 Ministers" and targeted for boycotts businesses that had no black workers, but were dependent on African Americans as customers and clients. Led by Rev. Leon Sullivan, pastor of Zion Baptist Church, representatives of the

400 Ministers met with company officials and asked that they begin hiring black workers. When there was no change in the company's hiring practices, the boycott or "Selective Patronage Campaign" was launched and remained in place until hiring practices were changed. Rev. Sullivan and others reported that as a result of the campaign, up to 300 businesses and industries in Philadelphia began to hire African American and other minority workers by 1963.[21]

Once these jobs opened for black workers in Philadelphia industries where they were previously denied employment, another problem arose. According to Rev. Sullivan, African Americans "had never been trained or prepared for the kinds of industrial employment opportunities created by the boycotts."[22] Sullivan had earlier formed a youth employment office in his church, but then decided that what was needed was vocational training. When he began to gather support for the creation of a training program, Sullivan appealed to those in the Philadelphia black community interested in self-help. He solicited funds from his congregation at Zion Baptist Church and other religious institutions in the city. School children collected "bags of pennies" to contribute and equipment was donated by various local businesses and companies, including Bell Telephone, Philco, Westinghouse, IBM, and the International Ladies Garment Union. In addition, Rev. Sullivan received a gift of $50,000 from an anonymous donor. A building was secured when members of the Philadelphia City Council, after much lobbying, agreed to allow Sullivan to rent an abandoned jailhouse in North Philadelphia for just one dollar per year. With regard to the name of this new program, Sullivan explained that "they could not be called *schools* because in the minds of the people, schools had failed them. So we decided to call them *centers*." The founders also wished to stress the commitment to providing new "opportunities" for advancement. Thus, the name settled upon was "Opportunities Industrialization Centers."[23]

On 26 January 1964, the first center was opened with great fanfare in North Philadelphia at 19th and Oxford streets. "Politicians, businessmen and businesswomen, community leaders, bands, choirs, Boys and Girls Scouts were in attendance."[24] The following day 135 men and 165 women began their classes. However, once the classes began in stenography, electronics, drafting, machine tooling, as well as food services, the instructors soon realized that most of the enrollees were lacking in basic literacy and mathematical skills. "The median age of those who came for training was about twenty-five, though most had dropped out of school by the eighth grade. Many lacked basic communication skills. Their poor hygiene not only testified to low self-image, but limited their ability to succeed in the business world."[25] Thus the OIC training program was soon divided into two phases: the feeder program and skills training. The feeder program included courses in basic grammar, etiquette, hygiene, black history, and an intensive counseling program. Enrollees moved through the feeder program at their own pace, and counselors helped to determine when they were ready to transfer to "skills training" and what particular skills they should pursue.[26]

Collective cultural capital from the black community allowed a second OIC to be opened in West Philadelphia a little over a year later, and additional fund-raising allowed three more OICs in other sections of the city. "The program's slogan was 'We Help Ourselves,' and our symbol was a key with the message 'To Open Any Door.'" In these early years the churches were a major source of support for establishing OICs. "Nothing has been more crucial to OIC's success than its ties to the church. . . . OIC would never have gotten off of the ground in the first place" if not for the prayers and support from church congregations.[27]

The continual exposure of "poverty in the midst of plenty" beginning in 1962 with the publication of Michael Harrington's *The Other America* meant that the Kennedy administration had placed antipoverty legislation and programs high on its agenda, but very little was accomplished before the president's assassination in November 1963.[28] The issue of poverty in the United States was then taken up by President Lyndon Johnson and the U.S. Congress with the passage of the Economic Opportunity Act in 1964. The legislation called for the creation of the Office of Economic Opportunity (OEO) that would offer financial support and technical assistance to state and local governments and non-profit organizations for the development of antipoverty programs. Community Action Programs (CAPs) formed at the local level would be eligible for federal funding for antipoverty programs. As a vocational training program available to youth and adults in U.S. cities, the Philadelphia OIC applied for small job-training grants in 1965 and 1966 from the OEO totaling about $6.5 million to help to support its activities. Then in 1967 President Johnson, who had been informed about OIC's achievements in training and placing hundreds in skilled jobs, decided he wanted to visit OIC and learn more about its activities firsthand. On 29 June 1967, President Johnson visited the jailhouse-turned training center in North Philadelphia and was impressed by what he found. He then decided to "put the full force of his Great Society program behind OIC's efforts."[29]

By 1970 there were fifty-one local OIC programs in the United States that enrolled over 50,000 trainees, with more than 30,000 placed in training-related jobs. These local OICs were "autonomous entities."

The local OICs adopt the basic feeder program/skills training structure, receive technical assistance provided by the national OIC, and partake of the federal, state, and local funds available to OIC. Because affiliates remain free to use these building blocks in whatever way they feel will best address the needs of their local community, the community-based aspect of OIC, so vital to its success, has been maintained.[30]

Between 1964 and 1969, various federal agencies had provided OICs with funding that amounted to $45.9 million and private donations totaled $2.6 million.[31]

**President Lyndon B. Johnson visiting the North Philadelphia
OIC Center with Leon H. Sullivan, 29 June 1967. Photo courtesy of
Temple University Libraries, Urban Archives, Philadelphia, Pennsylvania.**

Many times, the OICs were able to expand first to cities where National Urban League (NUL) branches were located. In the early decades of the 20th century during the "Great Migration," many groups and organizations were formed to assist southern black migrants to northern cities in their adjustment to urban life. First women and then other black migrants were assisted in finding housing and employment. In New York City, the Association for the Protection of Colored Women (1905), the Committee for Improving the Industrial Conditions of Negroes in New York (1906), and the Committee on Urban Conditions among Negroes (1910) came together to form the National League on Urban Conditions among Negroes (National Urban League) in 1911. The NUL branches served as a liaison between the local businesses and black workers. Thus in its capacity as an employment agency, the NUL was well positioned to identify the areas of skilled training needed by local businesses and industries and to serve as the conduit for the opening of OICs in local communities.[32]

Various administrative units were also formed to facilitate the establishment of OICs in various locales. The National Extension Services and the Development Task Force were formed in 1966 and 1968 respectively to provide technical assistance to educators in other cities interested in opening an OIC. The task force assisted those educators who were interested in receiving federal funding for the OIC. The Office of Extension Services provided help in those places where non-federally funded OICs were to be located.[33] Another important program, funded this time by a grant from the Department of Health, Education, and Welfare (HEW) beginning in 1966, was the "Adult Armchair Education Program," in which OIC employees held information sessions about the vocational training programs available at OIC at various places in the local communities, including the homes of potential enrollees. And beginning in 1971, OIC developed linkages with the Neighborhood Youth Corps in which youth serving in the corps could choose to enroll in an OIC training program instead of public secondary schools. Youth Corps enrollees combined their training with work experiences for which they received a monthly stipend.[34]

**Rev. Leon Sullivan and OIC trainee Esther Davies
at OIC in North Philadelphia in June 1965.**

In 1966 Dr. Folorunso Salawu, a Lagos physician, read about the OIC program in a magazine article and was impressed by the fact that OIC represented the attempts of private individuals to initiate a program to deal with high rates of unemployment. With the support of a group of interested Nigerians, Dr. Salawu contacted Leon Sullivan to get his advice on setting up a similar program in Lagos. Contacts were established and information was shared. In September 1968 a "Steering Committee" was formed for the Lagos OIC, whose members were local professionals, Christian and Moslem religious leaders, businessmen, and "Market Women."[35]

Early in 1968, after having heard from a group in Accra, Ghana, interested in establishing an OIC, Rev. Sullivan sent OIC director Valfoulaye Diallo to visit Lagos, Accra, and several other African cities to discuss with local professionals the possibility of establishing OIC programs. This was followed by a tour of several African nations by Leon Sullivan in February–March 1969. When he visited Lagos in 1969 at the invitation of Dr. Salawu, he urged the Lagos directors to obtain some support from the Nigerian military government, and after several meetings, government officials granted OIC Lagos several concessions, such as exemption from customs duty on training equipment imported into the country, and special work visas for OIC technical instructors and administrative personnel coming from the United States. Upon his return to Philadelphia, Sullivan organized "OIC International" as a new division within OIC to assist Africans and others interested in establishing OICs outside the United States.[36]

From the beginning of the first collaboration in Africa, the financial responsibilities for OICI and OIC Lagos were spelled out. A board of directors or "Registered Trustees" was formed in Lagos with Dr. Salawu as chair, and it was established as a non-profit organization so that the group could solicit financial support from the public. The first public solicitation was made to the "White Cap Chiefs and Lagos Market Women" in December 1970. Membership in OIC Lagos was also offered for one pound annually.[37]

Following Nigeria, the next group of Africans who expressed interest in establishing an OIC was from Ghana. Individuals from Accra contacted Sullivan and he visited the city in 1969, and the OIC group in Ghana was organized in 1970. With the formation of these programs in Africa, OIC officials decided they needed to spell out the "Standards and Guidelines for OIC International Affiliation." These guidelines made it clear that the organization of OIC programs in African nations would have to be "community based" and "non-partisan," and would depend on collective cultural capital and philanthropy raised in those nations.

> OIC's mission is providing training and job creation services to low income persons, regardless of race, color, creed, national origin, etc. OIC believes in the desire and capability of all individuals to grow and be self-reliant if provided job skills, life skills, and proper motivation and personal development opportunities as exemplified by the "feeder" concept, and job opportunities.

OIC is community-based. Its board (local and national) must be representative of the community and be responsible to that community, particularly to the poor people. OIC serves [the community]. . . . OIC is non-partisan. . . . OIC is a volunteer-based program. Volunteers are the leaders of OIC. Maintenance of volunteer involvement is critical to OIC success and integrity.[38]

With regard to fund raising, OICI officials emphasized the need to raise collective cultural capital to support the launching of the OIC programs in African nations. "A broad base of community financial support shall be actively sought." At the same time, it was recommended that "fund-raising expenses shall be kept to a minimum" and should not exceed 20 percent of the funds raised.[39]

Beginning in 1969, OICI officials applied for grants from the U.S. Agency for International Development (USAID) to support the salaries of OIC administrators and instructors who would go to set up the programs in Nigeria and other nations. Initially, the grant was to cover the salaries of some Nigerian personnel as well. OIC Lagos was to supply buildings for training facilities, equipment such as desks, chairs, books, and stationary for the feeder program, and salaries for the Nigerian administrative, secretarial, and instructional staff. OIC Lagos began operations in March 1971 with a group of 54 trainees enrolled in the feeder program; the second group included 75 trainees. The vocational training programs included secretarial sciences, electronics, commercial baking, hotel service and catering, auto mechanics, and office machine repair. The goal was to phase out the participation of OICI personnel in OIC Lagos over a five-year period.[40]

The African nations that Leon Sullivan visited in 1969 and the early 1970s were encouraged to organize groups to plan for the opening of OICs. Once support from USAID was possible to cover the expenses of OICI officers and instructors who came to those countries to help set up the OIC programs, the role of the local board of directors was to make arrangements with government officials to facilitate that process.[41] Social and cultural capital became major resources for the support of OIC programs in Ghana, Kenya, Ethiopia, and other African nations. Funds for the training programs were solicited from the public through memberships and donations. Fund-raising drives were organized by the boards of directors of the OICs in these nations to fulfill their part of the agreement reached with OICI.[42]

Beginning in 1975 the initial support from USAID to the African nations creating OIC programs began to expire. OICI officials submitted reports and accounts for the funds received from USAID over those years, but in most cases the local OIC boards of directors in the African nations were not in a position to substitute local funds for the foreign aid coming from the United States. In letters to the inspector general for USAID, the officers for OICI explained that it should "not be insisted upon that their success be predicated on their demonstrating that they would become totally self-sufficient." They also pointed out that "it must be recognized that it must take time to accomplish this essential objective" of "developing the human resources in Less Developed Countries." For example, OICI officers pointed to Accra, Ghana, where there were nine local board members, and seventeen OIC Ghana staff members had been brought to Philadelphia for training using funds from USAID. Between 1970 and 1974, there were 230 trainees placed in jobs, with a 94 percent retention rate. Local in-kind and cash contributions totaled over $90,000; and in 1974, $30,000 was raised for the OIC in Ghana.[43]

In many instances USAID officers agreed to provide additional assistance through the foreign aid program to African nations to support OIC programs, but the stipulation was that they would have to become self-sustaining financially. In other words, OICI programs in African nations had to be supported by collective cultural capital, government funding, and philanthropy after funds from USAID were no longer provided. And this has been the case. OIC International programs are operating *currently* in Liberia, Ghana, Cameroon, Nigeria, Sierra Leone, Gambia, and eleven other African nations.[44]

Building on the success of OIC International, in 1981 Leon Sullivan launched the International Foundation for Education and Self-Help (IFESH) to provide information on "self-help methods for improving the conditions of the poor" in the developing nations concerning food production, health care, employment, business development, and other areas. Among the programs sponsored by IFESH is the "International Fellows Program" that funds health care workers, bankers, agricultural experts, and others to assist in development projects. The "Teachers for Africa" program supports the sending of "master teachers" to African nations to engage in teacher training activities. Since its founding, "IFESH has affected millions of lives with self-help projects and programs in Africa, Latin America, and Asia" and has become "a major player for education and human development needs in African and other countries."[45]

CONCLUSION

The Tuskegee expedition and opening of the school in Notse, Togo, in 1901, the introduction of Tuskegee-style industrial education programs and the funding of Jeanes teachers in African nations by the Phelps Stokes Fund in the 1920s and 1930s, and the opening of the Booker T. Washington Institute in Liberia are all examples of transnational educational programs that began with African Americans in the United States and were transferred to African nations and colonial territories. The opening of the Opportunities Industrialization Centers in over a hundred cities in the United States by 1980 and their transfer to many African nations through OIC International is another major example of the movement of educational ideas and practices by and for African Americans from the United States to Africa.

At the same time, the contrast in the reception by Africans of the African American-modeled educational programs is striking. The industrial education programs provided by the Phelps Stokes Fund in the 1920s and 1930s received little or no financial support or resources from the Africans themselves. Most Africans were hostile to the Phelps Stokes Fund sponsored industrial education programs offered by missionary and government schools and at Liberia's Booker T. Washington Institute, and preferred to open their own independent schools. In the case of the OIC programs, the Africans themselves raised the social and cultural capital collectively in the 1970s to provide financial support for the introduction of the OIC vocational training programs into their larger cities. Both Africans and U.S. African Americans historically mobilized their own financial resources—cultural capital—to provide schooling that would advance their social and economic conditions, irrespective of the educational programs offered by missionary, governmental, or philanthropic agencies and institutions.

In the 20th century, U.S. African Americans and Africans often rejected industrial education programs that sought to adapt them to the social, economic, and racial status quo and were willing to financially support educational programs that prepared children and adults for political and economic self-determination. Indeed, the programs sponsored by OIC International and established in African nations were eventually taken over financially by the Africans themselves. The introduction of OIC International's vocational training programs, supported by collective cultural capital at the local and national levels, represents "the road not taken" by the International Monetary Fund, the World Bank, and other international development agencies in promoting educational alternatives for economic development in Africa and other nations in the developing world in the late 20th century.

NOTES

[1]Leon H. Sullivan, *Build Brother Build: From Poverty to Economic Power* (Philadelphia, PA, 1969), 179.

[2]James D. Anderson, *The Education of Blacks in the South, 1860–1936* (Chapel Hill, NC, 1988), pp. 121–83.

[3]Frenise A. Logan, "India—Britain's Substitute for American Cotton, 1861–65," *Journal of Southern History* 24 (November 1958): 472–480; and "India's Loss of the British Cotton Market After 1865," *Journal of Southern History* 31 (February 1965): 40–50.

[4]Donald Spivey, "The African Crusade for Black Industrial Schooling," *The Journal of Negro History* 63 (Winter 1978): 1–17; Michael O. West, "The Tuskegee Model in Africa: Another Dimension of the African/African American Connection," *Diplomatic History* 16 (July 1992): 371–87.

[5]Andrew Zimmerman, *Alabama in Africa: Booker T. Washington, the German Empire, and the Globalization of the New South* (Princeton, NJ, 2010), 130–31.

[6]Ibid., 171.

[7]Ibid., 127.

[8]Ibid., 163.

[9]Thomas Jesse Jones, *Negro Education: A Study of the Private and Higher Schools for the Colored People in the United States*. 2 Vols. (Washington, DC, 1917); *Educational Adaptations: Report of Ten Years' Work of the Phelps Stokes Fund, 1910–1920* (New York, 1920).

[10]V. P. Franklin, "Introduction," *Cultural Capital and Black Education: African American Communities and the Funding of Black Schooling, 1865 to the Present* (Greenwich, CT, 2004), ix–xx.

[11]Heather A. Williams, *Self-Taught: African American Education in Slavery and Freedom* (Chapel Hill, NC, 2007); Christopher Span, *From Cotton Field to Schoolhouse: African American Education in Mississippi, 1862–1877* (Chapel Hill, NC, 2009); V. P. Franklin, "Recent Books in African American Educational History," *The Journal of African American History* 87 (Fall 2002): 446–49.

[12]Mary Hoffschwelle, *The Rosenwald Schools of the American South* (Gainesville, FL, 2006); see also Peter M. Ascoli, *Julius Rosenwald: The Man Who Built Sears, Roebuck, and Advanced the Cause of Black Education in the South* (Bloomington, IN, 2006), 135–65.

[13]Thomas Jesse Jones, *Education in Africa: A Study of West, South, and Equatorial Africa by the African Education Commission under the Auspices of the Phelps Stokes Fund and the Foreign Mission Societies of North American and Europe* (New York, 1922); and *Education in East Africa: A Study of East, Central, and South Africa by the Second African Education Commission under the Auspices of the Phelps Stokes Fund* (New York, 1925).

[14]Phyllis McClure, *Jeanes Teachers: A View of Black Education in the Jim Crow South* (Phoenix, AZ, 2009).

[15]James Hardy Dillard, et al., *Report of Twenty Years' Work of the Phelps Stokes Fund, 1911–1931* (New York, 1932).

[16]Kenneth J. King, *Pan-Africanism and Education: A Study of Race Philanthropy and Education in the Southern States of America and East Africa* (Oxford, UK, 1971).

[17]Ibid., 124–25.

[18]Ibrahim Sundiata, *Brothers and Strangers: Black Zion and Black Slavery, 1914–1940* (Durham, NC, 1940).

[19]Donald Spivey, *The Politics of Miseducation: The Booker T. Washington Institute of Liberia, 1929–1984* (Lexington, KY, 1986), 125.

[20]Ibid., quotes on 125 & 146.

[21]For the origins of OIC programs, see Sullivan, *Build Brother Build*, 10–35; Leon H. Sullivan, *Moving Mountains: The Purposes and Principles of Leon Sullivan* (Valley Forge, PA, 1998), 11–24; Guian A. McKee, *The Problem of Jobs: Liberalism, Race, and Deindustrialization in Philadelphia* (Chicago, IL, 2008), 126–38; see also Matthew J. Countryman, *Up South: Civil Rights and Black Power in Philadelphia* (Philadelphia, PA, 2007), 83–120; Thomas Sugrue, *Sweet Land of Liberty: The Forgotten Struggle for Civil Rights in the North* (New York, 2009).

[22]Sullivan, *Moving Mountains*, 13.

[23]Ibid., 15.

[24]Ibid., 17.

[25]Ibid., 18.

[26]For information of the activities of the "Feeder Program," see "Feeder Program: OIC comprehensive service model—providing basic academic skills, as well as counseling to ensure that students were prepared emotionally to undergo intensive vocational and technical course instruction" (1965), box 76, Opportunities Industrialization Centers of America Papers, Urban Archives, Temple University, Philadelphia, PA (hereafter OICA Papers).

[27]Sullivan, *Moving Mountains*, 21; Sugrue, *Sweet Land of Liberty*, 279; McKee, *The Problem of Jobs*, 137–66.

[28]Michael Harrington, *The Other America: Poverty in the United States* (1962; rept. New York, 1997).

[29]Sullivan, *Moving Mountains*, 18; see also John C. Donovan, *The Politics of Poverty* (New York, 1967).

[30]Sullivan, *Moving Mountains*, 20–21.

[31]OICA, "Government Relations Office," box 33, OICA Papers. For example, "OIC accounted for more than 12 percent of the 91,000 people who received job training through the [War on Poverty's] Community Action

Programs (CAP) in 1968," McKee, *The Problem of Jobs*, 169.

[32]For information on the history of the Urban League, see Guichard Parris and Lester Brooks, *Blacks in the City: A History of the National Urban League* (Boston, MA, 1971); and Nancy Weiss, *The National Urban League, 1910–1940* (New York, 1974).

[33]"OIC National Extension Services, 1966–1971, Progress Reports," boxes 37 and 38; Developmental Task Force, "Reports on Activities in Chicago, Atlanta, Dallas, and San Francisco, 1968–1971," box 76, OICA Papers.

[34]Adult Armchair Education Program (HEW), 1966–1971, box 71; "OIC Linkage with Neighborhood Youth Corps, 1971–72," box 35, folder 34 & 38, OICA Papers; see also V. P. Franklin, "Opportunities Industrialization Centers: Collective Cultural Capital, Philanthropy, and Public-Private Partnerships in the Provision of Supplementary Education," in *Educating Comprehensively: Varieties of Educational Experiences,* ed. Linda J. Lin, Herve Verenne, and Edmund W. Gordon (Lewiston, NY, 2011), forthcoming.

[35]Correspondence between Dr. Folorunso Salawu and Valfoulaye Diallo, OICI director, box 1, folder 36, OIC International Papers, Urban Archives, Temple University, Philadelphia, PA (hereafter OICI Papers).

[36]Valfoulaye Diallo, OICI director, correspondence, 1967, 1968, 1969 Press Release—14 February 1969—"Trip to Africa," box 1, folder 40; Memo: 7 May 1969: "A Rendezvous with Rev. Leon H. Sullivan—The African Gathering: Report on Trip to Africa," box 2, folder 31, OICI Papers.

[37]Dr. F. Salawu to C. P. Johnston, Chair, Standard Bank of Nigeria, Lagos, 26 August 1971 (This letter included a request to serve as Chair of OIC Lagos National Advisory Board), box 1, folder 35, OICI Papers.

[38]OICI, "Affiliation Agreement—Standards/Guidelines: Recommended Affiliate Standards," box 2, folder 30, OICI Papers.

[39]OICI, "Board Standards—Fund Raising," box 2, folder 30, OICI Papers.

[40]V. Diallo to F. Salawu, 1 October 1970, Lagos, Nigeria; problems arose with the Nigerian Embassy providing two-year visas for OIC instructors to come to Lagos. Salaries of several Nigerian employees were to be covered by OICI, box 1, folder 42, OICI Papers.

[41]Executive Director Diallo to Leon H. Sullivan (LHS), correspondence, 1969; Tom Mboya, minister of economic planning and development, Nairobi, Kenya to LHS, 3 March 1969. W. A. Onyango-Ayoki to LHS, 10 March 1969, Nairobi, Kenya, offering support for OIC in Kenya. Draft of proposal for OIC in Kenya. B. A. Bentum, secretary general, Ghana Trades Union Congress to LHS, 13 March 1969; offers support from organized labor in founding of OIC in Ghana. L. D. Reddick, OIC coordinator of policies and programs, to Dr. Robtert Gardner, chief, U.N. Economics Commission, Addis Ababa, Ethiopia, 20 January 1969; on Rev. Sullivan's visit to Ethiopia, 19–24 February 1969; Other letters from Nigeria, Ghana, and Liberia from individuals wishing to receive information on employment in OIC in their country, box 1, folder 53, OICI Papers.

[42]For information on fund-raising activities in the African nations, see newspaper clipping from Accra, Ghana, 2 August 1973; "Cash for OIC," F. I. Andoh, treasurer of the Ghana National Chamber of Commerce to J. E. Kwamina Moses, chairman OIC Ghana. OIC provides "free skills training and job placement for unemployed and underemployed persons," box 2, folder 28, OICI Papers. For information on activities in Ethiopia, see Ethiopia OIC—Correspondence, 1969–1971. Asefa Gabregiorgis, Imperial Ministry of Education, Addis Ababa to LHS, 8 July 1969: Report on meeting of OIC Ethiopia, 30 June 1969. Membership list, Steering Committee. V. Diallo to Diallo Telli, administration secretary general OAU, Addis Ababa, 21 April 1971. Diallo to Robert Gardner, 17 May 1971. LHS met with Haile Selassie during trip to Ethiopia in May 1971. USAID interested in supporting financially OIC Ethiopia. Diallo Telli and Addis Ababa to LHS, 1 June 1971; Selashe Kebede, chair, OIC Ethiopia Steering Committee to LHS, 14 June 1971 box 5, folder 2, OICI Papers.

[43]"OIC International Response to the Office of the Inspector General's Foreign Assistance Report on the OIC International Activities submitted to the U.S. Congress, U.S. Secretary of State, and the U.S. Agency for International Development," February 1975, box 2, folder 35, OICI Papers.

[44]For information on current activities of OIC International in seventeen African nations and Haiti, see site map: http://www.oici.org/sitemap.

[45]Sullivan, *Moving Mountains*, 114–15. Dr. Julie Sullivan, the daughter of Leon Sullivan, is the president and CEO of IFESH. For detailed information on IFESH's current activities, see the IFESH website: www.ifesh.org.

AMANDLA! THE SULLIVAN PRINCIPLES AND THE BATTLE TO END APARTHEID IN SOUTH AFRICA, 1975–1987

James B. Stewart

Rev. Leon H. Sullivan, pastor emeritus of Zion Baptist Church in Philadelphia, was present in New York City when United Nations Secretary-General Kofi Annan formally introduced the Global Sullivan Principles of Social Responsibility (GSP) at a special session at the UN headquarters on 2 November 1999. Like the original "Sullivan Principles," the Global Sullivan Principles constituted a voluntary code of conduct for business activities, and over 120 companies, including most signatories to the original Sullivan Principles, endorsed Kofi Annan's initiative. In essence, the GSP restated the original objectives of the Sullivan Principles while broadening their applicability beyond the Republic of South Africa and modifying them to reflect contemporary challenges of "globalization" on the eve of the 21st century. The initiative declared: "The objectives of the Global Sullivan Principles are to support economic, social, and political justice by companies where they do business; to support human rights and to encourage equal opportunity at all levels of employment, including racial and gender diversity on decision-making committees and boards; to train and advance disadvantaged workers for technical, supervisory, and management opportunities; and to assist with greater tolerance and understanding among peoples; thereby, helping to improve the quality of life for communities, workers, and children with dignity and equality."[1]

The original Sullivan Principles, a corporate code of conduct formally announced in 1977 by Rev. Sullivan, became a focal point of debate about U.S. foreign policy and the behavior of multinational corporations during the heyday of the struggle against apartheid laws calling for the "separate development" of designated "racial groups" in South Africa. Rev. Sullivan fully intended the principles to serve as a catalyst for ending apartheid, and the Soweto rebellion beginning in June 1976 provided an important impetus for their development.[2] This uprising, led by black South African students opposed to the requirement that instruction in public and private schools be conducted in the Afrikaans language, also ushered in the first major phase of the divestment movement on U.S. college campuses.

James B. Stewart is Professor Emeritus of Labor Studies and Employment Relations at Pennsylvania State University in University Park, PA.

Student activists were calling on university officials to end investments in U.S. corporations operating in South Africa. Ironically, suspicion was aroused among anti-apartheid activists by the timing of the announcement of the Sullivan Principles, and their quick adoption by U.S. businesses and universities to justify maintaining their investment policies.[3]

Rev. Leon H. Sullivan received national and international attention in 1971 when he became the first African American appointed to the Board of Directors of General Motors Corporation, the largest automobile manufacturing company in the world. The origin of Sullivan's initiative can be traced to a tour of African nations in June 1975 when he was asked by anti-apartheid activists to take on the issue of South African apartheid. He issued a public statement in September 1975 describing the basic operating approach that would become associated with the principles, representing "a concerted double effort on the part of the government of the United States, and American based businesses [to change] operating [practices] in . . . South Africa."[4] The statement outlined what would later become the formal set of principles and expressed support for passage of the resolution submitted to the U.S. Congress by Congressman Charles Diggs of Detroit: "In the spirit of the Diggs Resolution dated April 22, 1975, businesses operating in South Africa that fail to comply with such equal fair employment practices, and equal opportunity provisions, should have all United States government contracts...cancelled, terminated, or suspended absolutely, or their continuance conditioned upon an accepted program by the United States government of compliance along these lines."[5] Sullivan's original position regarding the next course of action should these conditions not be met was that "all American companies operating in South Africa should withdraw formally and completely from that country."[6]

This September 1975 declaration contained most of the elements that shaped the trajectory of the Sullivan Principles. Rev. Sullivan wrote to the heads of various corporations in December 1975, inviting them to attend a meeting to be held in January 1976 "to informally discuss some of the activities and programs that different companies have utilized at their South African operations."[7] Twenty-one companies were invited to the meeting at Sands Point, New York, and fifteen sent representatives.[8] Only six of these attendees were among the twelve original signatories to the principles. GM's chief executive officer (CEO) Tom Murphy and Frank Cary, CEO of IBM, were the major endorsers of Sullivan's effort as a result of earlier involvements with Sullivan. Frank Cary had been a member of the National Industrial Advisory Council (NIAC) of Opportunities Industrialization Centers of America (OIC) since the council's formation in 1968; and Sullivan had worked closely with Tom Murphy from his appointment to the GM board of directors in 1971. In an article in *Time* magazine in September 1976 about Sullivan's activities, it was reported that when former President Lyndon B. Johnson, who had been a major supporter of Sullivan's OIC programs since 1967, learned of the Sullivan's GM appointment, he exclaimed, "Now what's good for General Motors really is good for America."[9]

This set of events raises several fascinating questions to be explored in this essay. How was Sullivan able to maintain the cooperation of these magnates of American industry in support of his principles? What was Sullivan's vision for U.S. businesses operating in South Africa and what strategies were deployed to realize his objectives? How successful was Sullivan in avoiding cooptation of the initiative by multinational corporations? And finally, what did the principles accomplish?

Given the eventual demise of South African apartheid, it is reasonable to ask: Did the implementation of the Sullivan Principles hasten or retard its end? Such a query must proceed with caution, however, because Sullivan was well aware that the adherence to these principles alone would not bring about the dismantling of apartheid. Thus, it is critical to understand how Sullivan's initiative interfaced with other efforts to confront the white racist regime. Donald R. Culverson's *Contesting Apartheid: U.S. Activism, 1960–1987* offered a retrospective assessment of anti-apartheid activities in the United States; and Francis Nesbitt's *Race for Sanctions: African Americans Against Apartheid, 1946–1994* described African Americans' efforts to combat apartheid, but both works minimize the impact of Leon Sullivan and the principles.[10] Many of Sullivan's critics who championed disinvestment, and the cessation of operations and exit of U.S. businesses from South Africa, viewed the principles as providing cover for overt and covert corporate support of the apartheid regime. These critics were heartened when many companies finally began to leave South Africa in the late 1980s, and celebrated this exodus as a refutation of the logic underlying the principles. However, the findings of Bernard Feigenbaum and Anton Lowenberg suggest the need for a more nuanced interpretation.[11] These researchers maintain that disinvestment was "most frequent among Sullivan signatory firms that . . . experienced rapid price appreciation, but [had] low profit margins" and that corporations with large South African operations were less likely to divest.[12] They concluded that "U.S. interest group pressure, mediated through institutional investment, seems to have [had] an effect on U.S. firms in South Africa." They found that "business operations [were] at least as important as anti-apartheid interest groups' political or moral preferences in determining the decision to disengage from South Africa," and "to the extent that interest groups insist[ed] on disinvestment, the most socially responsible firms . . . [were] weeded out and the least progressive firms . . . tend[ed] to remain."[13]

The primary focus for the Sullivan Principles was the plight of black South African workers and this was reflected in the design of the annual reporting process agreed to by those U.S. corporations that became signatories. However, opponents were understandably skeptical of self-reporting by U.S. firms, especially since Sullivan was not able to institute an on-site monitoring program. In fact, the evidence is mixed. The employment outcomes for black South Africans were positive, although less robust than claimed by some signatory firms. Alexandra Bernasek and Richard Porter indicate that the signatories to the Sullivan Principles "expanded their employment more rapidly than South African manufacturing as a whole, and they did it almost entirely with nonwhite labor."[14] They caution, however, that in other respects the signatories "behaved very much like typical non-signatory South African firms in their wage and employment growth patterns."[15]

Some researchers have sought to extract lessons from the implementation and operation of the Sullivan Principles useful for guiding contemporary efforts to monitor the behavior of multinational corporations through specific codes of conduct. Gay Seidman offered a somber assessment of these lessons: "Above all, the Sullivan experience reminds us that corporate codes of conduct offer only a feeble substitute for nationally based systems of corporate regulation."[16] In contrast, S. Prakash Sethi and Oliver Williams, who have written extensively on this topic, discerned more positive responses to the principles' regime.[17] They argued that "the Sullivan Principles have provided us with a plethora of experiences in terms of how to craft a good set of principles to guide business conduct that must be based on a combination of strong moral reasoning and economic feasibility."[18] In addition, they insist that "the Sullivan Principles also provide us with a rationale for how to create viable and defensible systems and procedures for monitoring and verifying corporate compliance with a given code of conduct, and the hazards and pitfalls that must be avoided for such a system to engender public trust."[19]

In formulating this view, Sethi and Williams drew upon the extensive, but virtually untapped, collection of primary and secondary documents detailing Sullivan's efforts to promote the principles through the formation of the International Council for Equality of Opportunity Principles (ICEOP).[20] However, Sethi and Williams's account disproportionately foregrounds the business community, and unfortunately, limits the recognition of the manner in which Sullivan creatively used traditional protest and mobilization strategies to extend the scope of black activism. Their limited attention to the ICEOP, and in particular its relationship to Sullivan's other anti-apartheid activities, unintentionally reinforces the tendency to be dismissive of the principles as a manifestation of black activism, as was the case in the study by Francis Nesbitt. This unfortunate impression is amplified by Sethi and Williams's failure to include a discussion of the Global Sullivan Principles, one of Sullivan's subsequent international initiatives that took full advantage of the lessons learned from the original principles.

"Amandla" is a Xhosa and Zulu word meaning "power" that served as the popular rallying cry for members of the African National Congress during the struggle against apartheid. This discussion provides the context and the details on the strategy pursued by Leon Sullivan to position the principles as a vehicle to influence the activities of U.S. businesses in South Africa. It was in his role as an insider and the creative use of "amandla" that allowed Sullivan to mobilize U.S. corporate interests against the apartheid regime. This reexamination of the principles sheds new light on the scope and possibilities of black activism in the international arena, a particularly salient issue in the current era of globalization.

THE SOUTH AFRICAN ECONOMY AND FOREIGN INVESTMENTS

Sullivan's corporate partners were well aware of his intentions and were decidedly cautious about his activities. Nevertheless, there were good reasons for them to explore strategies to justify continuing investments in South Africa. Multinational corporations from the United States and Europe played an increasingly important role in the South African economy in the post–World War II period. Visions of cheap and tractable labor led to a dramatic inflow of foreign capital between 1946 and 1950 and foreign investment accounted for about 40 percent of gross domestic investment in those years. The inflow of new foreign capital averaged about $308 million annually, and by the end of the 1960s, 40 percent of the South African manufacturing sector was controlled by foreign interests. Between 1970 and 1976 the annual net inflow of foreign capital had mushroomed to $1 billion per year. This accounted for about 13 percent of gross domestic investment, and by 1976 the total value of foreign investment was on the order of 20 billion Rand (R20 billion), compared to R2.8 billion in 1956. The United States, the United Kingdom, and other European nations were South Africa's principal foreign investors. U.S. direct investment increased from $140 million in 1950 to $750 million in 1970, and by 1975 the value had doubled to $1.56 billion. In 1970 over half of U.S. direct investment was in the manufacturing sector, 25 percent in petroleum, and 10 percent in mining. In addition, by the mid-1970s U.S. banks held approximately $2 billion in outstanding loans in South Africa, accounting for one-third of all foreign loan claims against South African interests.[21]

This extensive economic engagement was layered on top of a particularly pernicious system of overt and institutionalized racial discrimination. Political and social arrangements paralleling the U.S. "separate, but equal" Jim Crow regime were already in place prior to the Afrikaner Nationalist Party's victory in 1948. However, with the ascendance of the Nationalists, an unprecedented process of racial segregation took place, including legal prescriptions limiting the rights and opportunities for "non-white" groups. These new laws laid the foundation for modern apartheid in South Africa. The Population Registration Act of 1950 established a rigid racial classification system, while the 1953 Reservation of Separate

Amenities Act provided governmental authorization for the enforcement of racially separate public accommodations and other facilities. Interracial property transactions were outlawed under the Group Areas Acts of 1950 and 1957. Companies, other than banks, mines, and large factories, were assigned a "group character" according to the race of persons holding the controlling interests.[22] Various enactments facilitated the mobilization and exploitation of black South Africans. The Native Laws Amendment Act of 1952 established a registration process and labor bureau to control the movement of black South Africans seeking work in "white areas." Laws were passed outlawing strikes by black workers and prohibiting legally registered trade unions from having black members. The reservation of particular types of work for persons of specific racial groups was enshrined in the Industrial Conciliation Amendment Act of 1956.[23]

ORGANIZING A PLAN OF ACTION

The pervasive nature of the legal apparatus supporting South African apartheid contributed to the skepticism about the potential of Leon Sullivan's "code of conduct" for mounting an effective assault on racist practices. The idea of a corporate code of conduct was not new, however, and the British had adopted a code in 1974 "designed to encourage British firms in South Africa to improve their treatment of black employees."[24] A special attaché to the British Embassy was appointed to monitor implementation. This move prompted the appointment of a U.S. embassy official to monitor the treatment of black South Africans employed by U.S. firms, although no code existed at that time.[25]

The centerpiece of Sullivan's strategy was what was to become the International Council for Equality of Opportunity Principles (ICEOP), originally named the International Council for Minority Equality of Opportunity Principles (ICMEOP). Attorney Ira J. K. Wells, Jr., notified Rev. Sullivan on 6 October 1978 that the ICMEOP had been authorized to operate as a non-profit corporation in the Commonwealth of Pennsylvania.[26] Sullivan, Wells, and Rev. Gus Roman, the only officers listed in the application for non-profit status, were the original signatories to the ambitious effort to bring about social change in the Republic of South Africa.[27] The ICMEOP sought to "promote the human rights of all persons in all parts of the world and therefore help create an environment in which the definite worth and well being of persons can be developed to full potential by persuading those with the power of decision-making to share in a process to make available to all persons the equality of opportunity in areas of: employment . . . , education . . . , housing, transportation, recreational and health facilities . . . [a]nd improving the quality of employees' lives outside the work environment . . . [a]nd by establishing a monitoring system to assure implementation of the techniques of equal opportunity."[28]

In forming this council, Sullivan drew heavily on his experience in shaping Opportunities Industrialization Centers of America (OIC), the community-based organization providing vocational training and employment services to disadvantaged youth and adults. OIC was organized in Philadelphia in 1964 while Sullivan served as pastor of Zion Baptist Church. During the 1950s he gained national recognition for his efforts to combat juvenile delinquency, and the establishment of a Youth Employment Service in Zion Baptist Church. The OIC job training program grew out of these activities and was originally supported financially through the "collective cultural capital" raised in the African American community, as well as through donations of equipment and other materials from local businesses. Shortly after the opening of the first OIC, the Ford Foundation also provided some important financial support.[29]

With the launching of the "War on Poverty" in 1966, OIC programs were opened in over fifty cities, expanding to locations where National Urban League branches were located and engaged in job placement activities. OIC was built on the belief that industry would accept trainees who were "job ready." This meant that "the training program staff would have to develop a close association with the business community to know what job skills must be taught, what type of equipment is used on the job, and what types of new jobs might be expected to emerge."[30] OIC programs trained disadvantaged workers in the new skills needed by local business owners and industries.

There were several aspects of OIC's linkage to its business and governmental partners that are especially relevant for understanding how Sullivan managed his relationship with corporate partners in promoting the principles in South Africa. Initially, there was a cultural disconnect to overcome because members of the clergy were greatly overrepresented within the OIC leadership. Although there are certainly similarities between managing a church and managing a business, there are important cultural and operational differences. As Sonja Stone has observed, Sullivan learned both church administration and politics during the years he worked at Abyssinian Baptist Church with Rev. Adam Clayton Powell, Jr., who also served as the U.S. Congressman representing Harlem from 1945 to 1967.[31] Sullivan characterized Congressman Powell as "the greatest teacher of politics that Black people have ever produced."[32] This tradition often emphasized "speaking truth to power," rather than practicing the staid communication styles associated with the corporate world where status and hierarchy defined privilege and access. The divergent perspectives of the black ministerial leadership and corporate executives often resulted in a communication gap that Sullivan had to bridge.[33]

At the same time, Sullivan's organizations sometimes encountered difficulties in working with corporations due to insufficient attention to logistical and fiscal details typically emphasized by businesses. The ministerial overlay also meant that very few women were in OIC leadership positions, a gender bias replicated among corporate decision makers. As a consequence, women were largely absent in the history of the formation and implementation of the Sullivan Principles. This is essentially a story of the interaction between black clergymen and white male corporate executives. Despite the potential problems, however, the OIC clergy-business partnership endured due to multilevel linkages facilitated by the formation of the "National Technical Advisory Committee" and the "Industry Technical Assistance Contact Network." While the latter group managed interaction between industry representatives and local OIC managers, the membership on the advisory committee consisted of a mix of OIC officials and business people, and this multilayered structure not only facilitated cooperation, it also provided each member of the alliance a means to obtain on-going intelligence about the effectiveness of collaborative efforts. These assessments could be communicated upward through regular organizational channels to provide input for negotiating modifications to the overall partnership arrangements.[34]

Sullivan's close partnership with the business community created some resentment among other civil rights leaders. Economist Bernard Anderson noted that "OIC eschew[ed] the direct action tactics often employed by civil rights groups such as Rev. Jesse Jackson's Operation PUSH [People United to Save Humanity]."[35] While this strategy facilitated cooperation with the private sector, at the same time, it constrained Sullivan's ability to work effectively with some organizations less trusting of the business community. However, Sullivan generally maintained open alliances with civil rights leaders, and the featured speakers at OIC national convocations included the Southern Christian Leadership Conference's (SCLC) Joseph Lowery, the NAACP's Benjamin Hooks, the National Urban League's Vernon Jordan, and Jesse Jackson.[36] In addition, SCLC's Ralph David Abernathy joined the ICEOP board in July 1979.[37]

Sullivan was able to leverage the business partnership to access federal funds to support OIC and bridge the gap between the private sector and public programs designed to serve the needs of the unemployed.[38] OIC was designated as a prime national contractor for the delivery of manpower services in July 1971 and was funded at over $32 million for fiscal year 1972.[39] This unique status reflected Sullivan's influence in the highest governmental circles and his connection to Congressman Adam Clayton Powell, who sponsored the original legislation authorizing federal funding for OIC in 1966.[40]

Sullivan attempted to replicate characteristics of the tripartite OIC-business-government partnership in developing, implementing, and monitoring his principles for U.S. businesses operating in South Africa. At the same time, Sullivan relied heavily on his ministerial network in organizing the ICEOP. Five of the eight original board members had some affiliation with religious institutions, and no women were included.[41] He attempted to further consolidate a base of support among religious leaders by creating in 1979 an Ecumenical Clergy Support Committee. That same year the clergy support committee made an aggressive effort to deflect the criticism coming from other religious leaders attempting to discredit the Sullivan Principles. The minutes for the 13 September 1979 meeting indicate that a concrete action plan to deal with the opposition was outlined, including issuing a statement that any effort to attack Rev. Sullivan or the principles "would be dealt with in a strong fashion. . . ."[42] There is also mention of a potential "attempt to picket General Motors and a call . . . for Rev. Sullivan to resign from the GM Board."[43] Those in attendance felt that the group should assume an offensive posture. President Jimmy Carter had been supportive of OIC and the community development projects launched by Sullivan's "Progress Movement" in Philadelphia. It was suggested that a meeting be arranged with Sullivan, and Carter administration official Andrew Young, U.S. Ambassador to the United Nations, as well as Vernon Jordan, and Jesse Jackson. Rev. Sullivan agreed that such a meeting would be useful. "If we [orchestrate] the variables, they can work for us as they did in the case of Dr. Martin Luther King, Jr. . . ."[44]

President Jimmy Carter speaking at OIC-sponsored community development program in Philadelphia. Rev. Leon Sullivan seated at left. Courtesy of Leon H. Sullivan Charitable Trust, Philadelphia, PA.

Sullivan attempted to replicate the multilayered system of support that characterized the OIC-business partnership in establishing the infrastructure for the principles campaign. Sullivan established the "Industry Steering Committee" to seek out top-level corporate involvement and participation. In addition, representatives of Sullivan signatory companies were organized into "task groups" made up of executives below the CEO level. Mirroring the gender homogeneity of the ICEOP, no women were among the original task group chairpersons. Each task group was charged with developing implementation strategies to promote improvement in one of the areas targeted by the principles.

Recognizing the differences between working in an international as opposed to a domestic setting, Sullivan also attempted to duplicate the basic industrial support structure within South Africa. Conceivably, Sullivan could also have developed a communication network for local black managers to report on the concerns about their employers' activities in South Africa. Such a network would have provided him with inside information that could have been used to assess the level of institutional commitment to the implementation of the principles. However, no such mechanism was established. In a similar vein, Sullivan failed to take advantage of the expertise of U.S. academics or specialists in labor-management relations within nongovernmental organizations. The exceptions were the appointment of economist Andrew Brimmer as an original member of the ICEOP board, and the establishment of a consulting relationship with psychologist Kenneth Clark.[45]

IMPLEMENTING AND MONITORING THE SULLIVAN PRINCIPLES

The original version of the Sullivan Principles contained six requirements and committed signatories to (1) non-segregation in all eating, comfort, and work facilities; (2) equal and fair employment practices for all employees; (3) equal pay for all employees doing equal or comparable work for the same period of time; (4) initiation and development of training programs to prepare black and other non-white South Africans for supervisory, administrative, clerical and technical jobs; (5) increasing the number of blacks and other non-whites in management and supervisory positions; and (6) improving the quality of employees' lives outside the work environment in such areas as housing, transportation, schooling, and recreation and health facilities. Each of these general principles was supported by detailed statements of expected indicators of progress.[46]

Only the sixth principle asked corporations to do more than what was expected of businesses in the United States in the late 1970s. However, in the South African setting these principles had truly revolutionary potential. Sullivan originally proposed the following language to be contained at the end of the sixth requirement: "Where implementation requires a modification of existing South African laws or customs, we will seek such modification through appropriate channels."[47] Instead, the signatories insisted on eliminating the references to "laws and customs" and instead substituted "South African working conditions."[48] Even with these modifications, the original twelve signatories were still uncomfortable with the role that Sullivan envisioned for them as "warriors in the battle against the apartheid regime."[49] Their level of commitment was limited to efforts to improve working conditions in the plants that they owned and operated. The signatories summarily rejected a proposed amendment offered by Sullivan that would have tied future investment decisions to an assessment of progress in implementing the principles.[50] Thus, even at the outset of this venture, U.S. companies were unwilling to link issues of improved working conditions to the broader issue of whether their presence and investments in South Africa should be reconsidered.

Even with the more reserved language, neither the original corporations from which Sullivan sought support, nor the larger group of U.S. multinational corporations, enthusiastically embraced the Sullivan Principles. There was great unease about Sullivan's plans to advocate for the use of the principles as an instrument of U.S. foreign policy. For example, an internal memorandum to the chairman of General Motors Tom Murphy from T. S. Daniel discussed a planned meeting between Sullivan and the U.S. Secretary of State Cyrus Vance, in the following terms: "As I have indicated to you, there is a very strong negative feeling among the companies regarding Sullivan acting as their spokesman. Most (including IBM) have said they want two or three company officials to participate in any discussions with government officials."[51]

Within six months of the formal promulgation of the principles, fifty-four firms had become signatories. The design of a viable monitoring process to assess firms' implementation efforts was critical for establishing any sense of credibility among skeptics. The firm of Arthur D. Little (ADL) was selected to conduct a pilot survey of signatories to ascertain the extent of compliance with the principles. This initial report, along with the next two, was designed to capture progress in implementing the principles at six-month intervals. Subsequent reports would be submitted on an annual basis, a change formally announced by Sullivan at the 29 November 1979 meeting of the CEOs of the signatory companies hosted by Secretary Cyrus Vance. Sullivan had also used that occasion to announce his plans for "on-site" monitoring.[52]

The first ADL-prepared report contained no categorizations and was based on fifty-seven responses to questionnaires sent to 105 signatories. While it provided baseline data related to each of the principles, the narrative openly acknowledged that changes would be needed.[53] Paul Gibson, president of Envirotech, had written to Sullivan on 17 November 1978 recommending a three category classification scheme: "(i) companies that are implementing the Statement of Principles (satisfactorily); (ii) companies that are not implementing the Statement of Principles (satisfactorily), but which after being notified that you do not feel that they are implementing the Statement of Principles (satisfactorily), have submitted to you an acceptable plan with a specific time schedule to bring them into line, i.e., Category A(i); and (iii) companies that are not implementing the Statement of Principles (satisfactorily) and have not agreed to bring themselves into line as per Category A(ii) above."[54] Gibson went on to recommend how Sullivan should respond to inquiries about the compliance of individual companies.

Sullivan's corporate partners were especially concerned with his insistence on specifically identifying non-signatory companies. In a memorandum dated 26 February 1979, T. S. Krzesinski, who worked in the treasurer's office at General Motors, described an intense meeting over "Sullivan's absolute insistence that there be some form of public disclosure on the progress of individual companies'—in the current reporting cycle—compliance as of December 31, 1978 to be released by Sullivan and Arthur D. Little [in] late March 1979." Krzesinski complained that Sullivan had reneged on an earlier agreement to "defer public categorization until the semi-annual reporting period ending June 30, 1979." He believed that "despite intense resistance by industry representatives, Sullivan presented the group with no [a]lternative. In fact, he brought the meeting to a premature ending with his departure and emotional announcement that i[f] an acceptable manner of disclosure was not available to him prior to the next morning's meeting, he would terminate his involvement with the principles."[55]

The second ADL report, which covered the period 1 July to 31 December 1978, indicated there were 117 signatories and 165 non-signatory U.S. firms that were not listed individually. Confusion about reporting deadlines and appropriate responses necessitated the creation of several temporary categories for signatories such as "Reports Arrived Late," "Plan to Submit Report," and "Exceptional Situations."[56] The categories used in the second report for evaluating companies were: "making acceptable progress," "cooperating," and "non-respondent." To qualify as "making acceptable progress," it was only necessary that a company had submitted a completed first questionnaire for the period 1 January to 30 June 1978; submitted a completed second questionnaire for the period 1 July to 31 December 1978 by March 1979; committed to major facility modifications to enable non-segregation; and shown substantial commitment to implement the other principles. All other respondents were classified as "cooperating."[57]

In the 15 October 1979 press release announcing the release of ADL's third report, it revealed that "three-fourths of all reporting units of participating American corporations indicate that all facilities are now non-segregated, all signs are removed, and facilities are open to all races. This has happened in spite of

South African laws demanding separate provisions for persons of different races. The report further indicated some progress in the implementation of all parts of the 'principles.'"[58] This report reflected an amplification of the second principle announced by Sullivan in May 1979 to include the wording: "Support the elimination of discrimination against the rights of Blacks to form or belong to government registered unions, and acknowledge generally the right of Black workers to form their own union or be represented by trade unions where unions already exist."[59] The sixth principle had also been amplified, incorporating the wording: "Support changes in influx control laws to provide for the right of Black migrant workers to normal family life."[60] Sullivan's earlier attempts to obtain these changes had been unsuccessful.[61] As in the second report, the number of non-signatories (164) exceeded signatories (135). This time, however, the individual non-signatory companies were specifically identified.[62]

The reporting requirements associated with the Sullivan Principles differed from other codes of conduct, including those of the European Economic Community (EEC) and Canada. The EEC code, unlike the Sullivan Principles, was mandatory. However, although the EEC code mandated reporting, the performance of individual companies was not evaluated. The Canadian code also had a reporting requirement, but the compliance rate was usually extremely low.[63] The annual reporting process became a major enterprise in itself, and the requirements for managing it were well beyond the capabilities of ICEOP. In addition, the cost of this operation was borne by the signatories, who paid an annual fee which covered the operating costs of the administrative structure to support the implementation of the principles. Unfortunately, the ICEOP had no independent source of financial support that could be used as leverage, given the possibility of corporate control. Absent the type of leverage available through independent sources of income, an on-going pattern of fiscal dependence was created when the principles' "Industry Support Unit" (ISU) was incorporated in Pennsylvania in April 1979 as a non-profit group. This agency was established to "provide Sullivan with a conduit for obtaining funds to assist in the support of an Administrative Staff Unit (ASU), which will assist him broadly in facilitating promotion and implementation of the six principles."[64] Provisions for two classes of ISU directors were included in the articles of incorporation. Two "Class A" directors were to be appointed by Sullivan; and four "Class B" directors were to be elected by a majority of those corporations represented on the "Statement of Principles Industry Advisory Committee" (SOPIAC). The membership of the SOPIAC consisted of the chairs of the seven task groups, plus two at large members. Sal Marzullo of Mobil Oil would become the most important and active member of this advisory committee.[65]

In obtaining this commitment, Sullivan had to agree to limit the activities of the administrative staff funded by the ISU. The document recommending creation of the ASU stated: "It is recognized that Sullivan's personal objective, the destruction of the system of apartheid in the Republic of South Africa, goes beyond the issues of social and economic discrimination to which the Six Principles are addressed. It is understood between Sullivan and the companies that will support this effort that the use of such support will be limited to the ASU's activities involved with the promotion and implementation of the Six Principles as amplified by the guidelines."[66]

Sullivan fought the proposal to establish an ISU administrative structure separate from the ICEOP. As a compromise, the ISU provided support for an executive director of an administrative support staff for the ICEOP. Daniel Purnell was appointed to this position. Formerly director of the Community Resource Center of Cuyahoga Community College, Cleveland, Ohio, immediately prior to this appointment, Purnell had also served as an administrator in the office of public school desegregation in Cleveland.[67] While the ICEOP staff and board would be plagued by high turnovers over the years, Purnell would remain for the duration.

Despite the presumed understanding about staff roles, there was continuing disagreement between Sullivan and ISU's corporate supporters over how funds were to be used, the relationship to the ICEOP, and the high cost of the annual reporting process. Sethi and Williams's examination of the implementation of the Sullivan Principles focused almost entirely on the ISU staff and its interaction with D. Reid Weedon of ADL, with little mention of the ICEOP. At the same time, the elaborate reporting process and the credibility of the Arthur D. Little Company were insufficient to mollify many in the activist community who looked askance at the annual reports, in part, because they were based primarily on the self-reporting by U.S. companies. Sullivan sought to develop an on-site monitoring mechanism controlled completely by the ICEOP that would include regular visits to the signatory companies' operations to gather information and direct feedback from black workers. Unfortunately, Sullivan was never able to acquire external funding to establish such a monitoring system and the ISU's funders refused to support this activity. The lack of a ground-level intelligence network placed Sullivan at a distinct disadvantage in addressing specific problems for black workers seeking union representation. For example, Sullivan received a letter from W. M. Menze, a union organizer, dated 12 May 1981, requesting assistance in regaining employment at Firestone Company following what was described as an "illegal dismissal." This dismissal was apparently associated with Firestone's sale in 1981 of a majority interest to Federale Volksbeleggings Beperk, a South African holding company. There is no record of any intervention by Sullivan on the behalf of dismissed black workers.[68] Such experiences weakened the commitment of black workers to Sullivan's initiatives during a period when the black unionization movement was becoming the major force driving the South African government's labor reforms.

Sullivan's own visits to South Africa were only partially successful in broadening his support base. "Reverend Sullivan Visits S. Africa," was the headline of the ICEOP newsletter in October 1980 and included a photo of Rev. Sullivan and Bishop Desmond Tutu. On 4 September 1980 Sullivan was in Johannesburg to deliver the Hoernle Memorial Lecture, sponsored annually by the South African Institute for Race Relations. The newsletter reported that "press coverage before, during, and after the visit was heavy." A Johannesburg *Daily Mail* editorial was reprinted in the newsletter with the observation that Sullivan "is having to cope with considerable criticism, both in South Africa and in America, that the guidelines bearing his name are not doing what they are supposed to do, and indeed that they are being used as a prop for apartheid. . . . Mr. Sullivan has returned home vowing to set up an effective monitoring system and threatens disinvestment action against companies that do not come up to the mark."[69] However, the report in the newsletter included no information about specific plans for on-site monitoring.

The minutes for the ICEOP board meeting on 27 October 1980 indicated that Sullivan characterized his trip to South Africa as "very difficult." Nevertheless, he declared,

We are going in the right direction, but intensification and broadening are necessary, more vigorous dealing with legal aspects, which means separate development. We are changing conditions, but not the basic situation. We must change the ground rules of society; sessions between Whites and Blacks to change these rules are needed. These rules include: exile, prisoners, and Nelson [Mandela]. Problems must be confronted through economics. Difficult.[70]

THE SULLIVAN PRINCIPLES VERSUS
CONSTRUCTIVE ENGAGEMENT

Following the inauguration of Ronald Reagan as president in January 1981, there was a significant shift in U.S. foreign policy toward South Africa. The new policy of "constructive engagement" emphasized evolutionary social change in South Africa that would be pursued through non-confrontational means. This was seen as appropriate, given the common strategic interests of the United States and South Africa, and it justified unilateral action by the United States, as opposed to multilateral approaches through organizations such as the United Nations. This policy focused on confronting communism throughout southern Africa, with the issue of human rights in South Africa a secondary concern. Chester Crocker, assistant secretary of state for African affairs, was the policy's chief architect, and an official visit by South African military officials in March 1981 was one of the early and most visible manifestations of the change in policy. In November 1983 the Reagan administration heaped praise on the P. W. Botha regime for conducting a constitutional referendum that granted limited parliamentary participation to the "Coloured" (mixed race) and Asian populations, while black South Africans remained disfranchised.[71]

Leon Sullivan began to harden his position on apartheid in South Africa as early as October 1979 when he initiated a campaign to halt loans by U.S. banks to the South African government. Sullivan attempted to mobilize clergy across the United States to visit banks and attempt to convince the officers to adopt a proposed statement refusing loans to South Africa, but only a handful of banks were willing to endorse the statement. Sullivan's effort to mobilize grassroots support to force compliance also failed. At the same time, many of his corporate allies in the principles movement did not take kindly to this new initiative. What is especially important, however, is the difference in the approach toward the banks compared to other types of businesses. This difference was emphasized in a communication that Sullivan received 25 March 1980 from a banking executive: "What puzzles me most . . . is the distinction you apparently draw between banks and other business concerns in what you want us to do. . . . In negotiating with the banks . . . you seem to have taken a near-boycott approach."[72]

A broad-based movement opposing the Reagan administration's policy of constructive engagement began to crystallize early in 1983. On the legislative side, several attempts were made in Congress to derail the approach. William Gray, the Democratic representative from Philadelphia, introduced H.R. Bill 1392 that would require the president to use the authority of the War Powers Act to ban new investments in South Africa. Democratic representative from New York City Stephen Solarz introduced H.R. Bill 1693 that would require all U.S. firms operating in South Africa to comply with the Sullivan Principles, and banned new loans from U.S. banks to the South African government.[73] To the chagrin of his corporate partners, Sullivan actively supported both bills.

On 6 June 1983 Sullivan testified before the U.S. House Banking Sub-committee on Financial Institutions Supervision, Regulation, and Insurance in support of the Solarz bill.[74] The substance of his testimony appeared earlier in a 10 May 1983 article in the *Washington Post*, "It's Time to Step Up the Pressure on South Africa."[75] Sullivan mentioned his earlier testimony before the Foreign Affairs Subcommittee on Africa on 2 March 1982 in which he had called for "mandatory requirements for full compliance with the principles . . . backed up with embargoes, tax penalties, sanctions, loss of government contracts and any other effective means."[76] Sullivan also noted that "although the voluntary support of the principles has been effective, it has not been able to get the desired results quickly enough," and thus "I support the [Solarz] bill in its entirety."[77]

At the 20 May 1983 ICEOP board meeting, Sullivan proposed "A Five Step Action Plan" to his institutional supporters.[78] The plan called for (1) divestment of all funds in non-signatory companies; (2) divestment of funds in signatories that have received failing grades and have not provided written assurance that efforts to improve ratings will be undertaken; (3) withdrawal of funds from banks failing to give written assurance of cessation of loans to the South African government and its agencies; (4) the seeking of agreements from companies to forego new investments in South Africa; (5) the encouragement of similar actions by other investors.[79] Increasingly, Sullivan began to apply elements of the strategy used to oppose bank loans to attack the broader issue of corporate investments in South Africa. He spoke forcefully about the need for sanctions if the principles failed to yield concrete results. Information included in the fifth and sixth report of the signatories provided a solid rationale for his more militant actions. For example, the fifth report was much more candid in acknowledging problem areas than the earlier ones. It indicated that "[i]n spite of the progress, there are still problems. This year [1981] there was an increase in the number of companies not meeting the basic requirements."[80]

> While it is encouraging that the average pay increases for Blacks, Coloreds, and Asians have been more each year, it is still not clear that this rate of increase is sufficient to have a significant impact on the large wage gap between Whites and Blacks, Coloreds, and Asians. It has been hoped that much of this problem would be corrected as more Blacks, Colored, and Asians advance to the higher-paying supervisory and managerial jobs (Principle 5). But . . . the pace of this advancement has been slow. For senior managerial jobs hardly any such advancement has occurred since the Third Report.[81]

The reason for this was the "sluggish growth in the rate of participation of Blacks, Coloreds, and Asians in training programs designed to prepare them for supervisory and managerial positions."[82] This pattern was explained by educational inequities and inappropriate design of some training programs.[83] In a similar vein, the sixth report in November 1982 noted, "The proportion of Blacks, Coloureds, and Asians in supervisory positions has dropped, indicating a lack of progress in this area."[84] Continuing barriers to unionization of black workers were also highlighted.[85]

Sethi and Williams found that as the reporting process became more complex, the ICEOP became increasingly superfluous. It was easier for the ISU to work directly with the ADL's D. Reid Weedon to maintain the annual reporting process, rather than using the ICEOP as an intermediary. Financial uncertainties created by the ICEOP's dependence on funding from the signatories prevented actions to improve the reporting procedures and better connect ADL's activities to Sullivan's "task groups" in the United States and South Africa.[86] Moreover, some of the ICEOP's inadequacies also stemmed from internal managerial problems and the business practices of Daniel Purnell, the ICEOP executive director. Complaints from U.S. businesses operating in South Africa were sent to the ICEOP board of directors in September 1982 about the failure to meet U.S. tax filing deadlines to avoid penalties and the need for appropriate documentation for travel and entertainment expenses.[87] Specific recommendations were made because, according to one CEO, "it is apparent that ICEOP (specifically Mr. Purnell) is having difficulty strengthening internal accounting and financial operating controls."[88]

A significant decline in the number of signatories occurred between the completion of the sixth and seventh reports in 1983 as a result of the decision to require the payment of assessments to the ISU *before* designation as a signatory to the Sullivan Principles. As a result, the seventh report noted, "Twenty-nine signatories, mostly endorsers or *non-reporters*, have dropped out of the program rather than pay. Although the total number of signatories has decreased significantly, no such change has occurred in the total number of *reporting* signatories."[89]

By the mid-1980s Leon Sullivan's position on U.S. investments in South Africa was clearly in conflict with the policies of the Reagan administration and the economic interests of many U.S. businesses operating in South Africa. In March 1984 Secretary of State George Schultz hosted a meeting of eighteen representatives of Sullivan signatory companies and fourteen representatives of non-signatories. Schultz took the position that "in a sense" the cooperation of U.S. businesses in the Sullivan initiatives had "anticipated constructive engagement." This linkage of the Sullivan Principles to "constructive engagement" was designed to stem a tide of mounting public criticism, but it significantly damaged Sullivan's credibility with anti-apartheid activists. However, any potential gains in public support for constructive engagement were negated on 20 July 1985 when South Africa's president P. W. Botha declared a "state of emergency" for several regions of the country, and delivered his infamous "Rubicon" speech on 15 August 1985. Botha ruled out the possibility of power sharing with black South Africans and announced that he "had crossed the Rubicon" and would pursue change "at his own pace and on his own terms." However, even prior to Botha's speech the American Chamber of Commerce in South Africa had sought to distance itself from the apartheid regime. In a news release dated 7 March 1985 U.S. business groups condemned government policies such as "influx control, forced removals," denial of citizenship rights, and inadequate housing for non-whites, and called for negotiations between black South African leaders and the apartheid regime.[90]

With the hardening of the position of the South African government and the increasing demands for U.S. divestment, President Reagan issued an executive order in September 1985 banning the importation of South African gold coins, the Krugerrands, and mandated that U.S. corporations operating there adhere to the Sullivan Principles. The order also put some restrictions on technology exports to South Africa and directed the secretary of state to establish an "Advisory Committee on South Africa." GM's Roger Smith, IBM's Frank Cary, and Leon

**Rev. Leon H. Sullivan and Secretary of State George Schultz.
Courtesy of Leon H. Sullivan Charitable Trust.**

Sullivan were eventually appointed to that committee.[91] At the same time, Botha's speech and the South African government's actions intensified the momentum for divestment at many colleges and universities and in state and local governments. Until Botha's speech, many university and government officials had resisted the increasingly vociferous calls for divestment. TransAfrica, the African American lobbying group headed by Randall Robinson, had been especially instrumental in organizing opposition to the U.S. policy in South Africa. The "Free South Africa Movement" was launched in November 1985 when Robinson, Mary Frances Berry, Walter Fauntroy, and Richard Hatcher were arrested after staging a sit-in at the South African embassy in Washington, DC. The four were the first to be arrested at the embassy for protesting the arrest of black labor leaders and members of the African National Congress (ANC), and the murderous tactics employed by the South African government. Between November 1984 and the enactment of sanctions legislation in October 1986, up to 6,000 people were arrested while picketing at South African embassies and consulates around the world. Demonstrators included eighteen members of the U.S. House of Representatives and Connecticut Senator Lowell Weicker, who became the first Senator in U.S. history to be arrested for an act of civil disobedience.[92]

Leon Sullivan agreed to join the Presidential Advisory Committee on South Africa at a time when there appeared to be some movement toward resolution of the racial conflict. The British Commonwealth nations launched a peace initiative in late 1985 spearheaded by a seven-person international delegation that became known as the Eminent Person's Group (EPG). This group spent approximately six months attempting to create a dialogue between anti-apartheid leaders and the South African government. The June 1986 EPG report concluded that the South African government had demonstrated no genuine intention to dismantle apartheid, or enter into negotiations with ANC leaders. The Commonwealth leaders met in August 1986 and with the exception of the British agreed to impose limited economic sanctions on South Africa.[93]

President Reagan's failure to take more decisive action led Robert Dole, Richard Lugar, Nancy Kassebaum, and other Senate Republicans to join Democratic congressmen Howard Wolpe and Stephen Solarz and members of the Black Caucus in pushing for stronger sanctions. The result of this alliance was the passage of the Comprehensive Anti-Apartheid Act (CAAA) over a presidential veto on 2 October 1986. The legislation "set forth a comprehensive and complete framework to guide the efforts of the United States in helping to bring an end to apartheid in South Africa and lead to the establishment of a nonracial, democratic form of government." In effect, the law was intended to establish a new U.S. policy to replace "constructive engagement."[94]

Along with these developments, South Africa's economic instability was intensified by the refusal of major U.S. banks, beginning with Chase Manhattan in July 1985, to roll over the short-term loans of the South African government. As a result, South African officials were forced to temporarily freeze repayments of foreign loans and halt currency transactions, as well as close its stock market, after the value of the rand plummeted.[95] Economist Pauline Baker noted that "an international debt mediator had to be appointed, and protracted negotiations for rescheduling ensued."[96]

By 1986 the number of Sullivan signatories had increased to 183. This growth was impressive because it had occurred simultaneously with further tightening of the guidelines required to achieve a top rating. Signatories were now subject to the seventh requirement introduced in 1985: "Working to Eliminate Laws and Customs That Impede Social and Political Justice." This forward movement was disrupted by the decisions of some major signatories to terminate altogether their operations in South Africa. Coca-Cola announced plans to terminate operations in September 1986, followed closely by General Motors and IBM in October.[97]

Earlier that year at the 18 June 1986 ICEOP board meeting, in a last ditch effort to salvage the principles initiative, Rev. Gus Roman proposed the updating of the Sullivan Principles on "a theological basis." The board agreed to have Dr. Lawrence Jones, dean of Howard University School of Theology, develop the update. Jones attended the 31 July 1986 ICEOP board meeting and offered suggestions regarding the theological update, and several clergy were to be invited to a September plenary session.[98] However, Daniel Purnell was unsuccessful in obtaining foundation funding for this initiative. Instead, what was termed a "Call to Conscience Conference" was held on 30 September 1986, but the focus of this event was much different, and the news release announcing the conference indicated that the purpose was "to gain support for legislation in the U.S. Congress concerning welfare reform and to call for an end to the system of apartheid in South Africa."[99]

The Schultz Advisory Committee Report, mandated in President Reagan's September 1985 executive order, was released in 1987, entitled "A U.S. Policy Toward South Africa," and concluded that "constructive engagement" was a failed policy. The first priority of U.S. policy recommended in this report was to promote negotiations between the apartheid regime and legitimate black representatives. It also recommended that the administration distance itself from Pretoria's recently announced policies and attempt to internationalize existing sanctions. In addition, it advised administration officials to consider applying additional pressure on the South African government to lift the state of emergency, release all political prisoners, and end its ban on the ANC and other black political parties. In essence, the report not only reaffirmed, but in some cases recommended more stringent sanctions than authorized in the Comprehensive Anti-Apartheid Act of 1986.[100]

By the beginning of 1987 Leon Sullivan was operating under a self-imposed deadline for an end of apartheid in South Africa that he first announced in May 1985. It appeared on 7 May 1985 as an editorial in the *Philadelphia Inquirer* and was entitled "A Deadline for Ending Apartheid." There he indicated that "[i]t is my view . . . that if apartheid has not, in fact, ended legally and actually within the next 24 months, there should be a total U.S. economic embargo against South Africa, including the withdrawal of all U.S. companies to be followed, I hope, by other nations."[101] A somewhat modified version of the statement was published in the *Washington Post* on 28 May 1985.[102] While many had expected him to modify this position as the deadline approached, Sullivan held fast to the original plan and, at the same time, he participated in the Reagan advisory committee. In fact, he increased the pressure on his business colleagues, calling for commitments from universities, colleges, and various other institutions to divest their holdings in South Africa, totaling over $100 billion, if his 31 May 1987 deadline was not met. In May 1986 Sullivan even challenged corporations to initiate a campaign of "corporate civil disobedience" that would entail use of "the full strength of your company legal departments to challenge existing laws."[103]

Although Sullivan was fully prepared to follow through on the threat to dissociate himself from the principles, he approached this possibility with trepidation. At the 17 March 1987 ICEOP board meeting, he discussed three issues: "(1) The role of ICEOP if he [Sullivan] calls for withdrawal from South Africa, (2) a general assessment of the situation in South Africa, and (3) the activities he [Sullivan] has undertaken to bring change in South Africa."[104] Sullivan reported that "the companies had already begun contingency planning in case he [Sullivan] decides to call for withdrawal"; that "ICEOP would no longer be funded by the Industry Support Unit (ISU)"; and "the ICEOP-ISU relationship would end."[105] Sullivan characterized the situation in South Africa as tense and the South African government's posture as intransigent. "I need a sign, a glimmer of hope, to continue and I am still working with business leaders in Europe and the United States to help make the South African government budge. . . . I will determine what to do and whatever I decide, I can handle it." His decision was to be guided by the findings of a trip to South Africa planned for 22–29 May 1987. The minutes of the meeting indicate that the board agreed "to support Reverend Sullivan as he comes close to decision time."[106]

No such sign was forthcoming, and upon his return from South Africa, Sullivan delivered an obituary for his role in the principles movement at the June 1987 meeting with signatory company representatives: "Today, Wednesday, June 3, 1987, Leon Sullivan, Pastor of the Zion Baptist Church in Philadelphia, and author of the Sullivan Principles, a set of equal rights practices for American companies in the Republic of South Africa, called for withdrawal of all United States companies from the Republic of South Africa, and for a total United States embargo against South Africa, until statutory apartheid is ended, and Blacks have a clear commitment for equal political rights."[107]

By the late 1980s the international sanctions were having their effect and the South African economy was reeling. Between 1986 and 1988 after granting the right of black workers to unionize, abolishing the "pass laws," and allowing black South Africans access to previously all-white urban areas, P. W. Botha made it clear that white South Africans had to "adapt or die." After suffering a stroke in January 1989, Botha was convinced to resign and he was replaced by D. W. De Klerk, who announced on 2 February 1989 that he would work for the repeal of the remaining apartheid laws. On 11 February 1989 ANC leader Nelson Mandela was released from prison after twenty-seven years.

CONCLUSION

People from all over the world watched in amazement and with great expectations as Nelson Mandela was inaugurated President of South Africa on 8 May 1994. A large delegation of U.S. anti-apartheid activists and political dignitaries were in attendance. As would have been expected, Rev. Leon Sullivan was among those in attendance at these events, although his presence was not acknowledged in Francis Nesbitt's *Race for Sanctions*. Earlier efforts to distill lessons from the movement surrounding the Sullivan Principles have focused largely on implications for individual U.S. corporations. Unquestionably, the principles served as a catalyst for an extensive debate about corporate social responsibility and the role of various stakeholders in influencing the policies of multinational businesses. At the same time, however, one of the weaknesses of the Sullivan-ICEOP strategy was the over-reliance on his support network of black clergy to the exclusion of other potentially valuable partnerships. For example, Sullivan's close ties to corporations prevented the establishment of alliances with labor organizations both in the United States and South Africa. And the overdependence on corporations for funding and administrative support limited his ability to cultivate support in South Africa among black labor organizers.

On the other hand, the Sullivan Principles had an important indirect effect on the strategy used by other organizations and interest groups opposing apartheid. The Sullivan Principles' implementation process clearly influenced debates about divestment within the halls of academe and in corporate shareholder meetings. While the assessments are mixed on whether the Sullivan Principles contributed significantly to improving the well-being for all non-white workers in South Africa, there is little doubt that the employment conditions improved greatly for black workers in U.S. companies that were signatories to the principles. At the same time, it is important to note that the emergent black trade union movement successfully forced the South African government to introduce sweeping labor reforms during this period that improved the conditions for black workers in general.

Most importantly, the history of the Sullivan Principles tells the story of African American activism in the international arena. Along with the activities of long-time anti-apartheid activists, TransAfrica, the Free South Africa Movement, and the thousands who organized and participated in divestment campaigns and the demands for economic sanctions, Leon Sullivan and his supporters were instrumental in ending a system of government that denied people of African descent their political and economic rights and full participation in the governing of South African society. In many ways the promulgation of the Sullivan Principles represented the internationalization of the goals and objectives of the U.S. Civil Rights and Black Power movements in the 1970s and 1980s.

NOTES

[1] http://www.thesullivanfoundation.org/gsp/principles/gsp/default.asp.

[2] The Soweto Rebellion began on 16 June 1976 and escalated into a major human tragedy in which South African police killed approximately 600 young people. See Mosegami Mosala, *Soweto Explodes: The Beginning of the End of Apartheid* (Dubuque, IA, 2009).

[3]Hkan Thrn, *Anti-Apartheid and the Emergence of Global Civil Society* (New York, 2009).

[4]"Sullivan's United States Government and American Business South African Requests," September, 1975; "Publications—Press Releases, September 1975," box 13, file 24, International Council of Equality of Opportunity Principles Records, Urban Archives, Temple University, Philadelphia, PA (hereafter, ICEOP Records).

[5]Ibid.

[6]Ibid.

[7]Ibid.; Letters to invitees were dated 17 December 1975 and indicated that the meeting would be held at the IBM Development Center on 29 January 1976.

[8]The fifteen firms represented at the meeting were Burroughs Corp., Caltex, General Electric, Goodyear, Honeywell, Ingersoll-Rand, IBM, International Harvester, ITT, Mobil Oil, Motorola, Otis Elevator, 3M, Firestone, and General Motors.

[9]"The Black on GM's Board," *Time*, 6 September 1976, p. 54.

[10]Donald Culverson, *Contesting Apartheid, U.S. Activism, 1960–1987* (Boulder, CO, 1999); Francis Nesbitt, *Race for Sanctions, African Americans against Apartheid, 1946–1994* (Bloomington, IN, 2004).

[11]Bernard Feigenbaum and Anton Lowenberg, "South African Disinvestment: Causes and Effects," *Contemporary Policy Issues* 6 (October 1988): 105–17.

[12]Ibid., 114.

[13]Ibid., 115.

[14]Alexandra Bernasek and Richard Porter, "Private Pressure for Social Change in South Africa: the Impact of the Sullivan Principles," *Review of Social Economy* 55 (Summer 1997): 182.

[15]Ibid., 183.

[16]Gay Seidman, "Monitoring Multinationals: Lessons from the Anti-Apartheid Era," *Politics and Society* 31 (September 2003): 403.

[17]S. Prakash Sethi and Oliver Williams, "Creating and Implementing Global Codes of Conduct—An Assessment of the Sullivan Principles as a Role Model for Developing International Codes of Conduct—Lessons Learned and Unlearned," *Business and Society Review* 105, no. 2 (2000): 169–200; S. Prakash Sethi and Oliver Williams, *Economic Imperatives and Ethical Values in Global Business: The South African Experience and International Codes Today* (Notre Dame, IN, 2001).

[18]Sethi and Williams, "Creating and Implementing Global Codes of Conduct," 197.

[19]Ibid.

[20]These materials are housed in the Urban Archives at Temple University.

[21]These data are taken from Richard W. Hull, *American Enterprise in South Africa* (New York, 1990); Lawrence Litvak, et al., *South Africa: Foreign Investment and Apartheid* (Washington, DC, 1983); and Barbara Rogers, *White Wealth and Black Poverty: American Investments in Southern Africa* (Westport, CT, 1976).

[22]James B. Stewart, "Historical Patterns of Black-White Political Economic Inequality in the United States and the Republic of South Africa," *The Review of Black Political Economy* 7, no. 3 (1977): 266–95.

[23]There are several sourcebooks containing descriptions of apartheid legislation that can be consulted. This discussion is based on *South Africa: Human Rights and the Rule of Law,* ed. Geoffrey Bindman. International Commission of Jurists (London, 1988).

[24]See John Kane Berman, "Recent Political and Economic Developments in South Africa and Their Effects on U.S. Firms," in *Business in the Shadow of Apartheid,* ed. Jonathan Leape, et al. (Lexington, MA, 1985), 3–38.

[25]Ibid.

[26]Letter from Ira Wells to Rev. Leon Sullivan, 6 October 1978, Acc. 654; "Articles of Incorporation and By-Laws, 1978," box 1, file 2, ICEOP Records.

[27]Articles of Incorporation, International Council for Minority Equality of Opportunity Principles," 22 August 1978, filed in the Department of State, 28 August 1978, box 1, file 2, "Articles of Incorporation and By-Laws, 1978," box 1, file 2, ICEOP Records.

[28]"Statement of Purpose to the Constitution and By-Laws of Sullivan Principles," "Articles of Incorporation and By-Laws," box 1, file 2, ICEOP Records.

[29]See Bernard E. Anderson, *The Opportunities Industrialization Centers: A Decade of Community-Based Manpower Services (OIC)*—Power and Human Resources Studies No. 6.—University of Pennsylvania, the Wharton School, Industrial Research Unit (Philadelphia, PA, 1976); V. P. Franklin, "Introduction," in *Cultural Capital and Black Education: African American Communities and the Funding of Black Schooling, 1860 to the Present*, ed. V. P. Franklin and Carter J. Savage (Greenwich, CT, 2004), ix–xx.

[30]Anderson, *OIC*, 32; see also Guian McKee, *The Problem of Jobs: Liberalism, Race, and Deindustrialization in Philadelphia* (Chicago, IL, 2008), 126–69.

[31]Sonja Stone, "On Their Shoulders: Foundations of OIC Leadership Implications," *Adherent* (Spring 1983): 54.

[32]Leon H. Sullivan, *Build Brother Build: From Poverty to Economic Power* (Philadelphia, PA, 1969), 50.

[33]V. P. Franklin, "Adam Clayton Powell: The Need for Independent Black Leadership," in *Living Our Stories, Telling Our Truths: Autobiography and the Making of the African American Intellectual Tradition* (New York, 1995), 391–417.

[34]Anderson, *OIC*.

[35]Ibid., 86.

[36]Stone, "On Their Shoulders," 55.

[37]International Council for Equality of Opportunity Principles, "Minutes," 26 July 1979, "Board of Directors Meetings, Minutes, 1979," box 1, file 43, ICEOP Records.

[38]Anderson, *OIC*, 91.

[39]Ibid., 107.

[40]Stone, "On Their Shoulders," 55.

[41]The original members of the board were Rev. Sullivan, Rev. Gus Roman, Dr. Andrew Brimmer, Bishop Alfred Dunston, Bishop Richard Hildebrand, Dr. William McGill, Rev. John Ridyard, and Dr. Paul Ylvisaker; "Minutes of the First Meeting of the International Council, 27 November 1978," ICEOP Records.

[42]"Meeting with a group of Clergy on activities of U.S. Clergymen in reference to Rev. Sullivan's activities in regard to human rights in South Africa, 'Notes,' 9/13/79," "Activities—Meetings—ICEOP Meeting Minutes with Philadelphia Clergy regarding possible areas of involvement, in the Activities of Reverend Leon Sullivan in South Africa, 1979," box 9, file 1, ICEOP Records.

[43]Ibid.

[44]Ibid.

[45]The appointment of Andrew Brimmer and engagement of Kenneth Clark by the ICEOP board is discussed in the minutes of the 17 November 1978 meeting; see box 1, file 43, ICEOP Papers.

[46]The "Sullivan Principles" were officially announced on 1 March 1977. Meetings to cultivate support among corporations were held on 17 March, 16 May, and 21 July 1977.

[47]This language is included in a handout that Dr. Sullivan distributed at a 9 February 1977 meeting attended by representatives of fifteen companies, ICEOP Records.

[48]This language is included in the official version of the press release announcing the principles, see ICEOP Records.

[49]The original twelve signatories were: American Cyanamid Company, Burroughs Corporation, Caltex Petroleum Corporation, Citicorp, Ford Motor Company, General Motors Corporation, IBM, International Harvester Company, Minnesota Mining and Manufacturing Company, Mobil Oil Corporation, Otis Elevator Company, and Union Carbide Corporation.

[50]This wording is reported in a memorandum to T. A. Murphy from T. S. McDaniel dated 4 February 1977, entitled "Sullivan Initiative Re: South Africa," ICEOP Records.

[51]Ibid.

[52]"Sullivan's United States Government and American Business South African Requests," September, 1975; "Publications—Press Releases," September, 1975, box 13, file 24, ICEOP Records.

[53]First Report on the Signatory Companies to the Sullivan Principles," "Pubs—ICEOP, Pubs—Published Reports—Reports on the Signatory Co's to the Sullivan Principles, 1978–Oct. 15, 1979," box 12, file 9, ICEOP Records.

[54]Letter to "Reverend Leon H. Sullivan from Paul R. Gibson, 17 November 1978," "Activities—Plenary Mtgs., February 23, 1979," box 9, file 5, ICEOP Records.

[55]"Memo to R. J. McCabe from T. S. Krzesinski, 2/26/79," "Orgs.—ISU—Statement of Principles Industry Support Unit—Misc. Minutes, 1978–1983," box 3, file 29, ICEOP Records.

[56]"Second Report on the Signatory Companies to the Sullivan Principles," 2 April 1979; "Pubs—ICEOP Pubs— Published Reports—Reports on the Signatory Co's to the Sullivan Principles, 1978–Oct. 15, 1979," box 12, file 9, ICEOP Records.

[57]"Signatory Companies' Categories for Second Questionnaire," 22 February 1979, "Activities—Meetings— Plenary Mtgs., Feb. 23, 1979," box 9, file 5, ICEOP Records.

[58]"Sullivan Principles Spur Non-Violent Business Initiatives to Crack Walls of Apartheid," box 13, file 43, "Publications—News Releases, October 18–19, 1979," ICEOP Records.

[59]"Third Report on the Signatory Companies to the Sullivan Principles," 15 October 1979; "Pubs—ICEOP Pubs—Published Reports—Reports on the Signatory Companies to the Sullivan Principles, 1978–Oct. 15, 1979," box 12, file 9, ICEOP Records.

[60]Ibid.

[61]Ibid.; Robert Copp, International Labor Affairs Manager of Ford, wrote to Task Group members on principles 1 and 2 on 9 February 1979 to report that Sullivan was requesting that the previously proposed (16 June 1978) objective related to migratory workers be reconsidered at the 23 February 1979 meeting. "Letter to Participants in Task Group Meetings on Principles 1 and 2 from Robert Copp, February 9, 1979," "Activities—The Sullivan Principles Task Groups, Group I—Equal & Fair Employment Practices, 1978–79," box 9, file 18, ICEOP Records.

[62]"Third Report on the Signatory Companies to the Sullivan Principles," 15 October 1979, box 12, file 9, "Pubs—ICEOP, Pubs—Published Reports—Reports on the Signatory Co's to the Sullivan Principles, 1978–Oct. 15, 1979," ICEOP Records.

[63]Berman, "Recent Political Developments in South Africa."

[64]"March 1 Meeting with Dr. Sullivan Regarding Funding of Administrative Support Staff," "ISU—Statement of Principles, Industry Support Unit—Misc. Minutes—1978–1983," box 2, file 12, ICEOP Records.

[65]A draft copy of the Articles of Incorporation is in "ISU—Industry Support Unit By-Laws + Articles of Incorporation, 1979, 1984," box 2, file 9, ICEOP Records. Documentation of the date of incorporation is provided in a letter from Rev. Harrison Trapp to the Office of Charities Registration of the State of New York dated 15 October 1984.

[66]"Statement of Principles Industry Advisory Committee Meeting," "ISU—Statement of Principles, Industry Support Unit—Misc. Minutes—1983–1986," box 2, file 12, ICEOP Records.

[67]International Council for Equality of Opportunity Principles, "Minutes, Thursday, July 26, 1979," "Board of Directors Meetings, Minutes, 1979," box 1, file 43, ICEOP Records.

[68]"Letter to Rev. Leon Sullivan from W. M. Menze," (received 12 May 1981), box 8, file 2, ICEOP Records.

[69]"Newsletter of the International Council for Equality of Opportunity Principles, Inc," volume 1, no. 4, 10 October 1980; "Pubs—ICEOP Pubs—ICEOP Newsletter, 1980," box 12, file 4, ICEOP Records.

[70]"International Council for Equality of Opportunity Principles, Inc., Board Meeting Minutes, 27 October 1980"; "Ad—Board of Directors—Meetings—ICEOP Board of Directors Meeting Minutes, 1980," box 1, file 44, ICEOP Records.

[71]Pauline H. Baker, *The United States and South Africa: The Reagan Years* (New York, 1989).

[72]"Letter to the Rev. Mr. Leon H. Sullivan from Roger E. Anderson," 25 March 1980, "Banks—General Correspondence with Banks, 1979–1982," box 8, file 2, ICEOP Records.

[73]"H.R. 1693—A bill requiring United States persons who conduct business or control enterprises in South Africa to comply with certain fair employment principles . . . ," introduced by Rep. Stephen Solarz, 25

February 1983; and "H.R. 1392—A bill directing the President to exercise authorities contained in the International Emergency Economic Powers Act to issue regulations prohibiting investment in South Africa," introduced by Rep. William Gray, 10 February 1983, appended to the "Agenda of the International Council for Equality of Opportunity Principles, Inc., Executive Board Meeting, May 20, 1983"; "Ad—Board of Directors—Meetings—ICEOP Board of Directors Mtg. Minutes, 1983," box 2, file 1, ICEOP Records.

[74]A copy of Sullivan's testimony was appended to the agenda of the 13 June 1983 meeting of the ICEOP board; see "Ad—Board of Directors—Meetings—ICEOP Board of Directors Mtg. Minutes, 1983," box 2, file 1, ICEOP Records.

[75]Leon H. Sullivan, "It's Time to Step Up the Pressure on South Africa," *Washington Post*, 10 May 1983.

[76]Ibid.

[77]Ibid.

[78]"ICEOP Executive Board Meeting, March 14, 1983," appended to the "Agenda of the International Council for Equality of Opportunity Principles, Inc., Executive Board Meeting, May 20, 1983," box 2, file 1, ICEOP Records.

[79]Ibid.

[80]"Fifth Report on the Signatory Companies to the Sullivan Principles, October 8, 1981," "Pubs—ICEOP Pubs—Published Reports—Reports on the Signatory Co's to the Sullivan Principles, Nov. 1, 1979—Dec. 5, 1986," box 12, file 10, ICEOP Records.

[81]Ibid.

[82]Ibid.

[83]Ibid.

[84]"Sixth Report on the Signatory Companies to the Sullivan Principles, Nov. 1, 1982," "Pubs—ICEOP Pubs—Published Reports—Reports on the Signatory Co's to the Sullivan Principles, Nov. 1, 1979—Dec. 5, 1980," box 12, file 10, ICEOP Records.

[85]Ibid.

[86]Crawford's appointment is noted in a letter from D. Reid Weedon dated 12 January 1983, "Consultants—Arthur D. Little—Correspondence—1983," box 2, file 15, ICEOP Records.

[87]Letter to Board of Directors, International Council for Equality of Opportunity Principles, Inc. from Leon A. LaRosa, Jr., 1 September 1982, "Ad—Board of Directors—Correspondence—Daniel Purnell, 1982," box 1, file 17, ICEOP Records.

[88]Leon A. LaRosa, Jr., to Sal G. Marzullo, 15 December 1982, "Ad—Board of Directors—Correspondence—Daniel Purnell, 1982," box 1, file 17, ICEOP Records.

[89]"Seventh Report on the Signatory Companies to the Sullivan Principles, October 25, 1983," "Pubs—ICEOP Pubs—Published Reports—Reports on the Signatory Co's to the Sullivan Principles, Nov. 1, 1979—Dec. 5, 1986," box 12, file 10, ICEOP Records.

[90]The release indicates that the memorandum addressed sensitive government policy issues. The issues of political representation and negotiation between black South Africans and the apartheid regime were also addressed "so that collectively the memorandum deals with virtually all of those issues which currently form the basis of the disinvestment lobby's arguments." The complete report is included as "Appendix A," in International Peace Academy, *Southern Africa: Prospects for Peace and Security—The Second International Conference on Peace and Security* (Hingham, MA, 1987).

[91]"Statement of Briefing by the Honorable George P. Schultz, Secretary of State on the Appointment of Advisory Committee on South Africa, Thursday, December 19, 1985," (No. 298), "Publications—Press Releases—12/19/85," box 13, file 47, ICEOP Records.

[92]Baker, *The United States and South Africa*, 29. See also Nesbitt, *Race for Sanctions* and Culverson, *Contesting Apartheid*.

[93]Baker, *The United States and South Africa*, 41–42.

[94]Ibid., 44–45. See also Nesbitt, *Race for Sanctions* and Culverson, *Contesting Apartheid*.

[95]Baker, *The United States and South Africa*, 33.

[96]Ibid.

[97]Paul Lansing and Sarosh Kuruvilla, "Business Divestment in South Africa: In Whose Best Interest?" *Washington Post*, 18 September 1986; Merrill Perlman, "WEEK IN BUSINESS: GM and IBM Exit from South Africa," *New York Times*, Financial Desk, 26 October 1986, 20.

[98]"ICEOP Board Meeting Minutes of August 7, 1986," box 2, file 4, ICEOP Records.

[99]"News Release, Call to Conscience Conference, September 14, 1986," box 2, file 4, ICEOP Records.

[100]U.S. Dept. of State, Advisory Committee on South Africa, *A U.S. Policy Toward South Africa: The Report of the Secretary of State's Advisory Committee on South Africa,* Office of Public Affairs, Bureau of African Affairs (Washington, DC, 1987).

[101]"A Deadline for Ending Apartheid," *Philadelphia Inquirer*, 7 May 1985, clipping in box 13, file 7, ICEOP Records.

[102]"Give the Sullivan Principles Two More Years," *Washington Post*, 28 May 1985, clipping in box 13, file 7, ICEOP Records.

[103]A generic version of the letter sent to chief executive officers can be found in box 1, file 35, ICEOP Records.

[104]"ICEOP Board Meeting Minutes, March 17, 1987," box 2, file 5, ICEOP Records.

[105]Ibid.

[106]Ibid.

[107]"Statement to Signatory Company Representatives on the Sullivan Principles on June 3, 1987 at 10:14 a.m.," box 2, file 8, ICEOP Records.

THE PROGRESS MOVEMENT AND COMMUNITY DEVELOPMENT: THE ZION NON-PROFIT CHARITABLE TRUST

Nathaniel Bracey

One of America's greatest leaders arrived in Philadelphia, Pennsylvania, in 1950 to begin what would become one of the nation's most successful community development initiatives, the Progress Movement. Born in Charleston, West Virginia, on 16 October 1922, the young Rev. Leon Howard Sullivan spent time as assistant pastor at Abyssinian Baptist Church in New York City, under the leadership of Rev. Adam Clayton Powell, Jr., and in East Orange, New Jersey, as pastor of the First Baptist Church before coming to Philadelphia. When the 28-year-old minister accepted the position as pastor of Zion Baptist Church, the first hint of his audacity and forward thinking was when he asked the church's board of deacons to pay on his behalf a $100 membership fee for the Philadelphia Chamber of Commerce.

One deacon who was on the board at the time recalled how stunned the board members were at this request. When asked about it, Sullivan responded, "The Chamber of Commerce has advance knowledge of major economic trends, and membership would allow me to take immediate action on actions potentially beneficial to the congregation and our people." Thus from the beginning Rev. Sullivan was considered an unusual preacher. Indeed, several years ago one preacher confided to this writer that initially he did not respect Sullivan's approach because "I hardly heard him preach about Jesus in his sermons, it was always about money and economics." Today, that preacher is a convert and has incorporated Sullivan's economic approach in his ministry.

One might ask: Why did Rev. Leon Sullivan concentrate on economics as the basis for African Americans realizing full citizenship, along with civil and political rights? Sullivan himself traced this particular concern to the sermon he delivered to his congregation on 15 June 1962.

> One day I preached a sermon at Zion Baptist about Jesus feeding the five thousand with a few loaves and a few fishes. Everybody put in their little bit and you had enough to feed

Nathaniel Bracey is Executive Director of the Leon H. Sullivan Charitable Trust (formerly the Zion Non-Profit Charitable Trust) in Philadelphia, PA.

everybody with some left over. So I said, that is what I am going to do with the church and the community. I said, "I am going to ask 50 people to put $10 down for 36 months of loaves and fishes and see if we could accumulate resources enough to build something that we would own ourselves."[1]

The response was overwhelming and over 200 families joined the plan that Sunday morning and that was the beginning of the "10–36 Plan" that formed the basis of his far-reaching community economic development programs.

The funds contributed to the 10–36 Plan accumulated rapidly and Sullivan launched Zion Investment Associates (ZIA), which after 1977 was renamed the Progress Investment Associates, a for-profit corporation that would undertake income-generating projects. At the end of thirty-six months, subscribers would receive shares of the common stock and would be entitled to participate in yearly shareholders' meetings. Given the lack of access to adequate housing in Philadelphia's racially divided neighborhoods, in 1964 ZIA's first investment was in an apartment complex. This was the beginning of the "Progress Movement" in Philadelphia. It was followed by the building of Zion Gardens, a middle income apartment complex in North Philadelphia. Financed by ZIA with assistance from the U.S. Department of Housing and Urban Development (HUD) and a loan from the Federal Housing Administration (FHA), this $1 million project was completed in 1966.

The next project funded by ZIA through funds generated from the investors in the 10–36 Plan was the building of a shopping center in North Philadelphia, "Progress Plaza." Working with the Philadelphia Council for Community Development (PCCD), a private group focused on economic development, and the Philadelphia Recovery Authority, a municipal department, Sullivan was able to obtain prime land on Broad Street, near Temple University. To get the project started, the ZIA went to the local branch of First Pennsylvania Bank to seek out a construction loan. Initially, the loan officer was taken aback and rebuffed the request. However, by 1968 there were over 3,300 members of the 10–36 Plan so when Sullivan showed him the documentation for $400,000 worth of assets held by the ZIA, the banker immediately changed his tune. Sullivan concluded, "I found that $400,000 makes a difference in race relations in America."[2]

In the construction of Progress Plaza, the ZIA officers insisted that black-owned firms obtain contracts and that black workers be employed. In January 1964 the first Opportunities Industrialization Center (OIC) was opened with great fanfare and large crowds in North Philadelphia to provide disadvantaged workers with the training and skills needed in the local workforce. This became one of the most successful programs nationally and internationally to come out of the Progress Movement. Funded by donations from members of Zion Baptist Church and others and using equipment donated by businesses in Philadelphia, OIC trainees were offered a wide variety of programs including sheet metal work, machine tool operations, electronics, plumbing, and welding. A second OIC was opened in West Philadelphia in 1965. Many of the graduates of the OIC programs were employed by the companies that built Progress Plaza, considered the first black-owned and financed shopping center in the United States.[3]

Dedication ceremony for the first OIC, in a renovated jail at 19th and Oxford streets in North Philadelphia, 26 January 1964. Photo courtesy of Temple University Libraries, Urban Archives, Philadelphia, Pennsylvania.

Opened in October 1968, Progress Plaza contained sixteen stores, half of them black owned; the plaza included branches of Bell Telephone Company, Philadelphia Savings Fund Society, North Carolina Mutual Insurance Company, and an A & P Supermarket. Many of the store managers and black business owners would eventually receive their training through the "Entrepreneurial Development Training Center" that was sponsored by Zion Non-Profit Charitable Trust (ZNPCT), which was established in 1966. The ZNPCT was organized because Rev. Sullivan believed that the investors in the ZIA, who were receiving dividends from their investments, also needed to get used to giving something back to community in the form of charity and philanthropic activities. According to the papers of incorporation, the Zion Trust was a "faith-based initiative" whose mission was to "create economic and community development opportunities, using our resources to advocate on behalf of impoverished people based on Reverend Leon H. Sullivan's principles of self-help, social responsibility, and human rights."[4]

In March 1967, the officers of the Zion Trust submitted a proposal to the Ford Foundation for a grant for the development of a "training center for black entrepreneurs." After winning the grant of $400,000, the ZNPCT established at Progress Plaza the Entrepreneurial Development Training Center. Then the ZNPCT used some of these funds to construct the "Progress Human Services Center Building," located on Broad Street, adjacent to Progress Plaza. The building served as the central location for a wide variety of programs and services, including the headquarters for OIC of America, Spectrum Health Services, the Progressive Life Center for Foster Care Parent Recruitment, and the Philadelphia office of the National Caucus of Black Aging.[5]

In the late 1970s the ZNPCT entered into a partnership with local developers to construct Progress Plaza II in West Philadelphia, also known as Progress Haddington Plaza, which opened in 1980. The shopping center became home to over a dozen retail businesses, including a supermarket, restaurants, bank branches, and clothing stores. As was the case with Progress Plaza, the second shopping center achieved Zion Trust's major economic objectives of creating jobs, developing businesses, and expanding economic development in black neighborhoods. Sullivan's vision was to increase business ownership and management skills, providing black entrepreneurs with the opportunity and experience of working with budgets of hundreds of thousands or millions of dollars in both the public sphere and private enterprise.[6] The businesses supported by ZIA and the Zion Trust also included Progress Aerospace Enterprise, incorporated in May 1968, which had contracts from General Electric, Boeing, Philco-Ford, and Westinghouse Company. By February 1970 Progress Aerospace Enterprise had 107 employees.

The Garment Progress Manufacturing Company was started in August 1968 and was financed by ZIA and the Zion Trust. The company produced its own clothing lines by February 1970 was employing fifty workers. Rev. Sullivan's Zion Baptist Church was destroyed by fire in November 1970, and the Progress Construction Company was formed to assist in its rebuilding. ZIA also sponsored the four "Our Markets," large and much-needed grocery stores that opened in black neighborhoods beginning in the spring of 1971. In the case of the Mill Creek Housing Complex, the officers of the Zion Trust worked with tenants to secure loans to purchase and rehabilitate their homes. Opportunities Towers, a housing complex for the elderly and disabled, was another project assisted by loans provided by ZIA and the expertise and skills from employees and managers trained by the management programs sponsored by the Zion Trust.

Leon Sullivan, "The Chief," 1980.
Courtesy of Leon H. Sullivan Charitable Trust, Philadelphia, PA.

More recently, the ZNPCT concentrated its efforts and major assets on the 66,000 square foot Leon H. Sullivan Human Services Center in North Philadelphia (formerly the Progress Human Services Building); and the 75,000 square foot retail center, Progress Haddington Plaza, in West Philadelphia. Most appropriately, in 2005 the name of the Zion Non-Profit Charitable Trust was changed to the "Leon H. Sullivan Charitable Trust" and continues its educational and community development activities, serving as a model of self-help, cooperative enterprise, and economic advancement for groups and organizations throughout the United States. In 2011, Progress Haddington Plaza will be undergoing a $2.1 million upgrade and makeover, and the Sullivan Human Services Center will undergo a $38 million upgrade and expansion in a project to be named the "Leon H. Sullivan Living and Learning Center." The center will contain commercial retail shops and student residences, and will house the "Leon H. Sullivan Leadership Institute." This new institute will serve as the training center for leaders and community groups interested in pursuing Leon Sullivan's principles and approaches to education, management training, and community development.

NOTES

[1]"The 10–36 Plan—History," undated document, Papers of Leon Sullivan Charitable Trust, Philadelphia, PA (hereafter, LSCT Papers).

[2]Ibid., see also Leon H. Sullivan, *Build, Brother, Build: From Poverty to Economic Power* (Philadelphia, PA, 1969), 166–70.

[3]Sullivan, *Build Brother Build,* 170–79; V. P. Franklin, "Opportunities Industrialization Centers: Collective Cultural Capital, Philanthropy, and Public-Private Partnerships in the Provision of Supplementary Education," in *Educating Comprehensively: Varieties of Educational Experience*, ed. Linda J. Lin, Herve Verenne, Edmund W. Gordon (Lewiston, NY, 2011), forthcoming.

[4]"Brief History and Description of the Trust," 2, undated document, LSCT Papers. The original ZNPCT board members and trustees were Leon Sullivan, chairman; Eustace Gay, vice chairman; Ira J. K. Wells, Jr., secretary; William V. Downes, treasurer; Carl Hairston and Alfonso C. Jackson, trustees; and Judge Allen, executive director.

[5]"Black Capitalism at Work: What's Happening in Philadelphia," *U.S. News and World Report*, 17 February 1969, 63.

[6]Phyl Garland, "The Unorthodox Ministry of Leon Sullivan," *Ebony*, May 1971, 116–118.

BOOK REVIEWS

Douglas Walter Bristol, Jr., *Knights of the Razor: Black Barbers in Slavery and Freedom*. Baltimore: The Johns Hopkins University Press, 2009. Pp. 232. Cloth $50.00.

Despite the overtly racist atmosphere in the United States in the 19th century, black barbers spent an extraordinary portion of their working hours with a straight razor to the throats of their mainly white clientele. This ritual, however shocking it may have been to unfamiliar observers, was an ordinary occurrence, and it illustrated the tensions at the heart of U.S. race relations. Though many white men would have recoiled at the touch of an African American in their day-to-day interactions, in the barbershop these same men freely bared their throats to a razor-wielding black man. These encounters are the subject of Douglas Walter Bristol's *Knights of the Razor: Black Barbers in Slavery and Freedom*.

According to Bristol, these scenes offer a new vantage point for examining race relations in the 19th century. He argues that from barbershops where white men reclined beneath a black man's finely honed razor comes a fascinating abundance of historical detail that helps illuminate social and racial meanings. As white men enjoyed a shave and the experience of being waited upon, black barbers used their trade to navigate the treacherous shoals of white racism.

In the colonial and revolutionary era, enslaved barbers used the close ties they developed with slaveholders and their familiarity with elite European-American culture to create unique opportunities to gain their freedom and sometimes even their own barbershops. However, these men were often forced to occupy the position of plantation lieutenant for their masters, enforcing discipline over their fellow bondsmen, thus complicating their allegiances. In the era of the early republic, African American barbers took advantage of the stigma that whites increasingly associated with personal service to consolidate their control of the barbering trade. As was also true of their counterparts in the maritime trades, African American barbers secured a respectable status and achieved a life of relative ease, compared to most black workers who toiled in physically demanding manual labor. Despite the existence of restrictive laws and enduring racial discrimination, black barbers ran luxurious barbering "saloons" in prominent locations in all parts of the United States.

Even as many skilled trades excluded black men during the antebellum period, African Americans continued to find prosperity in the barbering profession. Though they sometimes had to compete with white barbers for white clientele, black barbers most often won the loyalty of white elites. In doing so they gained unprecedented access to the most affluent white men in the United States. Sectional tensions threatened to frustrate black barbers' place in American society in the late 1850s and Civil War years. Once the war ended, many southern barbers maintained and depended upon their ties to white elites. Their northern counterparts, however, began to serve an increasingly black clientele. The segregation of their business activity reflected the larger trend towards separatism and self-help in northern African American communities. Reconstruction reestablished barbers' place among the African American leadership. Black barbers enthusiastically occupied the forefront of Reconstruction politics, and the relationships they had cultivated in earlier years enabled them to continue to serve as mediators between the races.

Even as white Americans' commitment to racial equality diminished in the Gilded Age, black barbers continued to occupy the roles of mediators and ambassadors to elite men and organizations. However, as race relations reached what historian Rayford Logan has termed its "nadir" at the turn of the 20th century, white clients became scarce, and black barbers altered their tradition to serve the expanding African American populations in urban areas. Here was the origin of the modern black barbershop, and proprietors often grew their businesses into major corporations and placed themselves at the top of black enterprise.

Bristol's history of black barbering skillfully reveals the tortuous daily experience of living and coping with extreme racial prejudice. He captures a powerful black voice through his expert treatment of the records of his subjects' innermost feelings, found in books, journals, letters, newspaper articles, and speeches. These insights allow Bristol to pierce the veil of white stereotypes and offer a fascinating glimpse into the conflicted world of these racial "go-betweens." As black men barbered white clients, they had to project a merry submissiveness and stifle any anger they may have felt at the condescension and insults shown them by clients. Black barbers, more often than African Americans who were not so intimately associated with white men, had to conform to the humiliating standards of 19th-century racial protocol. This requirement magnified their experience of white racism.

At the same time, Bristol reveals that these men dealt with racism by developing an empowering group identity around their trade. They dubbed themselves "knights of the razor," and rather than internalizing the white stereotype of the menial black service worker, barbers claimed for themselves the barbering tradition of the European aristocracy. They developed a sense of respectability and virtue around their status as small businessmen, and often enjoyed the privileges of middle-class respectability. Their wealth and good reputations also made them vital African American community leaders.

Bristol is careful not to overlook many troubling questions raised by the black barbers' privileged status. Indeed, his work is meant to confront the scholarship that dismisses barbers as men who accepted and accommodated racial inequality. According to this line of thought, black barbers legitimated segregation by often refusing to serve black customers, reinforced the association of African Americans and servitude by applying their talents to the personal service industry, and seemingly validated racist stereotypes by consciously demeaning themselves for the sake of their white patrons. Bristol, however, views the role of black barbers as an important one in 19th-century racial negotiations. These men accommodated white arrogance to gain a significant degree of control over their own lives. Bristol argues that by successfully navigating volatile racial ground, "black barbers achieved truly remarkable success, took on the heavy burden of leadership, and exemplified both grit and ingenuity."

Knights of the Razor is an insightful and well-written analysis of race, racism, and the resourcefulness of black enterprise in the long 19th century. Douglas Walter Bristol has illuminated a history that well represents the process of African American men transforming themselves from enslaved workers and servants into successful businessmen and community leaders.

J. Brent Morris
Cornell University

Janice L. Sumler-Edmond, *The Secret Trust of Aspasia Cruvellier Mirault: The Life and Trials of a Free Woman of Color in Antebellum Georgia.* Fayetteville: The University of Arkansas Press, 2008. Pp. 171. Cloth $29.00.

Studies of free women of color in the antebellum United States have often examined the lives of female fugitives who created new lives in free territories and their affiliations with abolitionist groups. Historians Adele L. Alexander and Kent Leslie's biographies of free black women in the South focused on their white lineages and the social advantages they received. Far too often, free black women received notoriety as concubines of prominent southern white men. The life of Aspasia Cruvellier Mirault, a free woman of color who arrived in the United States with her family from San Domingue (later Haiti) in 1800, offers a very different perspective. By 1840 Aspasia Mirault had established herself in Savannah, Georgia, first by working with her sister in her sewing shop. Then, driven by an entrepreneurial spirit, Mirault opened a bakery that became very successful. Articles in the local white paper praised her pastries and homemade ice cream.

As her business expanded, Mirault decided to purchase a lot as a site to construct a home and business. But in 1818 the Georgia legislature passed a statute prohibiting free blacks from owning property, so Mirault entered into an agreement, "a secret trust," with a young white man, George Cally. Lot 22 in the Pulaski Ward would be purchased for her by Cally and he agreed to handle all legal transactions for the property. After the purchase, Cally, a carpenter, hired a construction crew and built Aspasia's home that allowed her to maintain her bakery business in the rear. In time this Whitaker Street address became the home for Mirault's family, some of her siblings and their families, and even George Cally.

Aspasia Cruvellier's marital relationship with Simon Mirault seemed to have evolved from a friendship related to their common West Indian heritage that blossomed into romance and marriage. In some parts of the text, Sumler-Edmond questioned their marital status, but in others she referred to them as a married couple. The couple had two daughters who proved to be successful businesswomen as well. It also appears that as her business grew, Mirault acquired enslaved workers to assist her in the business. Like other southern slaveholders, Mirault and her family were religious and she joined the St. John Baptist Catholic Church, giving generously to support the church's activities.

After the death of Simon Mirault, Aspasia met a wealthy black businessman, James Oliver. Though he was married, Aspasia gave birth to three sons, one dying during early childhood. Still Aspasia fared well and gained the favor of influential white men in Savannah, including the mayor. Aspasia Mirault became ill and suddenly died in 1857, and it appears that the death of the family matriarch seriously affected other family members. Although Letitia, Aspasia's oldest daughter, became the head of the family and business, she died within three years.

During the Civil War, Robert Oliver, Aspasia Mirault's oldest son, played in a black band that accompanied Confederate troops. After the war Robert Oliver, a trained brickmason, became head of the family, and on the basis of the foundation established by his mother, he and his children were considered part of Savannah's black elite. Unfortunately, the family members failed to maintain the Whitaker Street property, which was still in Cally's name. Cally failed to keep up with the taxes and fees on the property, and at a city-sponsored auction, the land was purchased by William Scholl for only $82.86. When one of Aspasia's grandsons learned of the situation, he filed a lawsuit on behalf of the heirs of Aspasia Mirault. One judge ruled in favor of the Mirault family, agreeing that George Cally and Aspasia Mirault had been in a "secret agreement" surrounding the land and the financial arrangements, and at no time did Cally own the property, though it was listed in his name. William Scholl appealed the verdict to the state supreme court, which reversed the earlier ruling upholding the legitimacy of the 1818 statute barring free black land ownership. However, Scholl's victory seemed bittersweet because problems with back taxes and other claims forced him to put the property up for sale.

Sumler-Edmond provides us an intriguing narrative on how a free black woman in a southern city created a strong economic foundation for herself, her family, and her descendants. Like other black and white immigrants, Mirault established herself among her fellow émigrés, and opened a business offering highly desirable products. She developed relationships with prominent whites in Savannah who served as guardians and protectors. She even became a slaveholder for the purpose of increasing her profits, rather than to free someone held in bondage, as was the case with most free black slave owners. There is little evidence that Aspasia Mirault was a "race woman," even though some of her descendants became social activists in Georgia. Mirault seemed to have little connection to Savannah's community of black women.

A major strength of Sumler-Edmond's narrative is the exposition of the laws and statutes passed in the early 19th century to restrict the rights of free people of color in the South. The twists and turns in the lawsuits and trials over the Whitaker Street property are fascinating. Sumler-Edmond constructs a compelling saga from court records, legal statutes, and other archival materials. Mirault's story forces the reader to acknowledge, if not commend, the varied ways this free black woman carved out a prosperous lifestyle in an antebellum southern city.

Jacqueline A. Rouse
Georgia State University

Carole C. Marks, *Moses and the Monster and Miss Anne.* Urbana and Chicago: University of Illinois Press, 2009. Pp. 224. Cloth $35.00.

Carole C. Marks's *Moses and the Monster and Miss Anne* is a fascinating, intellectually stimulating, and enlightening sociohistorical analysis. "Moses" is Harriet Tubman, "the Monster" is Patty Cannon, and "Miss Anne" is Anna Ella Carroll. Marks uses the introduction to establish a solid foundation for her historical narrative. Although slavery gave these women's separate struggles a common thread, the author provides arguments for four areas of convergence tying the lives of Tubman, Cannon, and Carroll together in various ways.

The first area of convergence is geography; all three women share roots in the Eastern Shore of Maryland. The Cannon-Johnson gang had its headquarters on the dividing line between Maryland and Delaware. Carroll grew up on her father's plantation located on the Eastern Shore, and Tubman escaped from enslavement in that region. The second area of similarity is that each of these women became in some way marginalized in Maryland's changing economy. The third area relates to the political/legal arena and each woman's opposition to specific forms of authority; and the last area of convergence relates to each woman's conscious rejection of gendered roles and expectations in the larger society.

Aside from presenting her arguments, Marks devotes the remainder of the introduction to explaining the importance of geography in this analysis. Marks points out that Maryland's Eastern Shore was an isolated peninsula rarely visited by strangers. The inhabitants developed their own distinct culture where qualities of independence and perseverance were valued. It was a region where slaveholding planters had grown rich off of tobacco production, Maryland's first staple crop. Maryland was also a border state that possessed a particularly large free black population.

Anna Ella Carroll was a prolific writer, and her father Thomas King Carroll served in the Maryland House of Delegates and as governor of Maryland. She was also related to Charles Carroll, one of the signers of the Declaration of Independence. We are told that Carroll was educated at home and studied law with her father Thomas Carroll. While Harriett Tubman is the most famous of the three women, Marks was able to unearth comparatively little about the early years of Patty Cannon. The first three chapters describe the women's social contexts and Marks situates each woman within the social, political, and economic environments of the times. Marks also sorts through the myths, legends, and documentary evidence surrounding the women, and painstakingly examines each biographical study, newspaper article, and other documents related to the women and then addresses their reliability.

In the discussion of "Political Economy and Marginalization," Marks describes how the changing political economy served to alter the life trajectory of each woman and moved each into the wage-labor market. With soil depletion ending the region's reliance on tobacco, many planters, including the Carroll family, lost much of their wealth. With the invention of the cotton gin at the end of the 18th century, enslaved laborers became the new "cash crop" for many Maryland planters, and the state ranked third in the sale of slaves to the western territories. Slave trading offered another way for Maryland's poor whites to get on the road to riches. After first opening, then closing, a school for girls, Anne Carroll assumed the role of a "political pamphleteer-lobbyist." She was able to support herself and help to defray her father's financial debts using her excellent writing skills and knowledge of the law to enter the political arena. Marks then focuses on the unstable financial situation of Tubman's owner and her fear of being sold to help settle his debts, which triggered Tubman's decision to escape to freedom. Once free, Tubman worked to help finance her return rescue missions to the South. Patty Cannon assembled a gang and moved into the slave trading business, a lucrative source of revenue.

"Rules, Laws, and the Rule of Law" examines these women's position in the antebellum social order where slavery and slave trading were increasingly defend-

ed by southerners and demonized by northerners. Whereas Anne Carroll manumit-
ted her enslaved workers and worked unsuccessfully to secure compensated emancipation for Marylanders and the colonization of formerly enslaved African
Americans in West Africa, Cannon, well aware that kidnapping was a crime, cap-
italized on the existence of a large free black population by kidnapping and sell-
ing many into slavery. Tubman pursued freedom for herself, her family, and her
people in the face of this illegal and legalized oppression.

"The Mantle of Domesticity" focuses on the disparate ways each of these
women challenged conceptions of the "proper woman's sphere." During the Civil
War Anne Carroll claimed responsibility for promoting the Union Army's
"Tennessee River Campaign" and self-identified as an "unrecognized member of
Lincoln's cabinet." Tubman worked as an armed rescuer of enslaved people and
also served as a spy and scout for the Union Army. Cannon's criminal exploits,
inconsistent with gender conventions, continued.

In the final chapter, Marks pulls these women's stories together, but this time
adds the religious dimension. She concludes by offering her assessment of the
contribution made by each of these Marylanders to U.S. history: Tubman's efforts
helped topple the institution of slavery; Cannon's notoriety helped "expose the
wicked practice of trafficking in human flesh"; and Carroll's activities helped to
preserve the Union. These women were often defined by those in the larger society as "dangerous" and "unruly." They were "unruly" because they were "not
afraid to challenge male authority"; and they were "dangerous" because they
"challenged the structure and content of a fragile American social system newly
separated from its colonial roots and struggling to invent itself." Marks's book is
a remarkable undertaking and adds to our understanding of women's complex
roles in American history by examining the intersections of race, class, and religion in the lives of women who might otherwise never be considered together.

Linda A. Causey
Youngstown State University

LeeAnna Keith, *The Colfax Massacre: The Untold Story of Black Power, White
Terror, and the Death of Reconstruction*. New York: Oxford University Press,
2008. Pp. 240. Cloth $40.00. Paper $15.95.

LeeAnna Keith tells of the Easter Sunday, 3 April 1873, Colfax, Louisiana,
massacre, "the deadliest incident of racial violence in the history of the United
States." The massacre has been called a riot in earlier racist accounts, but *The
Colfax Massacre: The Untold Story of Black Power, White Terror, and the Death*

of Reconstruction describes the origins and outcomes of the bloody incident that left 150 people dead. With illustrations, maps, and an abundance of relevant sources, Keith dissects the brutality of white supremacists and the impact of the violence on national politics. Keith begins the story with an account of the family background of William Smith Calhoun, one of the white witnesses of the massacre in Colfax. South Carolina senator William Smith, friend of President Andrew Jackson, moved to Alabama in the 1830s where he purchased land and slaves. After his death, his granddaughter and heir married Meredith Calhoun, and the couple lived the life of elite Huntsville planters, purchasing European art and titles as count and countess on European visits. The Calhouns shifted the family fortune to the Red River area in Central Louisiana in the 1850s and invested heavily in slaves and cotton and sugar plantations; they even entertained journalist Frederick Law Olmsted.

Their son, William Smith Calhoun, fell and broke his back when he was only three years old. Young "Willie" survived, and his parents arranged for him to receive the latest medical attention in France, where he lived in a chateau and learned French manners. Upon returning to Louisiana at age 15, although he was short and hunchbacked, he eventually rose in local society. His pro-Union views during the Civil War placed him at odds with his Confederate neighbors, and when the war ended, Calhoun came to be considered a "scalawag" because he rented land to formerly enslaved African Americans and opened schools for the freedpeople. Calhoun entered politics as a Republican and was soon elected to political office. William Calhoun's marriage to Olivia Williams, a black Creole woman, produced two children.

Following the war, Klansmen and other white vigilantes launched a reign of terror and violence against the freedpeople in Grant Parish, Louisiana, and its parish seat Colfax, as they did in many parts of the former Confederacy. The massacre of over 150 black men at the Colfax courthouse is one of the saddest days of the Reconstruction era. African American men, with a few white supporters, had assembled at the courthouse to rally for their civil rights. A group of ex-Confederate soldiers solicited support from surrounding parishes to attack the gathering. Pleas for help from William Smith Calhoun who witnessed the violence went unanswered. African Americans tried to defend the courthouse, but the larger force of militant whites with a cannon overwhelmed the defenders, forced them inside, and then set the building on fire. Those trying to escape were shot, and those who surrendered were executed "near a pecan tree" that was later memorialized in white supremacist folklore. Their bodies were mutilated as Governor William Pitt Kellogg declared a state of insurrection.

The federal grand jury originally indicted ninety-seven people, but the prosecutors were threatened, and charges were dropped against most of them. At the same time, all of the suspects were supported by local whites. By September 1873 federal officials decided to indict only the most prominent individuals, but unfortunately, the prosecuting attorney J. R. Beckwith failed to prepare the case properly, while the white defendants hired noted attorneys. Funds were raised throughout the area for the defense. The prosecutors had 240 witnesses to testify, but witnesses for the "Colfax prisoners" lied, and in two proceedings that followed, mistrials were declared. In the final trial the closing arguments by the defense attorneys lasted three days and they sought dismissal of the charges on "the ground that the Enforcement Acts that empowered the prosecution had been rendered void by the recent Supreme Court decision in the 1873 Slaughterhouse cases." The defense attorneys requested that Supreme Court Justice Joseph Bradley, who was a Louisiana native, attend the proceedings, alongside Judge John Woods of the circuit court who presided. Justice Bradley decided to take proceedings of the trials back to Washington, DC, studied the issues, and decided that the "power of Congress does . . . not extend to the passage of laws for the suppression of ordinary crimes within the states."

The defense attorneys had accused the black men of "assembling unlawfully," and the all-white jury's verdict of not guilty was rendered, with only three men convicted of conspiracy. As whites celebrated the victory in the courts, more black citizens were attacked and killed. This latest racial conflict coincided with the election of 1874, and General Philip Sheridan was sent to investigate the violence. Sheridan's report revealed that there were 2,500 political murders in Central Louisiana since the end of the Civil War, and he labeled those in white community "banditti."

The three men convicted of "conspiracy" in the Colfax massacre, William Cruikshank, J. P. Hadnot, and William Irwin, appealed their convictions and the case reached the U.S. Supreme Court in March 1876. By then the original efforts to press the case had greatly diminished. Attorney J. R. Beckwith had resigned, and the government's brief omitted "any reference to the racial identity or political rights of the Colfax victims, including the relevant protections of the 15th Amendment." The legacy of *U.S. v. Cruikshank,* written by Chief Justice Morrison Waites, came with the ruling that only states could protect rights of voters, not the federal government. Keith concluded that the decision in *U.S. v. Cruikshank* "spelled the end of federal intervention in southern civil rights and voting rights abuses" for generations. African Americans would eventually be removed from the political arena through violence and terrorism going from 130,444 in the electorate in Louisiana in 1870 to 5,320 in 1898. In 1876 William Smith Calhoun divorced his mixed race wife who died shortly thereafter, and their two children left the area.

Keith's *The Colfax Massacre* is an informative and important book, but one is surprised by the failure of the author to build upon the valuable insights into the violent overthrow of Reconstruction found in the works by Benjamin Quarles,

James McPherson, C. Peter Ripley, Mark T. Carlton, and William F. Messner. Along with Charles Lane's *The Day Freedom Died: The Colfax Massacre, the Supreme Court, and the Betrayal of Reconstruction* (2009), Keith's *The Colfax Massacre* provides important information on this terrible tragedy.

Charles Vincent
Southern University and A & M College

Christopher M. Span, *From Cotton Field to Schoolhouse: African American Education in Mississippi, 1862–1875*. Chapel Hill, NC: The University of North Carolina Press, 2009. Pp. 264. Cloth $35.00.

Christopher M. Span has written an illuminating account of how black Mississippians built institutions capable of sustaining their freedom during the Civil War and Reconstruction. In the first part of *From Cotton Field to Schoolhouse*, the years between 1862 and 1870 are the focus, from the military campaigns to control the state to the end of the Bureau of Refugees, Freedmen and Abandoned Lands, or Freedmen's Bureau's, operations in Mississippi. In three carefully researched chapters and an interpretation arising from a wealth of primary sources, Span highlights various aspects of the struggle for African American education and citizenship. African Americans valued literacy and created private venture and Sunday schools to safeguard their freedom. Formerly enslaved Mississippians aspired to exercise the full rights and responsibilities of citizenship. Span provides evidence that they organized many schools well before northern missionaries or agents of the Freedmen's Bureau arrived in the state.

African Americans sought to organize, staff, and control schools designed to raise their social, political, and economic status. They also sought to use property ownership, the vote, and their individual and collective agency to create collective social and cultural capital that would allow them to extend their personal and professional ambitions beyond menial labor. Because the black and white populations of the state were roughly equal, the ballot offered African Americans a potent tool for having a voice in local government. It also increased the likelihood that they would reap some benefit from state expenditures for schooling that previously benefited wealthy planters almost exclusively.

Span contends that northern missionaries working in Mississippi envisioned education as preparing the freedpeople for work as wage laborers, mainly for the planters who formerly enslaved them. The wealthy planters viewed African Americans, free or enslaved, as their property taken without compensation, thus unqualified for citizenship. Arguing that African Americans could not benefit from "book learning," the large landowners rallied to oppose free public education for black children arguing it was a waste of money. While some white Mississippians supported black Mississippians' educational goals, Span argues that most whites united across class lines in opposition to any schooling for black children. But some white Mississippians did risk ostracism, physical violence, or even death to help African Americans become literate, acquire property, and build schools.

In part two of *From Cotton Field to Schoolhouse*, Span chronicles the establishment of the dual system of public education in Mississippi between 1871 and 1875. The negative reaction of white Mississippians to racially mixed public schooling was even stronger than their animus toward schooling of African Americans at taxpayer expense. At the same time, African Americans used the separate public schools as a vehicle for improving their social and economic conditions. School attendance rose from less than 4,000 African Americans in September 1868 to more than 36,000 African Americans attending school in 1871.

Span demonstrates how inequality became an enduring feature of public education in Mississippi almost from the outset. Moreover, he showed how the conscious refusal of state officials to provide public high schools for African American youth limited the possibility of attending college. The lack of high schools, evident as early as 1871, frustrated many African Americans' hopes of using schooling for upward social mobility. Span is at his best in describing the collateral damage experienced by African Americans during the Civil War and the violent overthrow of the Republican-led government in Mississippi in 1875. With the upsurge of Ku Klux Klan violence in 1871, African American schoolhouses and teachers became prime targets, devastating the physical and intellectual infrastructure for educating black children and adults. Federal troops were dispatched to curtail the first phase of the violent reaction to African American progress. A second wave of reaction beginning in 1875 was even more virulent than the first. United in their opposition to the higher taxes levied to repair the destruction created by the war and to sustain public schools, white Mississippians revolted. While a poll tax raised significant revenue from African American voters to fund public education, importing progressive northern models of schooling proved to be expensive and socially destabilizing. Financing dual systems of public education required higher taxes from wealthy white Mississippians who uniformly favored private, not public, education.

Small landowners also felt the sting of high taxes. Span found that the tax rate on small farmers consumed "2 to 4 percent of their total cash income, and from 8 to 10 percent of their discretionary income." In 1873 when white Mississippians boycotted the elections, they were chagrined when the results produced unprecedented gains for African Americans. Voters elected African Americans as lieutenant governor, superintendent of education, speaker of the Mississippi House of Representatives, and as U.S. senator. Consequently, beginning in late 1874 white

Mississippians used violence to keep African Americans from voting and drove African American leaders out of their communities, a practice referred to as "bull-dozing." Whites used violence to drive northern Republicans from the state altogether, ending Reconstruction in Mississippi two years before the removal of federal troops from the South in 1877.

Span has written the first comprehensive history of black public education in Mississippi between 1862 and 1875. The interpretation is supported by a rich array of primary sources, including personal letters, newspapers, organization and governmental records, and a variety of secondary sources. His interrogation of earlier accounts of Reconstruction in Mississippi is particularly adept. *From Cotton Field to Schoolhouse* is an engrossing account of public education in Mississippi, a state synonymous with "King Cotton." The study offers a lens for interpreting public education during Reconstruction in other Deep South states with large African American populations. The book illuminates issues relevant to African American education in the 21st century such as adequate taxation, public versus private schooling, and educational equity. It is a welcome contribution to the historiography of southern black education.

Louis Ray
Fairleigh Dickinson University

Angela Hornsby-Gutting, *Black Manhood and Community Building in North Carolina, 1900–1930.* Gainesville: University Press of Florida, 2009. Pp. 244. Cloth $65.00.

The "construction of manhood" has been a topic of interest to historians for several decades. This interest, however, has generally not included African American men's efforts and activities in response to Jim Crow during the early decades of the 20th century. Most of the emphasis has been placed on the "great men" of the era. Examining how black men built communal institutions through grassroots activism, historian Angela Hornsby-Gutting offers a sophisticated analysis of not just black men, but also black women and their work of "uplifting the race" at the beginning of the 20th century. Hornsby-Gutting examines how African American men reconciled the growing influence of African American women during a period of disfranchisement and racial oppression, a time most scholars consider a low point in black life in the United States. The issues of middle-class respectability and raising black boys to be responsible "race men" occupied much time and work. Through their efforts, black men and women eviscerated the notion that African American men were powerless in the wake of Jim Crow.

Historians have documented the problems African Americans encountered from white supremacists at the beginning of the 20th century. As Hornsby-Gutting reports, "North Carolina's deteriorating racial climate," led to the exile of tens of thousands of African American North Carolinians who headed north. The racial transformation of northern urban areas and the larger effects of the Great Migration on the South have been dissected; however, few historians have actually examined how African Americans who remained responded to these social changes. In *Black Manhood and Community Building in North Carolina,* Hornsby-Gutting delivers a penetrating analysis that dispels the myth of black male impotence in the face of increasing white racism.

The book's four chapters examine how African American men confronted and responded to "the women's era"; the problems associated with young black males and how to raise them up; the black "secret societies" in North Carolina; and how African American men acted as "ambassadors of the race" within the community and to white political elites who acted as the enforcers of the racial caste system of the South. What is particularly interesting is that the author uses her analysis of gender identity as a window to view and understand how African American men strategized and moved to achieve middle-class respectability, improve race relations, and to define black manhood in an age when "boy" was a commonly used racial epithet. Hornsby-Gutting found that African American men often sought to "protect" African American women from violence from whites by enforcing a patriarchal system whereby the men intruded upon a woman's right to control her own affairs, thus, mimicking the practices in white society. Equally interesting is her examination of how the men closely observed the activities of women and sought to reassert their authority over "woman's work" despite their understandings of the "proper" role of women.

In the Victorian era there was increased emphasis on frugality and self-control. This cultural ethos reinforced African Americans' attempts to seek middle-class respectability through creating stable homes, practicing moral rectitude, and enforcing separate spheres for men and women. Hornsby-Gutting demonstrates that black clergy, educators, and businessmen played crucial roles in the development of young men, promoting healthy living standards, and responding to and shielding children from the degradation of Jim Crow segregation. In places such as Asheville, Greensboro, Raleigh, Durham, Charlotte, and other cities, Hornsby-Gutting traces the political and social activities of African American men and women, using a treasure trove of material. She demonstrates just how active the African American community was in developing standards for raising children and recovering their history. She demonstrates these practices by examining the life of Charles Hunter, who published books, pamphlets, and other materials on African American history in the state of North Carolina. Hunter and other African American men were prominent figures in the mounting of annual Emancipation Day ceremonies, state fairs, and other celebrations. These events allowed African Americans to debate and plot future directions and reconcile ideological differences.

In the very interesting discussion of "Gender and Fraternity in North Carolina's Black Secret Society," Hornsby-Gutting offers an analysis of the workings of the state's Masonic lodges and the chapters of the Order of the Eastern Star (OES). These institutions played a pivotal role in pooling resources, pushing for positive social change, and advancing African American social and economic interests. Hornsby-Gutting also explores the conflicts that arose between black men (lodges) and women (OES) over finances, institutional direction, and authority. She shows that "leaders of the OES sought a compromise between autonomy and dependence" in response to the attempts of African American men to circumscribe their power and independence. Disputes such as these provide important insights into gender and cultural differences in the context of the women's era and the debates over African American advancement.

Black Manhood and Community Building in North Carolina is thoroughly researched and well written. Using archival material from various sections of North Carolina, Hornsby-Gutting expertly weaves together a history previously lost. Persuasively, she notes that black men sought to move forward by "fashioning an African American manhood characterized by dignity and authority that would prove uplifting to their manhood and to the black community overall." Her analysis reveals that these values, standards, and activities fostered political projects for their descendants who were able to defeat Jim Crow. By analyzing the activities of black men through their interactions with black women, Hornsby-Gutting debunks the myth that African American men offered little in the way of leadership during these decades. She restores African American men to their rightful place as active participants in the struggle for racial equality. Historians, undergraduate and graduate students, and others would benefit from this informative work.

Daryl A. Carter
East Tennessee State University

Andrew Napolitano, *Dred Scott's Revenge: A Legal History of Race and Freedom in America.* Nashville: Thomas Nelson, 2009. Pp. 320. Cloth $25.99.

Barack Obama's election to the U.S. presidency was like seeing Haley's Comet—beautiful, amazing, brilliant, a once in a lifetime event that could leave you speechless. On the night of the election, I was caught up in the euphoria of what it would be like to live in a "post-racial society," where differences are respected and welcomed, and people are treated fairly no matter their race, ethnicity, gender, or sexual orientation. For one night, I indulged in the privilege of believing that none of the "isms" or "phobias" exists. I danced; I sang; and I hugged random strangers. Then, faster than it began, it was over, and I was back to reality.

The United States is not a post-racial society. Believing that is akin to playing make-believe. With even a basic understanding of American government and U.S. history, we know that the country was founded on several competing ideologies—Judeo-Christianity, capitalism, and the egregious practice of mistreating people of color, women, gays, the poor, and other marginalized members of society. So, being the critical young lawyer that I am, I begin to wonder: Is it realistic to believe, as many people do, that in four years (perhaps, eight) President Obama will end this country's continued practice of racial wrongdoing? It may not have been his intent, but Judge Andrew Napolitano's book *Dred Scott's Revenge* brings a welcome perspective to answering this question.

In *Dred Scott v. Sanford*, the U.S. Supreme Court ruled that people of African descent could not be U.S. citizens. Napolitano argues in *Dred Scott's Revenge* that the Supreme Court's decision was a significant turning point for race relations in the United States. The ruling, he explains, effectively constitutionalized the status of African people as slaves and non-citizens, and made black freedom and equal rights in the United States essentially unobtainable. Although the book's title elicits images of Dred Scott wielding a weapon against the forces of white racism like an epic character in a comic book or historical novel, that (thankfully) is not the book's premise. Instead, Napolitano argues that Dred Scott's revenge for the denial of his rights to citizenship is the catastrophic effect that the holding in *Dred Scott v. Sanford* has had on the United States since 1857.

Napolitano provides a well-researched and insightful examination of not only *Dred Scott v. Sanford*, but also the Civil War, the Tuskegee syphilis experiments, the 1954 *Brown v. Board of Education* decision, and the Civil Rights Movement; and he provides an excellent resource for young lawyers who want a basic understanding of U.S. history that does not read like a textbook. For example, Napolitano's discussion of Abraham Lincoln is the kind of blunt discussion that we need in historical discourse. In one chapter the dominant image of Abraham Lincoln as "the Great Emancipator" is shattered and replaced with that of a shrewd politician whose intent was not just to emancipate the enslaved, but to ship them to Liberia, West Africa, or Central America. Napolitano examines both past and contemporary issues of race in the United States, and at one point even acknowledges that, given the government's history of experimenting on African Americans (such as the Tuskegee experiments), it should not come as a shock that Rev. Jeremiah Wright and others believe that the government created Acquired Immune Deficiency Syndrome (AIDS) to kill black people.

It is exciting to read a book by a scholar who not only makes well-reasoned arguments, but also provides well-researched evidence. Even if you do not agree with his conclusions, you realize that you are not dealing with propaganda or arguments that lack substance. The major criticism of the book is the exclusion of African American women from the analysis. Certain parts of the book mirrored the traditional historical narrative that is confined to Abraham Lincoln, Martin Luther King, John F. Kennedy, Lyndon B. Johnson, and other "great men." However, African American women have had a significant impact on race relations in the United States, from the early slave revolts on plantations in Virginia and South Carolina to the modern movements to end poverty. Given Napolitano's penchant for challenging the normative view of U.S. history, in the future I would encourage him to explore the role of African American women in U.S. history.

Ultimately, Napolitano's book does not reveal anything that has not been discussed before. The book's brilliance lies in the original way that he presents the information. He ignites your curiosity, if not to challenge what he presents, then to enhance your understanding of American and African American history. The book made me want to learn more about the life of Abraham Lincoln, the politics of the Civil War, and the Tuskegee experiments in the 1930s and 1940s. This would mean not only revisiting aspects of U.S. history that make me angry, but also hopeful.

In the last chapter of *Dred Scott's Revenge*, Napolitano explains that the election of Barack Obama gives us hope for the dawn of a "new age." For Napolitano, it is a post-racial society where the social, economic, and political institutions operate in a "color blind" fashion. For others, a "new age" would be when the United States is a society where we acknowledge and appreciate each other's differences. Although Napolitano's vision of a "new age" may be different from others (including mine), Obama's election gave us hope that, despite the past, the country is headed for a better future. Perhaps the fact that we continue to hope and fight for that "new age" is Dred Scott's real revenge.

Zenobia V. Harris
Houston, TX

Amy Bass, *Those About Him Remained Silent: The Battle Over W. E. B. Du Bois.* Minneapolis: University of Minnesota Press, 2009. Pp. 232. Cloth $24.95.

Amy Bass's *Those About Him Remained Silent* is an impressive historical analysis of the complicated process of creating public memorials to W. E. B. Du Bois in his hometown in the Berkshire Mountains of Massachusetts. Bass reconstructs the hostile debates in the 1960s and 1970s over Du Bois's place in Great

Barrington's local history. Ultimately, residents overlooked their native son's accomplishments as a civil rights leader, educator, sociologist, and historian because of the controversial positions he took in the last years of his life. Du Bois left for Ghana, West Africa, at the end of his life because he was disillusioned by the persistence of racial and social injustice in the United States. His self-imposed exile to Ghana in 1963 and decision to join the Communist Party in the United States at the age of 93 made him guilty of treason in the eyes of many residents of his hometown. Bass adroitly uncovers the long journey to honor Du Bois and demonstrates how memorials to an amazing civil rights leader almost became a casualty of Cold War politics and American racism.

One of the major triumphs of this book, aside from its extraordinary historical detail, is the author's thorough methodology. Bass reconstructs local battles over Du Bois's legacy using local newspapers, especially editorials, to analyze the ways decisions about memorializing this nationally prominent African American figure were debated and decided at the local level. The *Berkshire Eagle* largely supported the Du Bois commemoration campaign, which was led by Walter Wilson. However, the *Berkshire Record* and the *Berkshire Courier* opposed the movement. Although Du Bois's boyhood home was eventually designated a "National Historic Landmark," the vitriolic local debates, in evidence primarily at public meetings and in editorials, almost kept Du Bois from being memorialized at all.

In 1968 the "Du Bois Memorial Committee" was formed. Bass pays close attention to the complex ways in which hysteria and the politics of fear created during the Cold War era fueled local opposition to the memorial committee, despite the achievements of the Civil Rights Movement. People were so scarred by the Cold War that for all Du Bois's greatness, his joining the Communist Party in 1961 sealed his fate for many as un-American and unworthy of commemoration. However, the local Berkshire residents who opposed the memorial committee's efforts were not just motivated by an irrational fear of communism. Prior to joining the Communist Party, Du Bois had indicted capitalism in *Black Reconstruction in America* (1935), and he was condemned for his associations with well-known "radicals" such as the singer and social activist Paul Robeson, and the communist politician William Patterson. In addition, his stance against the anticommunist origins of the Truman Doctrine, his subsequent dismissal from the NAACP for supporting the Progressive Party in 1948 over the Democrats, and his involvement in the Peace Information Center for which he was put on trial, but exonerated in 1950, led to increasing chastisement for his very public move to the left and overshadowed his scholarly achievements and longstanding work for black civil rights. The evidence from the newspaper editorials vividly shows how a national politics of fear can blindly shape how people behave at the local and national levels.

Racism also played a major role in the opposition movement. When the memorial committee attempted to organize the public celebration for the national historic park honoring Du Bois, rumors circulated that members of the Black Panther Party would attend and this fueled fears and more opposition. Walter Wilson, the committee's leader, argued that the Cold War rhetoric was really just a way to mask bigotry and racism. On 18 October 1969, after a·year of delays, 800 people attended the dedication ceremony at the memorial park created in Du Bois's name; the ceremony honored Du Bois's legacy and was held on the land where he grew up. However, locals tried to use frivolous zoning ordinances to stop the ceremony, while racism likely played an enormous role in explaining why the committee received so little support from local historical societies.

The memorial committee continued its efforts despite the local opposition. The members wanted to make the Du Bois Park a national landmark, award scholarships and prizes in his name, and refurbish Du Bois's boyhood home, which remained on the site, but was in need of repair. In 1976 the Du Bois site was named a National Historic Landmark. The horrific failure of the Vietnam War and the recent Watergate conspiracy made it hard for many locals to continue to play the patriotism card. To my mind, one of the most interesting findings in this study is that the FBI through its Counterintelligence Program (COINTELPRO) was involved in planting information, particularly among local veterans' groups and via editorials in the *Eagle*, to fuel the movement against the memorial committee. Despite continued opposition, on 20 October 1979, approximately 900 people finally came together to celebrate when the Du Bois Park was made a national landmark.

Bass only scratches the surface of an important theoretical issue with regard to the scholarship on public space and memory. Bass's research shows "how complicated the politics and culture of memory can be, and how public space can serve as the front line for battles regarding how various social groups are represented and defined." But who decides who will become part of public memory? Who dominates the conversations about whom to commemorate? Bass demonstrates that disgruntled citizens and newspaper editorialists had the power to thwart the commemoration of a national civil rights leader. She found that the controversy surrounding the Du Bois memorial "exemplified how history is generated and recreated at the most local and personal levels, by people passionately determined for their voices—and thus their ways of remembering—to be heard." That local Berkshire residents were able to prevent the memorializing of Du Bois for so long is extremely important.

Those About Him Remained Silent has enormous potential and undoubtedly raises many issues for future research. Debates over the nation's history take place at the national and local levels, and individuals construct history one public debate at a time. This conclusion is essential in thinking about how social change and history are crafted by individuals in the local arena, often through public debate and discussion.

Angela Jones
Stony Brook University

Edward J. Blum and Jason R. Young, eds., *The Souls of W. E. B. Du Bois: New Essays and Reflections.* Macon: Mercer University Press, 2009. Pp. 281. Cloth $45.00.

Among a number of widely accepted observations by scholars concerning the life and career of W. E. B. Du Bois is the conclusion that he became an avowed agnostic or even atheist. Until very recently, such conclusions have been widely accepted as verifiable truth. *The Souls of W. E. B. Du Bois: New Essays and Reflections*, coedited by Edward J. Blum and Jason R. Young, raises new questions and challenges long-held conclusions regarding the religiosity of one of the greatest American intellectuals of the 20th century. For Blum and Young, biographers and historians of Du Bois "might continue in their depictions of [Du Bois] as irreligious or antireligious," but in doing so scholars "wrongly underestimate Du Bois's spiritual power."

W. E. B. Du Bois, like most African Americans toward the end of the 19th century, grew up in Christian communities. First in the Congregationalist tradition of the Northeast, and later in the black Protestant traditions he experienced in the South. It was also while in the South that Du Bois witnessed firsthand the soul-numbing violence associated with white racist ideology and practice. It was during this period in the 1890s and early 1900s that Du Bois began, like many African Americans, to question openly the fundamental theological principles taught to him throughout his Christian upbringing.

The Souls of W. E. B. Du Bois is organized into four topical sections that are creatively reminiscent of Du Bois's sociopolitical and intellectual complexity and interests. These are: "Was W. E. B. Du Bois Religious?" "The Importance of *Souls*," "Rhetoric of Religion and Redeeming Lynch Victims," and "Islam, Judaism, and Buddhism." The essays contained in each section introduce scholarship that should be considered essential for both the casual student and the ardent Du Bois scholar. In the first essay Paul Zuckerman explores the "irreligiosity" of Du Bois and argues that Du Bois's break with traditional Christianity and religion in general is indisputable and cites a number of examples to support his thesis. He points to the absence of Christians in Du Bois's social circle, his lauding of "Soviet atheism," and his recanting of previously held Christian beliefs in a 1954 letter in which he revealed, "There is no religion of which I know whose dogma and creed is one in which I wholly believe." Some may think it odd to begin a volume that is largely an apologetic effort to establish the religiosity and spirituality of Du Bois with an essay that disputes this argument. Blum and Young's inclusion of this essay, and where it is placed, is appropriate and effective because it reminds the reader of the longstanding view among historians and Du Bois biographers of his irreligious worldview.

After reading these essays and reflections anyone who held the popular opinion regarding Du Bois's religiosity will be challenged to think very differently. Indeed, one could seriously begin to view Du Bois as one who embraced, or even helped shape, a theology of liberation within the parameters of the African American experience. For instance, acknowledging Du Bois's rejection of dominant Christian dogma and creeds, Dwight Hopkins presents a liberationist theological perspective and argues that Du Bois "maintained a firm belief in a God of love whose revelation expressed itself in his relentless, comprehensive work for other human beings." The nature of God for Du Bois, according to Hopkins, can be found in Du Bois's article, written later in life, entitled "On Growing Old." Here Du Bois declared, "I have loved a fight and I have realized that Love is God and Work is his Prophet." This notion of God for Du Bois appears again in his "Prayers for Dark People," in which he wrote, "God is Love and Work is His Revelation. Amen." Anthony Pinn presents his ideas on "veiled bodies" within the context of black religion, stating that Du Bois "was concerned with the aesthetic dimensions unleashed by religion, the manner in which religion served as a multipronged attack—when at its best—against the abuses faced by people of African descent." Michelle Kuhl examines Du Bois's effort to undo the psychological and emotional damage caused by the practice of lynching, which was used by whites to revive antebellum socioeconomic and political arrangements. In his "Martyr Tales" and other narratives, Du Bois transforms lynching, "the symbol of defeat[,] into a symbol of triumph." Du Bois skillfully associates the victims of lynching with the "broken body of Christ." For Kuhl, this association stands in a "rich tradition of black activists who transformed the grim horror of lynching into a Christian narrative of suffering and redemption." Craig Forney probes the religiosity of Du Bois by examining influential events during the period he penned *The Souls of Black Folk*. For Forney, this classic work illuminates numerous aspects of African American religion reflecting Du Bois's adoption of the "religious beliefs of African Americans from throughout the South."

Blum and Young's anthology is a rewarding and much-needed work that responds to the scholarly neglect of the topic it examines. Contrary to the dominant perspective among historians and Du Bois's biographers, *The Souls of W. E. B. Du Bois* offers fresh analysis and insights into the large body of work produced by Du

Bois and challenges the reader to revise previously held conclusions about Du Bois's religiosity and spirituality. The essays and reflections provide a significant contribution to multiple disciplines, including American and African American history, sociology, American religious history, liberation theology, and political science. Given the lack of scholarship on this subject, I fully agree with the editors that "Du Bois had so much to say about religion that it is time for his words to be heard and understood anew."

Lawrence A. Burnley
Whitworth University

Nathaniel Norment, Jr., ed., *The Addison Gayle, Jr., Reader.* Urbana and Chicago: University of Illinois Press, 2009. Pp. 454. Cloth $75.00. Paper $35.00.

In 1966 the Black Power Movement emerged, born of growing expectations and increasing frustrations among activists in the Civil Rights Movement. Contemporaneous with this resurgence of black nationalism was the cultural revival known as the Black Arts Movement. Addison Gayle, Jr., (1932–1991) was one of the leading figures of the Black Arts Movement. Gayle's career as educator, critic, writer, and editor spanned twenty-five years, and his voluminous writings revealed an extensive knowledge of philosophy, history, and the literary works of African, Irish, Russian, Chinese, Italian, French, German, Greek, English, Spanish, as well as African American and European American writers. Gayle was one of the first intellectuals to recognize that "Stokely Carmichael's injection of the phrase Black Power into the civil rights struggle was the most important accomplishment in the history of this ideological war [between integrationists and nationalists] in the last one hundred years"; and that the acceptance of the phrase "'Black is Beautiful' is the first step in the deconstruction [of the values of white aesthetics] and the construction of new ones . . . lying deep in the un-toured regions of the Black experience." Given his extensive knowledge of world literature, many literary historians consider him "the intellectual and theoretical architect of the Black Aesthetic Movement" and a "consummate critic."

The Addison Gayle, Jr., Reader reintroduces the world of scholarship to this man and his essential writings on "Black Aesthetics" and African American literature. The *Reader* is a collection of sixty essays and reviews by Gayle between 1967 and 1980. It consists of an introductory essay and six sections. The introductory essay by Temple University's Nathaniel Norment places Gayle and his writings in cultural and historical context, noting how Gayle attained the status of a "leading black literary and artistic authority," and it offers some insight into his personal life and the forces that shaped him, which is elaborated upon in the section devoted to "Autobiographies."

Part one, "Black Situations," contains nine "social essays" that offer cogent reasons for supporting Black Power politics, denounce so-called "responsible Negro leaders," and caution against the "professional black nationalist." After briefly recounting the history of black men's participation in U.S. wars from the American Revolution through the Korean conflict, yet still finding themselves socially and economically oppressed, Gayle's essay "Hell No, Black Men Won't Go!" explained why many young men, responding to Black Power appeals, refused to serve in the military during the Vietnam War years.

"Black Aesthetics," part two, includes ten essays, representative of the writings that established Gayle as the literary architect of the Black Aesthetic Movement. "The Harlem Renaissance: Towards a Black Aesthetic" provides the historical background for the "integrationist/nationalist" debates and examines the relationship between the New Negro Movement of the 1920s and the Black Arts Movement of the 1960s. Several essays, including "Separate, Not Mutual Estates," discuss the distinctness of people of African descent with regard to language, culture, worldview, and life experiences; and posit the responsibility of African American writers and critics to create an aesthetic that is true to the African American community and its history and culture.

The eleven essays in part three, "Literary Criticism," focus on Gayle's development of a blueprint for black literary criticism, defining its function in the context of the genesis of black cultural nationalism. In "Blueprint for Black Criticism," and "The Function of Black Criticism at the Present Time," Gayle declares that the realities of African American life require that black literature "mean and not be," and that literary criticism must offer new standards for judging African American literature, providing meanings and concepts free of white racist stereotypes. The latter point is discussed extensively in the essay "Cultural Hegemony: The Southern White Writer and American Letters." In his assessments and critiques of the writings of Paul Laurence Dunbar, Gwendolyn Brooks, James Baldwin, Langston Hughes, and Richard Wright, Gayle applies his literary insights and wide-ranging analytical skills to the works of these important literary artists. *Native Son* is held as a standard of black literature and Wright is quoted extensively in writings throughout the *Reader*.

"Book Introductions, Forewords, and Prefaces," and "Book Reviews," parts four and five, take up one-third of the selections in the *Gayle Reader*. These writings discuss the aspects of the "black aesthetic" found in the novels of John Killens, Paul Laurence Dunbar, Charles Russell, Claude McKay, Brenda Wilkinson, Ishmael Reed, Gayl Jones, William Demby, and Charles Cain. For Gayle the function of the "black novel" is "the liberation of black people," enabling them to be true to themselves and their heritage. The final section, "Autobiographies," includes some of the most intense, revealing, and poignant essays in the volume. They chronicle Gayle's own struggles over self-identity and manhood, and his journey toward personal liberation. The "Excerpt from 'Wayward Child: A Personal Odyssey,'" is especially revealing and thought-provoking, while "Black Fathers and Sons: Parts I and II" provides important insight into Gayle's intellectual development. By age 13 he had read "*The Souls of Black Folk,* autobiographies of Frederick Douglass and Booker T. Washington, poems by Langston Hughes, Carter G. Woodson's series on Life and History, and novels by Richard Wright, Claude McKay, and Jessie Fauset." He also had read works by Alexander Pushkin, Anton Chekhov, Fyodor Dostoyevsky, and other Russian writers. These works contributed to his efforts and commitment to contribute to the liberation of oppressed people all over the world.

Addison Gayle, Jr's writings support W. E. B. Du Bois's assertion that all art is, or should be, propaganda; and the *Addison Gayle, Jr., Reader* is an important addition to the literature on the Black Power, Black Arts, and Black Aesthetic movements. Nathaniel Norment has provided a valuable resource for students and scholars of African American history, literature, culture, and politics.

Barbara L. Green
Wright State University

Vanessa Siddle Walker, *Hello Professor: A Black Principal and Professional Leadership in the Segregated South.* Chapel Hill: The University of North Carolina Press, 2009. Pp. 312. Cloth $32.50.

Schooling for African Americans in the segregated South has been viewed historically through its deficits. As noted by Vanessa Siddle Walker, it is common to discuss segregated black schools in terms of funding inequalities, inadequate facilities, and the neglect of black educators' needs by white school board members and superintendents. *Hello Professor* offers a revisionist perspective by examining the experiences of Ulysses Byas, a black high school principal who worked in the Gainesville, Georgia, school system from 1957 to 1968. Using Byas's thoughts and writings, Walker portrays a sophisticated network of African American educators, parents, and community members working together nationally, regionally, and locally to craft an agenda that focused exclusively on the needs of African American children. At the forefront of this agenda were black intellectuals concerned with the plight of African American students, including Horace Mann Bond, Allison Davis, and W. E. B. Du Bois. Along with black school officials, these scholars developed a nontraditional pipeline that connected the best teaching practices of the era to black principals and communities in order to "address directly the limitations of their [black students'] segregated education and envision new possibilities."

One of the purveyors of the black intellectuals' agenda was Ulysses Byas who, like many black school principals of that period, was known as the "Professor." Byas's biography is interwoven into this historical ethnography of the complex social environment of the Jim Crow South. Byas's leadership style and methods allowed him to successfully navigate the rules and regulations of white school boards and superintendents to upgrade black schools, even when this was unpopular among white taxpayers. Byas was revered as "Dr. Jekyll and Mr. Hyde" as he masterfully "played the game" of outwitting school officials, using the local press to expose inequalities, while masking his agenda of seeking educational equality for his students.

Byas's creative and resourceful leadership style was traced to influences in his childhood. Born in 1924, he was one of eight children, raised in poverty by a single mother who insisted that all her children complete high school. As a young man, Byas struggled with his mother's request. At one time a high school dropout, Byas eventually received his master's degree from Teachers College, Columbia University, and his Ph.D. from University of Massachusetts, Amherst. As a youth, Byas thought school was a waste of time and he left at the end of eighth grade. Thankfully, Byas's negative attitudes towards education were short-lived, and he came to see the value of education once he experienced the harsh realities as a black male entering the workforce without a trade or a high school diploma.

After only four months of low pay and arduous work, Byas returned to school, and his mother insisted that he repeat the eighth grade to make up for the year he lost. Motivated to work and remain in school, Byas enrolled in Hudson Industrial School, where he excelled. After graduation, he joined the U.S. Navy where he worked as a cook. Byas was honorably discharged and used his veterans' benefits from the G.I. Bill to enroll at Fort Valley State College, where his experiences "turned the creative young man into an educator with conviction." While taking an adult education course, volunteering in a school-sponsored adult education program, and working as an in-service teacher in the business department, Byas found his passion for teaching. Upon graduation, he turned down a job as a school administrator, and instead headed to Columbia University's Teachers College.

In New York City, Byas was introduced to schooling without the oppressive constraints of legal segregation, and truly flourished when he began to view education as a tool for democracy. Byas took his new knowledge, infused it with his cultural heritage, and left New York for a teaching job in Elberton, Georgia. Before his departure, one of his professors warned that Georgia, one of the poorest states at the time, did not have the resources or facilities to implement Byas's lofty ideas for African American education. However, the black principals in Georgia were part of a national, regional, and local network of African American educators who collectively changed the trajectory of education for African Americans in the Jim Crow South. Walker documents this unique network of African American principals, college professors and presidents, parents, and community members who gathered annually on multiple levels as a consortium to push their agenda and find creative solutions to educating African American students despite inadequate resources.

Byas spent the bulk of his career as principal at Fair Street High School in Gainesville, Georgia, which was later rebuilt and named the E. E. Butler High School. Walker focuses on Byas's relationship with this school community and the way he implemented his new ideas within the boundaries of established cultural norms. During this era in the South, teachers functioned "in loco parentis" for their students. Black parents trusted teachers with their children's education and held teachers accountable for their children's success. Walker explains that as principal, Byas sought the support of the parents because they could assist him in preserving his autonomy as principal. As long as parents were happy and did not complain to the superintendent, Byas was able to run the school by his own high standards. Therefore, Byas attended the church services of all the religious denominations represented in his school and willingly embraced the cultural norms of the African American community, even when they differed somewhat from his own. Like many African American educators of his time, Byas geared the education of his students to meet the needs of the African American community.

Ulysses Byas is just one example from a cohort of resilient black principals whose experiences and activities counter the story of substandard and inadequate schooling for African American in the segregated South. Walker reintroduces this forgotten but influential world through Byas's notes, records, and conversations. Byas's story will inspire future educators and help them understand the importance of community, collaborative, and professional leadership in the transformation of public education.

Bettina L. Love
Northern Kentucky University

Sherman A. Jackson, *Islam and the Problem of Black Suffering*. New York: Oxford University Press, 2009. Pp. 232. Cloth $29.95.

Sherman A. Jackson makes a significant contribution to the scholarship on Islamic religious traditions and black theology in *Islam and the Problem of Black*

Suffering. In many ways the sequel to Jackson's earlier book, *Islam and the Blackamerican* (2005), this latest volume explores the essential elements of Sunni Islam to determine its applicability to the African American experience and the protest tradition in the African American religious history. Jackson focuses on the debate over black theodicy, triggered in the 1970s by the controversial book *Is God a White Racist?* (1973) by William R. Jones. As with all theodicy, black theodicy attempts to reconcile the existence of evil in a world created by "an all-good and all-powerful God." However, in its specificity, black theodicy focuses on the "historical and communal suffering" of African Americans and "begins by asking how an all-good and all-powerful God could sponsor and allow a moral evil that is as grand and sustained as the evil of American slavery and all that has come in its train." After the publication of James Cone's *Black Theology and Black Power* (1969) and *A Black Theology of Liberation* (1970), and other books by black liberation theologians, William Jones offered a critique, arguing that this new "black theodicy" offered a view of God as a racist who permits the suffering of African Americans and thus the "biblical concept of a just God who is the omnipotent judge of the world and the author of human history must be rejected."

Jackson argues that a similar critique should be leveled against traditional Sunni Islam, which also posits the existence of an all-good and all-powerful God. Sherman seeks "to present a theological perspective on the problem of black theodicy that the generality of religiously literate Muslims recognize as a valid representation of historical Sunnism." Jackson examines the rudimentary proto-Islamic tradition, orthodoxies, and authorities within the context of African American history. He discusses Edward Blyden's important book *Christianity, Islam, and the Negro Race* (1887), which promoted the positive impact of the orthodox and so-called heretical versions of the Islamic religion on African societies. However, individuals he describes as proto-Islamic leaders such as Noble Drew Ali, founder of the Moorish Science Temple, and Elijah Muhammad of the Nation of Islam "passed on the phenomenon of communal conversion to Islam among Blackamericans, a process whose beginnings . . . were dominated by heretical movements." Jackson is interested in interpreting traditional Sunni Islam as relevant to the African American experience because he believes that "Muslim tradition can contribute to one's ability to address contemporary issues without sacrificing one's sense of collective self, ideational community, or transcendent belongingness." African Americans could benefit by accepting or adopting Sunni doctrinal orthodoxy without losing their identity.

Islam and the Problem of Black Suffering consists of five chapters. The first chapter traces the development of Muslim theology from its embryonic stages to its more complex contemporary traditions, while chapters two through five are devoted to the four classical schools of Muslim theology: Mu'tazilism, Ash'arism, Maturidism, and Traditionalism.

Jackson's interdisciplinary approach, using theology, linguistics, historical and religious interpretations, allows him to examine methodically the classical schools of Islamic theology. Jackson argues that in the past African Americans who have become Sunni Muslims have accepted the faith and its traditions without questioning its relevance to African American historical and contemporary conditions. And given the understanding of Islamic religion as transcendent and all-encompassing, true believers would have little reason to question its relevance (or lack of relevance) to the particularities of the African American experience. However, Jackson emphasizes that none of the classical schools of Islamic thought "would bind God-fearing Blackamericans to a piety of quietism. For, again, all of them hold humans to be responsible for the evil they commit. As such, to revolt against the evil of suffering would not, according to classical Sunni Tradition, in any way amount to a revolt against God." Given that Jackson is committed to the principle that "Islam is essentially the sustained conclusions of those who are recognized by critical masses of Muslims as authorities," he believes that a Sunni tradition can be developed out of African Americans' communal experiences and history "and that grows out of and explicitly seeks to address [African American] reality." Jackson assumes that African American Muslims receiving traditional training in the Muslim world will import classical Islamic theology into the African American Islamic tradition. Ultimately, Jackson urges African American Islamic Sunnis to reevaluate the classical Islamic schools, and to examine their history and the experiences that brought them into existence. This would provide their theological interpretations with more substance as they seek to develop an African American Sunni Islam on a suitable experiential basis.

Islam and the Problem of Black Suffering is not just an examination of ongoing debates within the field of black theology, but an exposition of the Islamic worldview and its relevance to the African American experience. Jackson uses a wide range of primary and secondary sources, and students should pay close attention to the references because they provide in-depth information useful for future research. Jackson's earlier book *Islam and the Blackamerican* offers an analysis of classical Islamic theology and provides important background information on the issues addressed in this latest work. *Islam and the Problem of Black Suffering* warrants high praise for its scholarship and deserves the attention of Islamic jurists, imams, religious scholars, and converts.

Latif A. Tarik
American Public University

Alusine Jalloh and Toyin Falola, eds., *The United States and West Africa: Interactions and Relations*. Rochester, NY: University of Rochester Press, 2008. Pp. 477. Cloth $80.00. Paper $24.95.

Like many collections of essays, *The United States and West Africa* began life with a conference, held in 2005 at the University of Texas at Arlington, sponsored by the university's Africa Program, which seeks to promote economic ties between Texas and African nations. Accordingly, many of the chapters focus on matters commercial, not the least of them oil, a commodity in which Texans have more than just an academic interest. Both editors teach at the University of Texas, Alusine Jalloh at the Arlington campus and Toyin Falola in Austin.

This is a sizeable book, with twenty-two chapters divided into five parts, with a preface and introduction. There is no concluding chapter, which is not unusual in edited volumes, but which may have been useful in this case mainly because the introduction contains only summaries of the individual chapters, but attempts no larger overview of how the whole volume may be greater than the sum of its parts. History is the dominant field in the collection, but political science, anthropology, and sociology are also represented. The result is a text that is temporally wide-ranging, beginning with the early 19th century and continuing to the present. Spatially, the volume is less expansive, focusing largely on Anglophone West Africa, including Liberia. About half of the chapters range across national boundaries, discussing multiple colonial territories or nation-states. Each of the remaining chapters focuses on a single country, with Sierra Leone getting the most attention, followed by Liberia, Ghana, and Nigeria. Comparatively, Francophone West Africa is neglected. Just a single chapter is devoted exclusively to French-speaking countries, discussing the construction of an oil pipeline in Chad and Cameroon. Another chapter, on U.S. attempts to help foster entrepreneurship, discusses both Anglophone and Francophone nations.

Generally, the chapters are grounded in primary sources, mostly archival, but also oral. Taking the volume as a whole, the strongest chapters are in part one. There Ibrahim Kargbo and Ayodeji Olukoju discuss commercial relations between the United States and Sierra Leone and Nigeria from the early to the late colonial era. Hakeem Ibikunle Tijani offers a broader West African overview of the same subject. In one of the more interesting contributions, John Wes Grant, breaking with earlier discussions of the subject, argues that free African Americans in antebellum Virginia did not immigrate to Liberia in greater numbers because they were otherwise preoccupied with saving money to buy family members out of slavery. Still on Liberia, Ibrahim Sundiata attributes the "defeat" (not the "failure") of the Garvey movement there in the 1920s to a nefarious Americo-Liberian elite, "imbued with many of the values of Old Dixie."

In parts two and three the focus shifts from political economy to culture. Four of the six chapters in these two sections examine the interrelationships between African Americans and West Africans. Kwame Essien looks at African Americans residing in Ghana and their contributions to Ghanaian nation building since 1985. He concludes that, on balance, the interaction has resulted in "long-term, positive mutual relations" between African Americans and Ghanaians. Harold R. Harris takes up the same subject, also viewed from the Ghanaian side. But where Essien finds mutuality, Harris sees social distance, which he rather stereotypically attributes to differences between African American individualism and Ghanaian communalism. Fred L. Johnson III, in one of the volume's shortest pieces, goes much further than Harris. From his perch on the other side of the Atlantic (in the United States), Johnson sees a "wide chasm" and "unspoken antagonisms" (spoken ones too) between African Americans and West Africans. Bayo Lawal, also writing from the U.S. side, is more hopeful. Lawal, like the other three authors on the relations between African Americans and West Africans, deploys W. E. B. Du Bois's concept of "double-consciousness." Lawal suggests that the Du Boisian "twoness" is not just an African American condition, but one shared by diasporic communities worldwide. Seen through this lens, he argues, global black solidarity is not a given; it is not so much a cultural artifact as a historical process. Pan-Africanism, Lawal concludes, should be about building bridges.

In part four, *The United States and West Africa* returns to high politics, with one exception, Anita Spring's chapter on the "West African Enterprise Network," a U.S.-backed group that spreads the gospel of free enterprise in West Africa. The remaining five chapters in this part interrogate official U.S. policy—diplomatic, economic, and military—toward West Africa since the late colonial period. They show that during the Cold War, the United States had two paramount interests in West Africa: keeping the Soviet Union at bay and maintaining access to the region's natural resources, especially oil.

The final section is also concerned with matters of state, and brings the story of U.S. engagement with West Africa down to the time of Bush II, whose global "war on terror" did not spare West Africa. Three of the four chapters in part five deal in varying degrees of emphasis with the pursuit of Islamist radicals, who replaced the Soviet Union as the primary focus of U.S. diplomatic and military activities in West Africa. And then there is oil, which has lost none of its importance in the new dispensation. The fourth chapter in part five examines an Exxon Mobil pipeline, backed by the World Bank, that is being built to carry oil from Chad, through Cameroon, to the Atlantic Ocean. Tellingly, the last chapter in the volume is entitled, "U.S. Foreign Policy Agenda, 2005–2009: Why West Africa Barely Features," that is, with the exception of terror and oil.

What, then, to make of this volume? The emphasis on trade and politics likely means it will attract a specialized rather than a general audience, consisting of scholars, students, and policymakers. As already noted, this reviewer faults the editors for an inadequate introduction. Readers of a work like this, many of whom may only be interested in individual chapters, deserve a better roadmap to the volume as a whole, one that would offer a fuller discussion of points of agreement and disagreement among the various authors, along with situating the work within the larger literature. Since it is (in part, at least) a volume on Africa and its Diaspora, readers are also entitled to a text that does not refer to the *Universal* Negro Improvement Association (UNIA), that vitally important 20th-century global black movement, as the "*United* Negro Improvement Association." Especially is this the case when the book is published by a notable university press and, more to the point, coedited by Toyin Falola, the prolific author and a major authority on Africa and the African Diaspora. The misnaming of the UNIA begins in the introduction (p. 5), which is written by three authors, but in the first chapter by Adebayo Oyebade and Falola, the UNIA is indeed named correctly (p. 22), as it is in a later chapter (p. 75). On the next encounter, however, the UNIA is once more misnamed (p. 149), only to be named correctly in the following chapter (p. 196). To compound the problem, the index has no entry for the Universal Negro Improvement Association, just for the "United Negro Improvement Association," which includes the references to both names used in the text.

There are other instances of inattention to detail. This is not simply nitpicking. As the ones whose names appear on the dust jackets, editors of collections are responsible for carefully vetting the individual chapters, not least to avoid problems like the ones with the UNIA. Further, editors usually have multiple opportunities during the production process to fix such problems. Somehow, Jalloh and Falola missed them all. That said, *The United States and West Africa* is a welcome addition to the literature. Most notably the historical chapters, along with the ones on the African American–West African connection, should withstand the test of time.

Michael O. West
Binghamton University

Jehu J. Hanciles, *Beyond Christendom: Globalization, African Migration, and the Transformation of the West*. Maryknoll, NY: Orbis Books, 2008. Pp. 430. Paper $35.00.

The 2000 census indicated there were over one million foreign-born Africans living in the United States. This recent development, a distinct product of economic globalization, presents scholars across the academic disciplines with a seemingly endless number of exciting questions not only about origins, but also the future interactions of African immigrants with their new communities. Historian and globalization scholar, Jehu J. Hanciles does a commendable job of tackling this multifaceted topic from the religious perspective in *Beyond Christendom: Globalization, African Migration, and the Transformation of the West.*

The first part provides readers with a thorough review of popular globalization theory, which rightfully concludes that these economic processes, and their various demographic and cultural consequences, present us with a world full of possibility. This is in contrast to the rather simplistic narrative of homogenization in the form of the American "melting pot" concept. In particular, Hanciles notes that several studies have demonstrated that the encounter with modernity in Africa and the rest of the "global South" has not led to the wave of secularization witnessed in parts of the West, but rather an exponential increase in evangelical Protestant, Catholic, and Islamic religious activity. Hanciles traces the historical evolution of the Christian church and the concept of Christendom (from the conversion of Constantine), which like globalization, "also fostered the Western idea of a univer-sal civilization." Like the *Pax Americana* view of globalization, the author also rejects the Christendom paradigm not only for its Eurocentrism, but its failure to admit that the "global South" serves as the current center of dynamic Christian activity. In this section Hanciles also highlights how colonial mentalities not only corrupted the efforts of missionaries, but also how Christianity was transformed into a "non-Western religion . . . defined by local expressions and marked by cul-tural plurality." This last point is of particular importance in later parts of the text.

Part two of *Beyond Christendom* is a summary of some of the major religious, political, and economic causes of migration and immigration from the rise of European colonialism to the contemporary phenomenon of massive movement of peoples from the "developing" to the "developed" world. This section's greatest strength is the shift in focus to Africans' experiences within the larger dynamics of the modern (and postmodern) world of globalization. Some of the major cata-lysts of African immigration during the colonial and post-colonial eras have included Africa's unequal place in the international economy, weak nation-states, and civil conflict. This section also contains extensive statistical data on the num-ber of African migrants living in Western nations and their countries of origin. Finally, part two reviews the theories about how immigrants tend to function or assimilate into their new societies. The overall importance of this section is that the array of political and economic challenges presented by the "New World Order" have produced not only millions of refugees and asylum seekers, but also potential missionaries coming from particularly strong religious backgrounds.

Most of the new ground is covered in the third and final sections of the book, which profile African migrant pastors, their missionary activities, and the church-es they have established in the United States. It is here that readers benefit the most from Hanciles's extensive interviews with African church officials on both sides of the Atlantic. In this section Hanciles argues that African immigrant churches fall into four main categories: "Abrahamic," independent churches founded by an individual African migrant; "Macedonian," churches established by the initiatives of African-led or African-based ministries; "Jerusalem-type," African churches affiliated with Western denominations; and the "Samuel-Eli type," mainline churches rejuvenated by an influx of new African congregants. These types are discussed in the case studies of African immigrants turned missionaries and their vibrant congregations in the United States, which have roots in Kenya, Ghana, Nigeria, Liberia, the Congo, and other nations. Supporting these case studies is the inclusion of survey data from various congregations, which provides us some key insights into how these churches are tailored to serve the social and spiritual needs of the congregants. Also of note, Hanciles has thoughtfully included appendices listing his contacts among Ghanaian and Kenyan church officials, and a directory of over fifty African immigrant churches in the United States. For scholars interested in contemporary African Christianity, particularly Pentecostalism, or the African immigrant experience in the United States, this information should be invaluable.

One of the most promising and exciting directions the interdisciplinary study of globalization has taken is the focus on its relationship with organized religion. In *Beyond Christendom,* Jehu Hanciles has provided a solid starting point for casual readers seeking to understand the complex historical/global dynamics which have created mobile people, the mobile faiths they bring with them, and the impact both have on their new societies. Scholars will find the use of interviews of church officials, participant observation of Sunday services, and case studies to be most helpful in understanding how African immigrant communities have begun to create unique spaces for themselves in the United States.

After reading *Beyond Christendom*, it becomes clear that massive immigration will transform the West demographically, but the extent to which immigrants' missionary activities will reach outside their immigrant constituencies is unclear. More than anything, Hanciles has clearly demonstrated that people from the developing world are not powerless pawns in the face of the leviathan of globalization, but potential agents for a spiritual revival in Western societies. The old trope of the European missionary "civilizing the natives" is turned on its head here. To be sure, this fuller view of global interaction suggests that the explosive growth of the Pentecostal movement in West Africa can lead to the establishment of Nigerian mega-churches in the suburbs of Dallas, Texas.

Justin Williams
New York, NY

Mary Frances Berry, *And Justice for All: The United States Commission on Civil Rights and the Continuing Struggle for Freedom in America*. New York: Alfred A. Knopf, 2009. Pp. 339. Cloth $30.00.

Mary Frances Berry served as a member of the U.S. Commission on Civil Rights (CCR) for twenty-four years, and as its chair for approximately ten years. During her tenure she fought three Republican administrations to maintain the CCR's independence and viability as an agency monitoring the progress of civil rights for African Americans, Native Americans, Hispanic Americans, the disabled, women, and the elderly. Thus, no one is more qualified to write the history of the CCR and its successes and struggles than Berry.

Tracing the history of the CCR chronologically, Berry describes its origins from 1957 when President Dwight D. Eisenhower supported its creation by Congress as a response to the civil rights crisis that confronted him in Little Rock and other parts of the South. Despite the Supreme Court's 1954 *Brown* decision, Eisenhower did not want the federal government to force the desegregation of public schools upon white southerners; nor did he want to use the power of the federal government to protect the voting rights of African Americans in the South. By advocating the creation of the CCR, an agency that formed a barrier between the federal government and the enforcement of civil rights, Eisenhower found what he thought was an easy way out. As Berry notes, Eisenhower "proposed a temporary commission on civil rights as a safety valve to relieve discontent and make it possible for him to avoid tough decisions about racial issues." Thanks to the conscientiousness of some of the CCR's original members such as John Hannah of Michigan State University and Father Theodore Hesburgh of Notre Dame, the CCR went well beyond Eisenhower's political purpose and began to play a major role in the struggle for civil rights. The CCR followed its charge as defined by the Civil Rights Act of 1957 to subpoena witnesses and hold hearings, to investigate allegations of the denial of voting rights and equal protection of the laws, and to report findings and recommendations to the president and the Congress.

Berry shows that the relationship that Eisenhower formed with the CCR became the norm for most of the presidents under whom the CCR commissioners served. From Eisenhower through John F. Kennedy, Lyndon B. Johnson, Richard M. Nixon, Gerald Ford, Jimmy Carter, Ronald Reagan, George H. W. Bush, and Bill Clinton, none were strong advocates or supporters of the commission's work. These presidents felt that the CCR was a nuisance and tried to hinder its actions or prevent it from having any real significance or impact on activities within their administrations. Readers of Berry's history will be surprised to find that Democratic presidents such as Kennedy and Clinton were just as obstructionist and reluctant to support the CCR's work as the Republicans.

In addition to describing the lack of support that the Civil Rights Commission faced from most of the presidents, Berry also documents and dramatizes the often hostile political climate in which the CCR operated. She shows how Congress, particularly the southern members, sought to undermine the CCR and to prevent it from carrying out its work by reducing its funding and supporting the appointment of commissioners who did not support the enforcement of civil rights laws. In its earlier years the CCR barely survived because southern segregationists in Congress repeatedly cut its budget and refused to reauthorize and extend its existence if it acted too aggressively in holding hearings on civil rights violations or advocated too strongly that the federal government enforce civil rights laws. From the beginning of its existence the CCR and its staff had to deal with threats and attacks from conservative and racist politicians in Washington, DC, who attempted to undermine its work.

Despite the opposition, Berry provides numerous examples of how the CCR affected the enforcement of civil rights for American citizens. According to Berry, the CCR was instrumental in the passage of the Civil Rights Act of 1964, the Voting Rights Act of 1965, the language minority protection of the Voting Rights Act of 1975, the Age Discrimination Act of 1978, and the Americans with Disabilities Act of 1990. Over the course of this fifty-two-year history, the CCR held hearings throughout the country to focus the nation's attention on voting rights, racially motivated violence, disparities in education, and police brutality. It also issued numerous reports that made recommendations on controversial issues such as discrimination in housing, the impact of affirmative action, and the discrimination practiced by various agencies of the federal government. Indeed, the CCR often laid the groundwork for policies and actions that other enforcement agencies of the federal government undertook—such as the denial of federal funds to state and local government agencies and organizations that practiced discrimination on the basis of race, ethnicity, or gender.

Berry also describes how the Reagan and two Bush administrations attempted to destroy the CCR and compromise its independence not only by appointing commissioners who did not support its mission, but also by trying to fire commissioners who did not follow their anti–civil rights agenda. Berry documents how Republican appointees opposed affirmative action; did not want to address issues of discrimination against racial minorities, women, and gays; and used their majority votes to block the CCR from doing anything with which they disagreed. Republican appointees such as Linda Chavez, Abigail Thernstrom, Clarence Pendleton, and Robert Redenbaugh should never have served on the CCR because they were openly hostile to its goals and objectives, and attempted to use it to endorse and support the anti–civil rights stance of the Reagan and two Bush administrations.

Overall, Berry has written the definitive history of the United States Commission on Civil Rights. She has provided us both a scholarly history of the CCR as well as an insider's view of its work, successes, failures, and approaches to addressing the enforcement of civil rights legislation. She has skillfully linked the history of the CCR to the history of the Civil Rights Movement. Readers will also enjoy the numerous photos Berry has interspersed throughout the book to illustrate the CCR's work, to identify its members, and to document the history of one of the nation's most important federal agencies.

W. Marvin Dulaney
University of Texas at Arlington

BOOKS RECEIVED—2010*

Abdullah, Zain. *Black Mecca: The African Muslims of Harlem.* New York: Oxford University Press, 2010. Pp. 294. Cloth $35.00.

Abel, Elizabeth. *Signs of the Times: The Visual Politics of Jim Crow.* Berkeley: University of California Press, 2010. Pp. 391. Paper $25.95. Cloth $60.00.

Alexander, Adele Logan. *Parallel Worlds: The Remarkable Gibbs-Hunts and the Enduring (In)Significance of Melanin.* Charlottesville: University of Virginia Press, 2010. Pp. 375. Cloth $29.95.

Ashton, Susanna, ed. *I Belong to South Carolina: South Carolina Slave Narratives.* Columbia: University of South Carolina Press, 2010. Pp. 317. Paper $59.95.

Baker, Barbara A., ed. *Albert Murray and the Aesthetic Imagination of a Nation.* Tuscaloosa: University of Alabama Press, 2010. Pp. 249. Cloth $45.75. Paper $25.00.

Baldwin, Lewis V. *The Voice of Conscience: The Church in the Mind of Martin Luther King, Jr.* New York: Oxford University Press, 2010. Pp. 365. Paper $29.95.

Barnes, Jack. *Malcolm X, Black Liberation, and the Road to Workers' Power.* New York: Pathfinder Press, 2009. Pp. 413. Paper $35.00.

Beauchamp, Lincoln T. *Blues Speak: The Best of Original Chicago Blues Annual.* Urbana: University of Illinois Press, 2010. Pp. 161. Paper $24.95.

Berresford, Mark. *That's Got 'Em! The Life and Music of Wilbur C. Sweatman.* Jackson: University Press of Mississippi, 2010. Pp. 230. Cloth $50.00.

Braziel, Jana Evans. *Duvalier's Ghosts: Race, Diaspora, and U.S. Imperialism in Haitian Literatures.* Tallahassee: University Press of Florida, 2010. Pp. 308. Cloth $69.95.

Brown, Leonard L., ed. *John Coltrane and Black America's Quest for Freedom: Spirituality and the Music.* New York: Oxford University Press, 2010. Pp. 235. Paper $27.95.

Buick, Kirsten Pai. *Child of the Fire: Mary Edmonia Lewis and the Problem of Art History's Black and Indian Subject.* Durham, NC: Duke University Press, 2010. Pp. 297. Paper $24.95.

---

*Scholars and advanced graduate students interested in reviewing these or other books for *The Journal of African American History* should contact the editorial office at jaah@jaah.org.

Carter, Donald Martin. *Navigating the African Diaspora: The Anthropology of Invisibility.* Minneapolis: University of Minnesota Press, 2010. Pp. 362. Paper $30.00.

Davies, Sharon. *Rising Road: A True Tale of Love, Race, and Religion in America.* New York: Oxford University Press, 2010. Pp. 327. Cloth $27.95.

Dorsey, Mignette Y. Patrick. *Speak Truth to Power: The Story of Charles Patrick, A Civil Rights Pioneer.* Tuscaloosa: The University of Alabama Press, 2010. Pp. 130. Paper $16.00.

Edmonds, Ennis B. and Michelle A. Gonzalez. *Caribbean Religious History: An Introduction.* New York: New York University Press, 2010. Pp. 268. Cloth $75.00. Paper $24.00.

Garfield, Gail. *Through Our Eyes: African American Men's Experiences of Race, Gender, and Violence.* New Brunswick, NJ: Rutgers University Press, 2010. Pp. 250. Paper $24.95.

Ginwright, Shawn A. *Black Youth Rising: Activism and Radical Healing in Urban America.* New York: Teachers College Press, 2010. Pp. 178. Paper $25.95.

Glasrud, Bruce A. and Cary D. Wintz, eds. *African Americans and the Presidency: The Road to the White House.* New York: Routledge, 2010. Pp. 248. Paper $26.95.

Goudsouzian, Aram. *King of the Court: Bill Russell and the Basketball Revolution.* Berkeley: University of California Press, 2010. Pp. 423. Cloth $29.95.

Griffiths, Jennifer L. *Traumatic Possessions: The Body and Memory in African American Women's Writing and Performance.* Charlottesville: University of Virginia Press, 2009. Pp. 144. Cloth $39.50. Paper $19.50.

Henderson, George. *Race and the University: A Memoir.* Norman: University of Oklahoma Press, 2010. Pp. 248. Cloth $24.95.

Hicks, Terence and Abul Pitre, eds. *The Educational Lockout of African Americans in Prince Edward County, Virginia (1959–1964): Personal Accounts and Reflections.* Lanham, MD: University Press of America, 2010. Pp. 99. Paper $19.95.

Hill, Robert A. and Edmond J. Keller, eds. *Trustee for the Human Community: Ralph J. Bunche, the United Nations, and the Decolonization of Africa.* Athens: Ohio University Press, 2010. Pp. 205. Cloth $59.95. Paper $26.95.

Hunt, Darnell and Ana-Christina Ramón, eds. *Black Los Angeles: American Dreams and Racial Realities.* New York: New York University Press, 2010. Pp. 439. Cloth $75.00. Paper $26.00.

Li, Stephanie. *Something Akin to Freedom: The Choice of Bondage in Narratives by African American Women.* New York: SUNY Press, 2010. Pp. 162. Cloth $60.00.

Lipsitz, George. *Midnight at the Barrelhouse: The Johnny Otis Story.* Minneapolis: University of Minnesota Press, 2010. Pp. 235. Cloth $24.95.

Lubet, Steven. *Fugitive Justice: Runaways, Rescuers, and Slavery on Trial.* Cambridge: The Belknap Press of Harvard University Press, 2010. Pp. 367. Cloth $29.95.

Mackey, Frank. *Done with Slavery: The Black Fact in Montreal.* Montreal, Can.: McGill-Queen's University Press, 2010. Pp. 604. Cloth $49.95.

Mandela, Nelson. *Nelson Mandela: Conversations with Myself.* New York: Farrar, Straus, and Giroux, 2010. Pp. 454. Cloth $28.00.

Minutaglio, Bill. *In Search of the Blues: The Journey to the Soul of Black Texas.* Austin: University of Texas Press, 2010. Pp. 167. Cloth $50.00. Paper $24.95.

Morgan, Phillip, ed. *African American Life in the Georgia Lowcountry: The Atlantic World and the Gullah Geechee.* Athens: The University of Georgia Press, 2010. Pp. 311. Cloth $34.95.

Murphy, Gretchen. *Shadowing the White Man's Burden: U.S. Imperialism and the Problem of the Color Line.* New York: New York University Press, 2010. Pp. 279. Cloth $75.00. Paper $25.00.

Murrell, Nathaniel Samuel. *Afro-Caribbean Religions: An Introduction to Their Historical, Cultural, and Sacred Traditions.* Philadelphia, PA: Temple University Press, 2010. Pp. 431. Paper $39.95.

Norde, Gerald S. *Peculiar Affinity: The World the Slave Owners and Their Female Slaves Made.* Fairfax, VA: History4All, Inc., 2007. Pp. 163. Paper $18.00.

O'Dell, Jack. *Climbin' Jacob's Ladder: The Black Freedom Movement Writings of Jack O'Dell.* Edited and introduced by Nikhil Pal Singh. Berkeley: University of California Press, 2010. Pp. 319. Cloth $34.95.

O'Riley, Michael F. *Cinema in an Age of Terror: North Africa, Victimization, and Colonial History.* Lincoln: University of Nebraska Press, 2010. Pp. 198. Cloth $45.00.

Polyne, Millery. *From Douglass to Duvalier: U.S. African Americans, Haiti, and Pan Americanism, 1870–1964.* Tallahassee: University Press of Florida, 2010. Pp. 292. Cloth $69.95.

Riser, R. Volney. *Defying Disfranchisement: Black Voting Rights Activism in the Jim Crow South, 1890–1908.* Baton Rouge: Louisiana State University Press, 2010. Pp. 326. Cloth $40.00.

Ritchie, Andrew. *Major Taylor: "The Fastest Bicycle Rider in the World."* San Francisco: Cycle Publishing, 2010, 2nd edition. Pp. 208. Cloth $39.95.

Roediger, David, ed., with Martin Smith. *Listening to Revolt: The Selected Writings of George Rawick.* Chicago, IL: Charles H. Kerr Publishing Company, 2010. Pp. 194. Paper $14.00.

Rogers, Molly. *Delia's Tears: Race, Science, and Photography in Nineteenth-Century America.* New Haven, CT: Yale University Press, 2010. Pp. 350. Cloth $37.50.

Roman, Miriam Jimenez and Juan Flores, eds. *The Afro-Latina Reader: History and Culture in the United States.* Durham, NC: Duke University Press, 2010. Pp. 566. Cloth $99.95. Paper $29.95.

Root, Erik S., ed. *Sons of the Fathers: The Virginia Slavery Debates of 1831–1832.* Lanham, MD: Lexington Books, 2010. Pp. 345. Cloth $75.00.

Rosemont, Franklin and Robin D. G. Kelley, eds. *Black, Brown, and Beige: Surrealist Writings from Africa and the Diaspora.* Austin: University of Texas Press, 2009. Pp. 395. Cloth $65.00.

Rutkoff, Peter M. and William B. Scott. *Fly Away: The Great African American Cultural Migrations.* Baltimore, MD: John Hopkins University Press, 2010. Pp. 408. Cloth $45.00.

Schafer, Daniel L. *Anna Madgigine Jai Kingsley: African Princess, Florida Slave, Plantation Slaveowner.* Gainesville: University Press of Florida, 2010. Pp. 177. Paper $19.95.

Scott, Darieck. *Extravagant Abjection: Blackness, Power, and Sexuality in the African American Literary Imagination.* New York: New York University Press, 2010. Pp. 317. Cloth $49.00. Paper $22.00.

Sharpless, Rebecca. *Cooking in Other Women's Kitchens: Domestic Workers in the South, 1865–1960.* Chapel Hill: University of North Carolina Press, 2010. Pp. 273. Cloth $35.00.

Shellum, Brian G. *Black Officer in a Buffalo Soldier Regiment: The Military Career of Charles Young.* Lincoln: University of Nebraska Press, 2010. Pp. 360. Paper $19.95.

Shipton, Alyn. *Hi-De-Ho: The Life of Cab Calloway.* New York: Oxford University Press, 2010. Pp. 283. Cloth $29.95.

Sills, Vaughn. *Places for the Spirit: Traditional African American Gardens.* San Antonio, TX: Trinity University Press, 2010. Pp. 138. Cloth $29.95.

Sitkoff, Harvard. *Toward Freedom Land: The Long Struggle for Racial Equality in America.* Lexington: University Press of Kentucky, 2010. Pp. 240. Cloth $50.00.

Stricklin, David. *Louis Armstrong: The Soundtrack of the American Experience.* Chicago: Ivan R. Dee Publisher, 2010. Pp. 174. Cloth $26.00.

Taylor, Glenda R. and Mary J. Taylor. *Truth Beyond Illusion: African American Women, 1860s–1950s.* New York: AMH Publishers, 2009. Pp. 186. Paper $24.99.

Thompson, Garland L. *Unheralded but Unbowed: Black Scientists and Engineers Who Changed the World.* Charleston, SC: CreateSpace, 2010. Pp. 336. Paper $21.95.

Thurman, Howard Washington. *The Papers of Howard Washington Thurman.* Columbia: The University of South Carolina Press, 2009. Pp. 377. Cloth $59.95.

Trotter, Joe W. and Jared N. Day. *Race and Renaissance: African Americans in Pittsburgh Since World War II.* Pittsburgh, PA: University of Pittsburgh Press, 2010. Pp. 328. Cloth $29.95.

Whelchel, L. H., Jr. *The History and Heritage of African American Churches: A Way Out of No Way.* St. Paul, MN: Paragon House Publishers, 2011. Pp. 334. Cloth $24.95.

Woods, Clyde, ed. *In the Wake of Hurricane Katrina: New Paradigms and Social Visions.* Baltimore, MD: John Hopkins University Press, 2010. Pp. 422. Paper $30.00.

Wynn, Neil A. *The African American Experience During World War II.* Lanham, MD: Rowman & Littlefield Publishing Group, 2010. Pp. 184. Cloth $36.95.

The Journal of African American History

CARTER G. WOODSON
DISTINGUISHED LECTURERS
2010–2011

The Association for the Study of African American Life and History and *The Journal of African American History* are pleased to present the list of the Carter G. Woodson Distinguished Lecturers for 2010–2011. These lecturers are among the leading scholars in the field of African American history and culture.

We hope that you will begin to make plans to bring one of these speakers to your campus, institution, or fundraising activity for your ASALH branch or local cultural organization. Lecture sponsors agree to pay a $1,000 lectureship fee to *The Journal of African American History* ($500 of which will go to the speaker) as well as the lecturer's travel and lodging expenses (if any).

This is an important way to help support the ongoing activities of *The Journal of African American History.*

For more information contact:
Sylvia Cyrus, Executive Director
ASALH
2225 Georgia Avenue, Suite 331
Washington, DC 20059

Telephone: 202.865.0053

ASALH Office: info@asalh.net
ASALH website: www.asalh.org

Derrick P. Alridge, University of Georgia at Athens
* "W. E. B. Du Bois and the Education of Black People"
* "Hip Hop as a Social and Intellectual Movement"
* "Metaphors and Symbolic Representations of Blacks in U.S. History Textbooks"

Dr. Derrick P. Alridge is Professor of Education and Director of the Institute on African American Studies at the University of Georgia, Athens. His areas of scholarship include the history of U.S. African American education, civil rights studies, and Hip Hop studies. He is currently codirector of the Foot Soldier Project for Civil Rights Studies at UGA—a research project that produces historical documentaries on the Civil Rights Movement in Georgia. Professor Alridge's work has been published in a variety of journals, including *The Journal of African American History, The Journal of Negro Education,* and *The Journal of Human Behavior in the Social Environment.*

Felix Armfield, Buffalo State University/SUNY
- "Eugene Kinckle Jones and the Founding of Alpha Phi Alpha Fraternity"
- "Eugene Kinckle Jones and Black Social Work"
- "Black Social Work Education and the Supreme Court's Gaines v. Missouri Decision, 1938"

Dr. Felix Armfield is Associate Professor of History at Buffalo State University in the Department of History and Social Studies Education. He also was a member of the faculty of Western Illinois University from 1995 to 2000. Most recently, he published the book *Black Life in West Central Illinois* (2001), and he is presently working on a biography of Eugene Kinckle Jones, a pioneer in black social work in the early 20th century and the first executive secretary of the National Urban League, 1916–1940.

Deidre Hill Butler, Union College
- "Activist Mothering in African American Families"
- "The Split: A Womanist Interpretation of an Episode of Suburban Black Community Reconfiguration, 1904–1920"
- "Having Our Say: Teaching Black Studies to Our Community and Beyond"

Dr. Deidre Hill Butler came to Union College from Clark University in Worcester, Massachusetts, where she earned her Ph.D. Dr. Butler's research interests include the social geography of race, class, and gender in African American social institutions in New England, and the role of African American women in contemporary stepfamilies. She has received recognition for her scholarship from the New York African-American Institute and the Massachusetts Historical League. Dr. Butler has served on the program committees for the Association of Black Sociologists and the Association for the Study of African American Life and History, and she is a member of the American Sociological Association. She is an active member of the Black Women's Health Project, a national black women's grassroots health initiative. Dr. Butler contributed an essay to the 2003 ASALH Black History Month Kit, *The Souls of Black Folk: Centennial Reflections.*

De Witt S. Dykes, Jr., Oakland University
- "African American Family History and Genealogy"
- "The Underground Railroad in History and in Memory" (illustrated with slides)
- "How Africans Became African Americans: Family, Culture, and Continuity"

De Witt S. Dykes, Jr., is Associate Professor of History at Oakland University in Rochester, Michigan, specializing in African American history, family history, and genealogy. Dr. Dykes is the author of numerous articles in the *Dictionary of American Biography, Notable Black American Women, Notable Black American Men,* and *Black Women in America: An Historical Encyclopedia.* He has also published scholarly essays in various books on African American and family history.

Sheila Y. Flemming, Lemoyne-Owen College
- "Dr. Mary McLeod Bethune: The Public and Private Icon"
- "And Justice for ALL: Reparations for African Americans"
- "Women in the Anti-apartheid Movement in South Africa"

Dr. Sheila Y. Flemming is Vice President for Institutional Advancement at Lemoyne-Owen College in Memphis, TN. She received her Ph.D. degree from Howard University and is the author of *Bethune-Cookman College 1904–1994: An Answered Prayer to a Dream* (1995). Dr. Flemming has written and lectured extensively on Dr. Mary McLeod Bethune, women in Africa, reparations, and African American leadership, and she is past president of the Association for the Study of African American Life and History.

David Barry Gaspar, Duke University
- "Meaning, Purpose, and Practice: Carter G. Woodson and 'Scientific' Black History"
- "The Visible Hand: Carter G. Woodson and the Shaping of *The Journal of Negro History,* 1916–1926"
- "Carter G. Woodson, *The Journal of Negro History,* and the Early Scholarship of Eric Williams"

Dr. Gaspar was born in St. Lucia in the West Indies and pursued undergraduate studies at the College of the Virgin Islands and the University of the West Indies. He received his Ph.D. degree in history in 1974 from Johns Hopkins University. His research interests are related to the development of the Atlantic World since 1400, with particular emphasis on the significance of the African

Diaspora. Among his published works are *Bondmen and Rebels: A Study of Master-Slave Relations in Antigua* (1993), and the coedited volumes *More Than Chattel: Black Women and Slavery in the Americas* (1996) and *A Turbulent Time: The French Revolution and the Greater Caribbean* (2003). He recently (2003) founded and edits the academic periodical *Contours: A Journal of the African Diaspora.* Dr. Gaspar has taught at the University of the West Indies, the University of Virginia, Michigan State University, and since 1980 at Duke University.

Robert C. Hayden, University of Massachusetts at Boston
- "African Americans in Science, Technology, and Medicine"
- "Using Carter G. Woodson's Life and Work to Rethink and Revamp Public High School History Courses"
- "The Boston Riot of 1903: Booker T. Washington vs. William Monroe Trotter and the Radicalization of W. E. B. Du Bois"

Mr. Robert C. Hayden is a lecturer in African American history and urban studies at the University of Massachusetts at Boston. He taught in the Black Studies Program at Boston College from 1983 to 1993; in 2001 he retired as a Senior Lecturer in African American history at Northeastern University. Mr. Hayden is the author of sixteen books and publications, including *Mr. Harlem Hospital—Dr. Louis T. Wright: A Biography, African Americans in Boston: More Than Three Hundred Fifty Years,* and important books on African Americans in science, technology, and medicine. In 1994–1995 he was a scholar-in-residence at the Schomburg Center for Research in Black Culture. He formerly served as the secretary of the Association for the Study of African American Life and History and is the founding president of the Martha's Vineyard branch.

David Jackson, Florida A&M University
- "Reassessing America's Most Powerful Black Leader: Booker T. Washington and the Tuskegee Machine"
- "Charles Banks and African American Entrepreneurs in the Age of Jim Crow"
- "A Radical Preacher Activist: Bishop Henry McNeal Turner"

Dr. David Jackson received his B.S. degree in history and education and a master's degree in public administration from Florida A&M University. He earned his Ph.D. from the University of Memphis. He is currently Associate Professor of History at Florida A&M University where he won the Rattler Pride Award for Community Leadership and the Teacher of the Year Award (1999–2000). He has published several articles and books, including *A Chief Lieutenant of the Tuskegee Machine: Charles Banks of Mississippi* (2002).

Ida E. Jones, Howard University

- "Joel 2:28: Let Your Sons & Daughters Prophesy—African American Church Founders Bishop Mary Magdelena Tate and Bishop Ida B. Robinson"
- "Carter G. Woodson—from Education of the Negro to Miseducation of the Negro: Understanding the Internal Decline of African American Leadership"
- "The Light Within: African American Churches and Archives"

Dr. Ida E. Jones is a native of Cambridge, Massachusetts, and currently the senior manuscript librarian in the Moorland-Spingarn Research Center. She is a graduate of Howard University with a B.A. in journalism (1992), and a Ph.D. in history (2001). Her field of study centers around African American religion and historic records preservation, and her research examines the role of the church within African American culture and the American political economy. She has worked with a number of churches to preserve their records and promote understanding of their historical importance in American urban history. Dr. Jones is an adjunct faculty member in the Department of History at Howard University.

Benjamin Justese, GED Testing Service

- "George Henry White: The Man and the Myth"
- "Broken Brotherhood: The Rise and Fall of the National Afro-American Council, 1898–1908"
- "George White, Josephus Daniels, and the Showdown over Disfranchisement, 1900"

Mr. Benjamin Justese is the special projects director for the GED Testing Service, Washington, DC, and has been a print journalist, businessman, teacher, and U.S. diplomat. He completed graduate work in political science at North Carolina State University and in journalism at the University of North Carolina at Chapel Hill. He is the author of *George Henry White: An Even Chance in the Race of Life* (2001), which was nominated for a Pulitzer Prize in biography. He is currently compiling a collection of White's writings and speeches, and working on a biographical directory of North Carolina's African American officeholders from 1868 to 1901.

Tony Martin, Wellesley College

- "Marcus Garvey's Vision and Impact"
- "The Battle for Black History: Two Hundred Years of Struggle"
- "The Pan-African Movement"

Dr. Tony Martin is an Emeritus Professor of African American Studies at Wellesley College, Massachusetts, and has taught at the University of Michigan at Flint, Cipriani Labour College (Trinidad), and St. Mary's College (Trinidad). He has been a visiting professor at the University of Minnesota, Brandeis University, Brown University, and Colorado College. He also spent a year as an honorary research fellow at the University of the West Indies, Trinidad. Dr. Martin has authored, compiled, or edited eleven books, including *Literary Garveyism: Garvey, Black Arts, and the Harlem Renaissance,* and the classic study of the Garvey movement, *Race First: The Ideological and Organizational Struggles of Marcus Garvey and the Universal Negro Improvement Association.* Dr. Martin also qualified as a barrister-at-law at the Honourable Society of Gray's Inn (London) in 1965, and earned a B.Sc. honors degree in economics at the University of Hull (England) and an M.A. and Ph.D. in history at Michigan State University.

Audrey Thomas McCluskey, Indiana University

- "Lucy Craft Laney and Mary McLeod Bethune: Progenitors of Black Women Leadership"
- "Lucy Craft Laney: Early Black Feminist?"
- "Fredi Washington and Hattie McDaniel and the Embodiment of Black Female Performance in 1930s Hollywood"

Dr. Audrey Thomas McCluskey is an Associate Professor of African American and African Diaspora Studies, and Director of the Black Film Center/Archive at Indiana University. Her research bridges the intersections of historical and cultural studies to focus on women educators, particularly school founders, as cultural agents and institution builders. She examines their work as models for nation-building that reside in domestic and gendered notions of leadership, family, and race. Dr. McCluskey's research and teaching has also been in the area of cultural studies, specifically the embodiment of black female performance in early "race" and Hollywood films.

Gregory Mixon, University of North Carolina at Charlotte
- "African American Personhood and the Civil War"
- "The Community and Individual: Black Union History, Public Policy, and the Atlanta Riot of 1906"
- "The Atlanta Riot and the History of Race Riots in the United States"

Dr. Gregory Mixon is Associate Professor of History at the University of North Carolina at Charlotte. He received his Ph.D. in history from the University of Cincinnati. His research interests include African American and United States history, Latin American history, and community planning. He is the author of *The Atlanta Riot, "A Memorandum to Armageddon": Race, Class, and Violence in a New South City.* A new research project focuses on "Black Southern State Militias, 1865–1910." Dr. Mixon has published articles and reviews in *The Journal of African American History, Georgia Historical Quarterly,* and *Atlanta History: A Journal of Georgia and the South.*

Kim Pearson, The College of New Jersey
- "The Journalism of W. E. B. Du Bois"
- "(Re)Covering Hamlet: Lessons from the Imperial Foods Fire"

Dr. Kim Pearson is Assistant Professor of Journalism at the College of New Jersey and in 2000, Pearson was named the New Jersey Professor of the Year by the Carnegie Foundation for the Advancement of Teaching and the Council for the Advancement and Support of Education. She is the author of numerous articles that have appeared in *Emerge, The Crisis* magazine, and in *The Quarterly Black Review of Books.* Ms. Pearson was a contributor to *The Souls of Black Folk: Centennial Reflections,* the first interactive ASALH Black History Month Kit.

Brenda Gayle Plummer, University of Wisconsin at Madison
- "African Americans and U.S. Foreign Affairs"
- "Race and Gender in the Cold War Era"
- "African Americans in Diaspora Perspective"

Dr. Brenda Gayle Plummer teaches in the Department of History at the University of Wisconsin at Madison. She has also held positions at the University of Minnesota at Twin Cities, the University of California at Santa Barbara, and Fisk University. Plummer received her Ph.D. from Cornell University. She has published *Window on Freedom: Race, Civil Rights, and Foreign Affairs, 1945–1988*

(2003); *Rising Wind: Black Americans and U.S. Foreign Affairs, 1935–1960* (1996); *Haiti and the United States* (1992); and *Haiti and the Great Powers, 1902–1915* (1988).

Brenda E. Stevenson, University of California, Los Angeles
- "Sally Hemmings: Slave Maiden, Memory and Mystery"
- "Laboring Women: Slave Women and the Southern Economy"

Dr. Brenda E. Stevenson is Professor of History at the University of California, Los Angeles. She received her Ph.D. in American history from Yale University. Her work centers on the 18th- and 19th-century South, particularly the social and work worlds of slave men, women, and children. Her major publications include *Life in Black and White: Family and Community in the Slave South* and *The Journals of Charlotte Forten Grimke.* She is completing a book on slave women in the American South from the colonial to the antebellum era.

Rosalyn Terborg-Penn, Morgan State University
- "Black Women in the Woman Suffrage Movement"
- "Intersections of Identity and Politics: 1920s Elite Black Women"

Dr. Terborg-Penn is Emeritus Professor of History at Morgan State University, and the coordinator of graduate programs in history. She received her Ph.D. in Afro-American history from Howard University and is the cofounder of the Association of Black Women Historians. She is the editor of several books on African American women's history and is the author of *African American Women in the Struggle for the Vote, 1850–1920* (1998).

Richard Brent Turner, University of Iowa
- "Islam in the African American Experience: Past, Present, and Future"
- "Martin Luther King, Jr., Malcolm X, and Hip Hop Culture"
- "Black New Orleans and the African Diaspora"

Dr. Richard Brent Turner is Associate Professor in the Department of African American World Studies and the Department of Religious Studies at the University of Iowa. He holds M.A. and Ph.D. degrees in religion from Princeton University and an M.A. degree in Afro-American studies from Boston University, and he has been an associate at the W. E. B. Du Bois Institute for African

American Research at Harvard University. Professor Turner's publications include *Islam in the African American Experience* (second edition, 2003) and numerous articles, book chapters, and book reviews on African American religion that have appeared in *The Journal of Religious Thought, Journal of Ritual Studies, The Black Perspective in Music, The Journal of African American History, The Muslim World, Middle East Affairs Journal,* and *The American Historical Review.* He is currently working on a book on New Orleans and the African Diaspora.

Sheila S. Walker, Washington, DC
* "Okra, Gumbo, and Banjo: Everyday Africa in the Americas"
* "Gold, Rice, and Bugs Bunny: Africa's Brain Drain and the Creation of the Americas"
* "Scattered Africa: Faces and Voices of the African Diaspora" (with video presentation)

Dr. Sheila S. Walker served as the William and Camille Cosby Endowed Professor in the Social Sciences at Spelman College in the 1990s and has done extensive field research and participated in cultural activities throughout Africa and the African Diaspora in the Americas. She edited *African Roots/American Cultures: Africa in the Creation of the Americas* (2001) and the accompanying video documentary *Scattered Africa: Faces and Voices of the African Diaspora* (2002). In 1996 she organized the international conference "The African Diaspora and the Modern World" with the cosponsorship of UNESCO, and she is currently developing visual documentation of the African Diaspora in the Americas.

Lillian S. Williams, University at Buffalo, New York, SUNY
* "Mary Burnett Talbert: American Visionary"
* "African American Women and Reform"
* "Blacks in Urban America"

Dr. Lillian S. Williams is Associate Professor of African American Studies at the University at Buffalo, the State University of New York. Until recently, Dr. Williams was Associate Professor of Women's Studies at SUNY at Albany where she was also director of the Institute for Research on Women. She is the author of *Strangers in the Land of Paradise: The Creation of an African American Community, Buffalo, New York, 1900–1940.* Her current research is on African American women and the club movement and she is completing a book titled *Blacks in Green: African Americans in the Girl Scout Movement.*

Yohuru Williams, Fairfield University

- "Color, Features, and Hair: Rethinking Race in the 21st Century"
- "In Defense of Self-Defense: The Black Panther Party in History and Memory"
- "Permission to Hate: Lynching and the Law, 1865–1930"

Dr. Yohuru Williams is Associate Professor of History at Fairfield University in Connecticut. He received his Ph.D. from Howard University in 1998. Dr. Williams is the author of *Black Politics/White Power: Civil Rights, Black Power and Black Panthers in New Haven* (2000) and *A Constant Struggle: African-American History from 1865 to the Present—Documents and Essays* (2002). He also served as general editor for the ASALH's 2002 and 2003 Black History Month Kits, *The Color Line Revisited* and *The Souls of Black Folk: Centennial Reflections.* Dr. Williams's scholarly articles have appeared in the *Black Scholar, The Journal of Black Studies,* and *Black History Bulletin.* Dr. Williams is presently working on a book on African American political activism in Delaware.

Zachery R. Williams, University of Akron

- "Black Public Intellectuals, Past and Present (Including Black Religious Intellectuals)"
- "Africana Policy Studies"
- "Black Men's Studies: The Making of a Radical Tradition and Paradigm"

Dr. Zachery R. Williams is Associate Professor of African American History at the University of Akron and a minister with the African Methodist Episcopal Zion Church. Dr. Williams received his Ph.D. in history from Bowling Green State University. He has worked in the areas of "Black Masculinist Thought" and "Africana Policy Studies," and he is the author of *In Search of the Talented Tenth: Howard University Intellectuals and the Dilemmas of Race in Academia, 1926–1970.*

Call for Papers

"California on My Mind:
The Golden State in the African American Imagination"

The Journal of African American History is planning a Special Issue—"California on My Mind: The Golden State in the African American Imagination." We are seeking studies by historians, literary scholars, sociologists, and other social researchers engaged in theorizing about and documenting various aspects of the African American experience.

California has meant something utopian and specific in the history of people of African descent in the Americas. Indeed, California has been on the minds of African-descended people in the United States especially since its entrance into the union in 1850 as a "free state." The association of "California" with "freedom" meant that enslaved and oppressed African Americans felt an attachment, even though they never made it there. Another group with California on their minds would be those African Americans who actually visited and were impressed by the state's physical beauty, the racial diversity, and western lifestyle, but who never lived there, yet longed to stay. The third group would be the African Americans who migrated to the "Golden State" and created communities, institutions, and social networks. What has California meant to them?

It has been suggested that in the case of Los Angeles, for African-descended peoples the city was the stuff of dreams, but the realities were often harsh and disappointing. We have examined the process of racialization for African-descended people in Los Angeles, "the nature of the 'black' in *Black Los Angeles*." With the African American experience statewide taken into account, the "realities" under examination change, but the declension narrative could predominate and serve to explain at the state level the existence of the *Golden Gulag*. The racialization process occurring in Los Angeles was also taking place in other parts of California, but we still need to know if the declension narrative applies to the communities formed and institutions created.

In locating California as a site in the African American imaginary a good place to begin would be W. E. B. Du Bois's articles in *The Crisis* magazine in November 1913. "Here I had my first sight on the Pacific and realized how California faces the newest color problem, the problem of the relation of the Orient and Occident. The colored people of California do not realize the bigness of this problem and their own logical position." At the state-level it is imperative to move beyond the black-white binary and focus on meanings created as a result of interactions with Asians, Mexicans, Native Americans, and other "colored people of California." Looking throughout the state, we would document the individual and collective meanings of the oppression of the indigenous population to African Americans who were being oppressed by the same forces. Racially restrictive housing covenants aimed at maintaining segregation discriminated against Japanese Americans, Chinese Americans, Native Americans, Filipino Americans, and other "colored people of California." In challenging the racial restrictions in housing, employment, and education in various parts of the state, lawyers and plaintiffs for various peoples of color made common cause with the NAACP. And we would have to look beyond Los Angeles to understand the meanings of alliances for workers' rights and social justice. The alliance between Cesar Chavez's United Farm Workers union and Bobby Seale, Elaine Brown, and the

Black Panther Party has been documented in the JAAH. What does this incident tell us about the meaning of California in the African American and Chicano experiences?

For those who never visited, from the early 20th century imaginings about California were framed by Hollywood. Here there would be possible challenges to the declension narrative, though for many African Americans, Hollywood symbolized the lies being spread in the popular media about black people. The images of the beauty of the state inspired tributes, garnered awards, and were publicized broadly and African Americans imbibed them as did other sectors of the public. These imaginings of California, spurred by filmic images, were often confirmed and enhanced by the narratives and images of those who actually visited the state. Langston Hughes's California was in some ways similar to, but in many ways different from, James Baldwin's. How did we come to know California through the works of African American writers and other artists? The musical soundtracks, the film images, the architectural renderings, and the religious awakenings should all contribute to African American cultural meanings about California.

This Special Issue is inspired by *Harlem on My Mind*, the exhibition of 700 photos and explanatory texts and over 500 film images mounted in New York City in 1969 by the Metropolitan Museum of Art. In 1994 Allon Schoner, the curator for *Harlem on My Mind*, concluded that the exhibition "transformed museums, compelling them to open their galleries to subjects and audiences they had excluded." Harlem was the subject in images and narratives by and about African Americans. The reverence inspired beauty for artists from all over the world. The exhibition included the images of people from everywhere visiting or living in Harlem, and narratives about Harlem from everywhere covering five decades. Harlem as a grand and important cultural capital conjured up meanings to people of African descent around the world, as does California. "California on My Mind," the proposed JAAH Special Issue, seeks to offer new insights into the meanings of the Golden State in the African American imagination.

Essays should be no more than 35 typed, double-spaced pages (12 point font), including endnotes. The JAAH uses *The Chicago Manual of Style,* 15th Edition (Chicago, 2003) for citations. Guidelines for manuscript submission are available in *The Journal of African American History*; and on the JAAH website: http://www.jaah.org.

Submitted essays will be peer reviewed. Your cover letter should include the title of your essay, name, postal address, e-mail address, phone number, and fax number. Your essay should begin with the title of the essay and should NOT include your name.

Please send three (3) hard copies of your manuscript to:

Prof. V. P. Franklin, Editor
The Journal of African American History
University of California, Riverside
Graduate School of Education
1207 Sproul Hall
900 University Avenue
Riverside, CA 92521
E-mail: vpf1019@aol.com; or jaah@jaah.org

Submission Deadline: 2 April 2011

Call for Papers

"The History of African Americans and U.S. Criminal Justice System"

The Journal of African American History (JAAH) is planning a Special Issue on the history of African Americans and the criminal justice system in the United States since the Reconstruction era. Historically, police and other law enforcement agencies have targeted African Americans and accused them of "breaking the law," resulting in the incarceration of tens of thousands of black men, women, and children in U.S. prisons, penitentiaries, chain gangs, prison farms, and other correctional facilities. Police abuse has a long history and remains a major grievance in communities of color, but was usually justified by governmental officials. In addition to arrests, police abuse has taken many forms, including physical brutality, deadly force, verbal abuse, racial profiling, the targeting of African Americans in "law and order" campaigns, spying and surveillance of political activists, and racially discriminatory hiring practices by law enforcement agencies. Studies in the fields of history, law, and the social sciences have documented the racialization of the criminal justice system, which helps to explain the extreme disparities in incarceration rates between whites and people of color in the United States.

The JAAH Special Issue welcomes scholarly essays on the history of police–black community relations and how this relationship has changed (or remained the same) from the late 19th to the late 20th century. Topics include but are not limited to police brutality, racial profiling, black women and/or youth and the criminal justice system, the role of law enforcement agencies in maintaining white privilege, police abuse as a civil rights issue, national and local challenges to police practices, and the racial disparities in incarceration rates historically.

Essays should be no more than 35 typed, double-spaced pages (12 point font), including endnotes. The JAAH uses *The Chicago Manual of Style,* 15th Edition (Chicago, IL, 2003) for citations. Guidelines for the manuscript submission are published in the JAAH and on the JAAH web site: http://www.jaah.org; e-mail address for inquiries: vpf1019@aol.com or clarence.taylor@baruch.cuny.edu.

Submitted essays will be peer reviewed. Your cover letter should include the title of your essay, name, postal address, e-mail address, phone number, and fax number. Your essay should begin with the title of the essay and should NOT include your name.

Please send three (3) hard copies of your manuscript to:

Prof. Clarence Taylor, Guest Editor
c/o V. P. Franklin, Editor
The Journal of African American History
University of California, Riverside
GSOE—1207 Sproul Hall
900 University Avenue
Riverside, CA 92521

Submission Deadline: 1 July 2011

Call for Papers

96th Annual ASALH Conference • Richmond, VA • October 4–9, 2011

The Association for the Study of African American Life and History (ASALH) is soliciting papers and panels for its upcoming 96th Annual Convention. This year's conference theme is: "African Americans and the U.S. Civil War." Although the program committee welcomes papers and panels on any aspect of African and African American history and culture, special preference will be given to submissions directly related to this year's theme.

Using a wide variety of disciplines, this year's conference seeks to explore many aspects of African American involvement in the Civil War, 1861–1865. Important topics include African Americans and the abolitionist movement, African American women and life on the homefront during the war years, African American participation in the military and African American life and politics during the Reconstruction Era, 1865–1877. In addition, recent popular and scholarly debates over causes of the Civil War will be explored.

In 1861 as the United States stood at the brink of civil war, people of African descent, both slave and free, waited with a watchful eye. They understood that a war between the Union military and the Confederacy might bring about the "day of jubilee" and the destruction of slavery. When the Confederate troops fired upon Fort Sumter on 12 April 1861 and hostilities began, President Abraham Lincoln maintained that the paramount cause was to preserve the Union, not to end the practice of slavery. Frederick Douglass, the most prominent African American leader, declared that regardless of Union intentions, the war would bring an end to the South's "peculiar institution."

Over the next four years, the four million people of African descent in the United States sought to prove Frederick Douglass right. Free and enslaved African Americans rallied around the Union flag and the cause of freedom. From the cotton and tobacco fields of the South to the small towns and big cities of the North, nearly 200,000 black men joined the Grand Army of the Republic and took up arms to destroy slavery and the Confederacy. The ASALH convention theme for 2011 honors the role of people of African descent in ending slavery and preserving the Union.

Given the recent political and academic debates about the legacy of the Civil War, papers and panels offering interdisciplinary analyses and perspectives of the continuing legacy of the Civil War in American and African American life are particularly welcome.

The deadline for the submission of panel and paper proposals is 30 April 2011.
All proposals must be submitted electronically to ASALH through the All Academic online system at http://www.asalh.org/callforpapers.html. For **complete panels** that are submitted by March 30, day and time preferences will be given on a first come first served basis. Please refer to the FAQ page for what constitutes a complete panel at http://www.asalh.org/files/FAQs_sheet.doc.

Proposals should include title of the paper or panel, author(s) and affiliation(s), an abstract of paper or panel of 200–250 words, and all contact information. Only *panel* proposal submitters will receive complimentary audio/visual equipment on a first come first serve basis.

For information on how to make electronic submissions, please visit www.asalh.org/96thconvention.html, and visit the FAQ page at http://www.asalh.org/files/FAQs_sheet.doc for important information regarding submissions.

Academic Program Chair, Derrick P. Alridge
dalridge@uga.edu

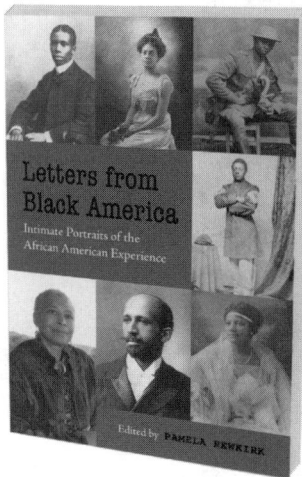

FROM THE ASALH PRESS

THE AUTHORITATIVE ORIGINAL VERSION

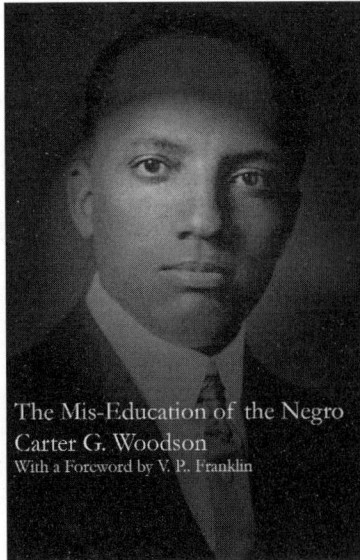

The Mis-Education of the Negro
Carter G. Woodson
With a Foreword by V. P. Franklin

Support ASALH!!
Use Our Version of Woodson's Classic Work
for your classes and study groups.
It is a central text for understanding black social thought.

Order from asalh.net/BooksforSale.html

ISBN: 0-9768111-0-3   Price $9.99

A
ASALH

96th Annual ASALH Convention · October 5–9, 2011 · Richmond Marriott ·Richmond, VA

ASSOCIATION FOR THE STUDY OF AFRICAN AMERICAN LIFE AND HISTORY

"Founders of Black History Month"

REGISTRATION DEADLINE:

June 17, 2011

Completed Applications

Require ALL of the Following:

1. **Completed Request Form** (with additional pages if necessary)
2. **Registration Fee of $40.00**
3. **Copies of the book (s) you intend to sell at the Book Signing**
4. **Name of the Representative attending to support the sale of your book (s)** (MAX. 1 person)
5. **Author must be member of ASALH by July 1, 2011**

AUTHORS BOOK SIGNING REQUEST FORM
PLEASE TYPE OR PRINT CLEARLY

Prefix_____ First_____ M.I.____ Last _____ Suffix_____

Address _____ City _____ State____ Zip_____

Day ( )_____ - _____ Evening ( ) _____ - _____ Mobile ( ) _____ - _____

Email _____ Website_____

Primary Contact Person _____ Rep. attending for book sales _____
(if different from author)

Please attach a list of additional titles, publisher information and how many copies you intend to bring of your publications. **PLEASE NOTE:** ASALH will not assume responsibility for the transportation of publications to and from book signing location at the time of the event and any damages incurred herewith. We reserve the right to reject books submitted that are contrary to the scholarly mission and tradition of ASALH.

I, (please print) _____, certify that the above information is complete and accurate.

X _____ Date_____

BOOK INFORMATION

Title 1:_____

Brief Description:_____

_____

Copyright Year:_____ # of Copies You Intend to Bring: _____

Title 2:_____

Brief Description: _____

_____

Copyright Year:_____ # of Copies You Intend to Bring: _____

PUBLISHER INFORMATION

Publisher Co. 1: _____

Contact Person:_____ Address 1_____

Address 2 _____ City _____ State ____ Zip _____

Day ( ) _____ - _____ Eve.( ) ___ - _____ Fax ( ) ___ - _____

Email _____ Website _____

Publisher Co. 2: _____

Contact Person:_____ Address 1_____

Address 2 _____ City _____ State ____ Zip _____

Day ( ) _____ - _____ Eve. ( ) ___ - _____ Fax ( ) ___ - _____

Email _____ Website _____

Method of Payment: ☐ Check or Money Order ☐ Visa ☐ MasterCard ☐ AMEX Code _____ *pay online at www.asalh.org* otal Amount $ _____

Card holder's name _____ Billing Address _____

Signature _____ Card number _____ Exp. Date_____

RETURN THIS FORM WITH PAYMENT TO:
ASALH Convention Ads/Exhibits • Howard Center • 2225 Georgia Ave., NW Ste. 331 • Washington, DC 20059
Phone: 202 - 865 - 0053 • Authors: exhibits@asalh.net • Website: www.asalh.org

Message in the Music: Hip Hop, History and Pedagogy
Edited by Derrick P. Alridge, The University of Georgia
James B. Stewart, Pennsylvania State University
and V. P. Franklin, University of California, Riverside

Forthcoming in 2010 from ASALH Press!

This volume examines the messages in Hip Hop music and culture from its beginnings in the early 1970s to the present. With a special focus on Rap music, the volume situates Hip Hop in African American and U.S. history and illuminates the messages and the meanings that Rap artists have conveyed in their music.

Contents: Introduction, *Derrick P. Alridge, James B. Stewart, and V. P. Franklin,* "Message in the Music: Hip Hop, History, and Pedagogy"; *James B. Stewart,* "Message in the Music: Political Commentary in Black Popular Music from Rhythm and Blues to Early Hip Hop"; *Derrick P. Alridge,* "From Civil Rights to Hip-Hop: Toward a Nexus of Ideas", *V. P. Franklin,* "Jackanapes: Reflections on the Black Panther Legacy for the Hip Hop Generation"; *Charise Cheney,* "In Search of the Revolutionary Generation: (En)Gendering the Golden Age of Rap Nationalism", *Edward Onaci,* "I can Be Your Sun, You Can Be My Earth: Masculinity and Gender in the Nation of Gods and Earths"; *Pero Gaglo Dagbovie,* "Of All Our Studies, History is Best Qualified to Reward Our Research: Black History's Relevance to the Hip Hop Generation"; *Layli Phillips, Kerri Reddick-Morgan, and Dionne Patricia Stephens,* "Oppositional Consciousness within an Oppositional Realm: The Case of Feminism and Womanism in Rap and Hip Hop, 1976–2004"; *Bryan Bracey,* "Crossover Collaborations: Towards Realizing Hip Hop's Political Potential"; *Bettina L. Love,* "Commercial Hip Hop: The Sounds and Images of a Racial Project"; *Ayanna F. Brown,* "Just Because I am a Black Male Doesn't Mean I am a Rapper! Sociocultural Dilemmas in Using "Rap" Music as an Educational Tool in Classrooms"; *R. Dianne Bartlow,* "Defying Gender Stereotypes and Racial Norms: Naming African-American Women's Realities in Hip Hop, and Neo-Soul Music"; *Paula Marie Seniors,* "Transforming the Carmen Narrative: The Case of Carmen the Hip Hopera"; *Ronald L. Jackson and Sakile Camara,* "Scripting and Consuming Black Bodies in Hip Hop Music and Pimp Movies"; *Lesley Feracho,* "Hip Hop and Global Politics in Caribbean Music: Debates in Transnationalism, Resistance, Culturalism, and Appropriation in Cuban and Puerto Rican Rap"; *Aimee Meredith Cox,* "That Supposed to Be Me?: Marginalized Young Black Women Talk Back to 'Hip Hop'"; *Bernard W. Bell,* "The Global Impact of Hip-Hop on Mainland China".

$19.99

MEMBERSHIP FORM

New Membership ☐   Renewal Membership ☐
The annual membership year is January 1 - December 31

(Please type or print legibly)

Name: Circle Prefix: Mr.   Mrs.   Miss.   Dr.   Rev   Min.   Pastor.   Bishop   TODAY'S DATE _____
Circle Prefix: Sr.   Jr.   II.   III.   IV.   Ph.D.   Ed.D.   M.D.   Esq.   Referred by _____

_____

First   Middle   Last

Address: _____ **City:** _____ **State:** _____ **Zip:** _____

Daytime Phone: _____ **Evening Phone:** _____ **Fax:** _____

Email Address: _____

ASALH Branch Affiliation (if you are currently a member of an ASALH Branch, please list here:
Students Membership Only, Indicate Name of School You Attend: _____

City where school is located _____ **State where school is located** _____ **Zip** _____

Major _____ **Degrees Pursued** _____

PLEASE CHECK ONE

INSTITUTIONAL MEMBERSHIP ☐   **$250.00 Enter name of institution on appropriate line below**

College/University - (Department) _____
Non-Profit Organization _____
Church/Religious Organization _____
Student Organization _____

INDIVIDUAL MEMBERSHIP

General ☐   **$65.00**   Senior (65+) ☐   **$45.00**   Student ☐   **$35.00**
All memberships include quarterly issues of ASALH publication, The Journal of African American History
(formerly the Journal of Negro History), voting privileges and discounts at the national conference and other events

DUAL MEMBERSHIP ☐ **$100.00** Payment includes $65.00 general membership and spouse will receive
membership for $35.00. A dual membership couple will receive one copy of all correspondence and publications.
The couple will have one vote. Discount privileges apply to both individuals.

LIFE MEMBERSHIP ☐ **$1000.00**   **JR MEMBERSHIP** ☐ **$500.00**
(Ages up to 18 years old)
(Also payable in $200.00 installments and must be completed in 5 years)   Installment # _____

Sustaining Life Member Yearly Contribution (Beyond Final Life Membership Payment)
- Heritage Hero *(for life Members who are Seniors only)*   ☐ *$50.00 - $75.00*
- Heritage Defender for Life Members   ☐ *$76.00 - $100.00*
- Heritage Guardian for Life Members   ☐ *$101.00 +*

INDIVIDUAL SUBSCRIPTIONS (Individuals may purchase additional subscriptions at rates below.)
The Journal of African American History ☐ $65.00/Year
The Black History Bulletin ☐ $50.00/Year

For more information on Dr. Woodson and the continuing efforts of ASALH visit www.Asalh.org, or call (202) 865-0053